ERA *of* PERSUASION

TWAYNE'S
AMERICAN THOUGHT
AND CULTURE SERIES

Lewis Perry, General Editor

ERA *of*
PERSUASION

American Thought and Culture, 1521–1680

E. BROOKS HOLIFIELD

Twayne Publishers • Boston
A Division of G. K. Hall & Co.

To Edmund Morgan
and
To the memory of
Sydney Ahlstrom

Copyright © 1989 by E. Brooks Holifield.
All rights reserved.
Published by Twayne Publishers
A division of G. K. Hall & Co.
70 Lincoln Street, Boston, Massachusetts 02111

Copyediting supervised by Barbara Sutton.
Book design and production by Janet Z. Reynolds.
Typeset in Janson by Compset, Inc., Beverly, Massachusetts.

First printing 1989

Printed on permanent/durable acid-free paper
and bound in the United States of America.

Library of Congress Cataloging-in-Publication Data

Holifield, E. Brooks.
Era of persuasion : American thought and culture, 1521–1680 /
E. Brooks Holifield.
p.   cm. — (Twayne's American thought and culture series)
Bibliography: p.
Includes index.
ISBN 0-8057-9050-0 (alk. paper).
ISBN 0-8057-9055-1 (pbk. : alk. paper)
1. United States—Intellectual life—17th century.   2. United
States—Civilization—To 1783.   3. Persuasion (Psychology)—
History—17th century.   I. Title.   II. Series.
E162.H64 1989
973.1—dc19
                                                        88-31272
                                                        CIP

Contents

ABOUT THE AUTHOR
FOREWORD
PREFACE
ACKNOWLEDGMENTS
CHRONOLOGY

ONE
Persuasion   *1*

TWO
Promoters   *18*

THREE
The Persuasive Past   *39*

FOUR
Persuasion Across Cultures   *62*

FIVE
Theologies of Persuasion   *90*

SIX
Dissenters   *110*

SEVEN
Rulers   *133*

EPILOGUE   155
NOTES AND REFERENCES   159
BIBLIOGRAPHIC ESSAY   188
INDEX   194

About the Author

E. Brooks Holifield is the Charles Howard Candler Professor of American Church History at Emory University, Atlanta, where he teaches in the Candler School of Theology, the history department, and the Graduate School of Arts and Sciences. A graduate of Hendrix College, the Yale Divinity School, and the Yale University Graduate School, he has written on a variety of topics in the history of thought in America. In *The Covenant Sealed* (1974), he traced the development of seventeenth-century English and American Puritan theology and piety; in *The Gentlemen Theologians* (1978), he examined religious thought in the Old South between 1795 and 1860; in *A History of Pastoral Care in America: From Salvation to Self-Realization* (1983), he studied the relationships between religion and psychology over a three-hundred-year period. He has twice received year-long research fellowships from the National Endowment for the Humanities, one of which made possible much of the reading for this book. He and his wife, Vicky, live in Decatur, Georgia. They have two children, Erin and Ryan.

Foreword

The American Thought and Culture Series surveys intellectual and cultural life in America from the sixteenth century to the present. The time is auspicious for such a broad survey because scholars have carried out so much pathbreaking work in this field in recent years. The volumes reflect that scholarship, as well as valuable earlier studies. The authors also present the results of their own research and offer original interpretations. The goal is to bring together books that are readable and well informed and that stand on their own as introductions to significant periods in American thought and culture. There is no attempt to establish a single interpretation of all of America's past; the diversity, conflict, and change that are features of the American experience would frustrate any such attempt. What the authors can do, however, is to explore issues of critical importance in each period and those of recurrent or lasting importance.

The culture and intellectual life of the United States are subjects of heated debate. While prominent figures summon citizens back to an endangered "common culture," some critics dismiss the very idea of culture—let alone *American* culture—as elitist and arbitrary. The questions asked in these volumes have direct relevance to that debate, which concerns history but too often proceeds in ignorance of it. How did leading intellectuals view their relation to America, and how did their countrymen regard them? Did Americans believe that theirs was a distinctive culture? Did they participate in international movements? What were the links and tensions between high culture and popular culture? While discussing influential works, creative individuals, and major institutions, the books in this series place intellectual and cultural history in the larger context of American society.

The scope of this first volume is panoramic. It begins with a ceremonial event among Puritan leaders of Massachusetts and returns to explore the arguments of New Englanders over history, faith, and governance. It follows similar arguments in other colonies. There are gripping descriptions of the contrasting worldviews of Indians and missionaries in New Mexico, and in general this account of the earliest stages of American culture is trans-Atlantic and multiethnic. Throughout, E. Brooks Holifield discovers an engagement with projects and a constant need to persuade, or try to persuade, that gave direction and energy to the intellectual endeavors of the age.

Lewis Perry

Preface

Seventeenth-century America was so diverse that it seems even now to defy all attempts to discern any unifying pattern of beliefs and ideas. Pueblo Indians in New Mexico, Hurons around the Great Lakes, Algonkian-speaking groups in New England, and scores of other autonomous native American cultures scattered from coast to coast; Africans from a variety of West African cultures; Franciscans, Dominicans, Jesuits, and conquistadors in New Spain; Recollects, Jesuits, and merchants in New France; Dutch traders and Dutch Reformed preachers in New Netherland; small farmers and Jesuit priests in Maryland; Swedish traders and Lutheran pastors in New Sweden; English tobacco planters and Anglican clergy in Virginia; farmers, merchants, and Puritan preachers in New England—they had little in common. They also had little liking for diversity.

No common set of ideas or values, no common nationality, no center of loyalty united the motley Americans of the seventeenth century. But when we turn away from the quest for a unified set of ideas and beliefs and look instead at the function of thinking and writing during the earliest period of the American experience, we discover one pervasive characteristic of early American thought: when men and women dealt with ideas, they were usually trying to persuade somebody to do something. Living on the periphery of European civilization, where European cultures encountered native American traditions, they formulated their ideas with practical aims in mind.

In referring to early colonial America as an era of persuasion, I have no intention of minimizing the coercion and violence that marked the period, especially in the relationships between European settlers and native Americans. The threat of violence always lingered in the background whenever men and women disagreed, and the limits of persuasion often became painfully evident. Rather than counterposing persuasion and coercion, I have simply defined persuasion in contrast to thought that was dispassionate, disinterested, or speculative.

The English colonies along the eastern coast held about 4,600 people in 1630 and over 151,000 by 1680 (Spanish and French settlements considerably increased that population), and perhaps several million native Americans inhabited the continent. I do not assume that the treatises and narratives of two hundred or so articulate colonists and explorers can reveal the innermost thoughts and motives of that mass of people. Yet I do assume that those men and women, writing and speaking in societies in which a sense of deference to the educated or the articulate remained strong, expressed the public vocabulary of their cultures. They elaborated many of the various ways in which it was possible for anyone in seventeenth-century America to think about the world.

I have not restricted myself to twentieth-century national boundaries. The ideas that I examine found expression in cultures north of the Rio Grande. I explore patterns of native American thought on both ends of the continent. I look at New Mexico, New Netherland, New Sweden, New France, Virginia, and Maryland, though the literate and prolific writers and speakers of New England rightly occupy a large portion of the narrative.

To venture into seventeenth-century America is to enter a world of thought vastly different from our own. I hope that I have maintained always that sense of difference and strangeness. And yet it was also recognizably a predecessor of our world. Some of its accomplishments and failures still help to shape who we are; some of its images and turns of phrase still inform our public discourse.

Acknowledgments

No one writes a book like this without accumulating ample debts. A grant from the National Endowment for the Humanities gave me a chance to immerse myself in the primary sources. I hope that the notes and bibliographical essay suggest the extent of my debt to the work of other historians. I also want to express my gratitude to colleagues who either criticized portions of the manuscript or discussed its ideas with me, especially to Lewis Perry, Athenaide Dallett, David Pacini, John Juricek, Jonathan Prude, and David Hall. I did not always convince them; I did profit greatly from their comments. Dean Jim Waits at Emory University helped me find the time to write. And the two historians to whom I dedicate the book—Edmund Morgan and the late Sydney Ahlstrom—taught me far more than this book can show.

Chronology

1521   Ponce de León returns to Florida.

1534   Jacques Cartier sails to New France. Henry VIII and the English Parliament separate the Church of England from Rome.

1537   Pope Paul III issues bull *Sublimis Deus* trying to halt the slaughter of American Indians.

1538   Expedition of Hernando de Soto begins.

1540   Expedition of Francisco Vásquez de Coronado.

1547   Accession of Edward VI in England.

1549   Dominican missionaries land in Florida.

1553   Accession of Catholic Queen Mary in England.

1558   Elizabeth I begins her reign.

1559   Elizabeth's Act of Uniformity draws Puritan protests.

1564   Laudonniére's expedition to Florida.

1565   Spanish found St. Augustine.

1572   Debate between John Whitgift and Thomas Cartwright over the nature of the church in England.

1581   Rodríguez expedition to New Mexico.

1584   Richard Hakluyt the Younger, *Discourse on Western Planting*.

1585   Settlement of Roanoke Island.

1588   English defeat the Spanish Armada.

1588 Thomas Hariot's *Briefe and True Report of the New Found Land of Virginia*.

1597 Guale revolt on St. Catherine Island.

1598 Don Juan de Oñate leads advance into New Mexico.

1603 James I reigns over England. Samuel de Champlain sails to New France.

1605 Francisco Escobar's expedition to California.

1607 Settlement of Jamestown.

1608 John Smith's *True Relation*.

1610 Sir Thomas Gates brings new laws to Virginia.

1611 Jesuit mission to New France.

1612 John Smith's *Map of Virginia*.

1613 Alexander Whitaker's *Good News from Virginia*.

1616 John Smith's *Description of New England*.

1619 Representative assembly in Virginia. Shipload of Africans to Virginia.

1620 Mayflower Compact and settlement of Plymouth Plantation.

1622 Powhatan uprising in Virginia.

1624 Settlement of New Netherland. Revocation of the Virginia Company Charter.

1625 Accession of Charles I.

1628 William Laud becomes bishop of London and begins anti-Puritan campaign.

1629 Charles I begins eleven-year period of personal rule without Parliament. Massachusetts Bay Company charter granted.

1630 Francis Higginson's *New-Englands Plantation*. John Winthrop leads first large body of Puritans to Massachusetts Bay.

1632 Edward Winslow explores Connecticut Valley.

1633 William Laud becomes archbishop of Canterbury and chancellor of London. John Cotton arrives in New England.

1634 Settlement of Maryland.

1636 Roger Williams founds Providence, Rhode Island after his banishment. Hooker's Newtown Congregation migrates to Connecticut. Harvard College founded. Pequot War begins.

1637 Synod of church leaders condemns Anne Hutchinson. Founding of New Haven colony.

1638 Founding of New Sweden.

1639 Fundamental Orders of Connecticut. Baptist congregation founded in Providence.

1640 *Bay Psalm Book.* Calling of Long Parliament. Migration to New England largely stops.

1641 Thomas Shepard's *Sincere Convert.*

1642 English Civil War begins.

1644 John Cotton's *Keyes of the Kingdom of Heaven.* Roger Williams's *Bloudy Tenent of Persecution for the Cause of Conscience.*

1646 Calling of the Cambridge Synod in New England.

1647 John Cotton's *Bloudy Tenent.* Nathaniel Ward's *Simple Cobler of Aggawam.* New England mandates grammar schools. Reassembling of the Cambridge Synod.

1648 Cambridge Synod produces Cambridge Platform. Thomas Hooker's *Survey of the Summe of Church Discipline.*

1649 Execution of Charles I. Maryland's Toleration Act. Thomas Shepard's *Theses Sabbaticae.*

1650 Anne Bradstreet's *Tenth Muse.*

1652 John Clarke's *Ill Newes from New-England.*

1654 Jewish settlement in New Netherland. Maryland act withdraws toleration from Catholics.

1655 Adriaen van der Donck's *Description of the New Netherlands.*

1656 Quakers arrive in Maryland and New England.

1657 Clerical assembly in Massachusetts meets to resolve disputes over admission to baptism. Flushing Remonstrance (protest against religious intolerance in New Netherland).

1659 Hanging of Quakers in Boston.

1660 Restoration of the monarchy in England: Charles II. Thomas Shepard's *Parable of the Ten Virgins.*

1662 Halfway covenant. Michael Wigglesworth's *Day of Doom.*

1663 John Eliot completes the translation of the Bible into the Algonkian language.

1664 English conquest of New Netherland.

1666 George Alsop's *Character of the Province of Maryland.*

1670   Founding of Charleston. Daniel Denton's *Brief Description of New York*.

1672   Quaker George Fox tours American colonies.

1675   King Philip's War begins. Covenant renewals begin in New England.

1676   Bacon's Rebellion. Increase Mather's *Brief History of the War with the Indians*.

1677   William Hubbard's *Narrative of the Troubles with the Indians*.

1679   Reforming Synod meets in New England.

1680   Pueblo Revolt.

one

_____

Persuasion

In 1677 Urian Oakes, the acting president of Harvard College, addressed the dignitaries assembled at the annual commencement. A local boy who had made his mark in England before returning home in 1671 to be the pastor of the church in Cambridge, he stood before the governor, magistrates, and ministers as a brilliant and versatile scholar, "one of the greatest lights that ever shone in this part of the world." When he arrived back in New England, a jubilant Cotton Mather composed an ode of celebration—"Welcome, great prophet, to New England shore, the fam'd Utopia of more famous More"—and the Harvard overseers had soon expressed a similar opinion of him. Judging him to be the "Master of the true, pure, Ciceronian Latin and Language" in America, they pleaded with him for two years to assume the permanent presidency of the college. His commencement address, delivered in flowing Latin eloquence, should have represented an undiminished triumph.[1]

Yet he betrayed little sense of triumphal optimism. Oakes complained that intellectual achievement counted for nothing in a colonial culture preoccupied with profit, pleasure, and ambition:

The Emperor Nero . . . when advised to sign a death warrant, used to say, "How I wish I knew not letters!" I'm afraid that no small number among us *eruditi*, men most highly deserving of State and Churches, condemned to a laborious life, exposed to the injuries and mockeries of artisans and workmen who are leading a profitable and pleasant existence, will say with Nero, "How *we* wish we knew not letters!" If there be one thing more lamentable in these times than aught else, it is that foolish fellows, good-for-nothings, mad nobodies, haranguers at street-corners, have more influence with the populace than reverent men, filled with singular gifts of the divine spirit.[2]

1

He feared that Massachusetts Bay had become an intellectual wasteland, cluttered by unlearned mechanics who pretended to be ministers, unlettered women who masqueraded as physicians, and unmanageable workers whose successful quest for affluence mocked the unrewarded exertions of the scholars who prepared themselves "through much labor, great expense, long experience."[3] If such laments accurately displayed the tribulations of the colonial scholar in Cambridge, the heavenly city of America's first Republic of Letters, what must have been the tone of intellectual life in the backwaters of New York, Williamsburg, and New Haven?[4]

When Oakes addressed the friends of Harvard at the August commencement, however, he was offering no dispassionate analysis of popular attitudes toward an intellectual elite; he was asking his auditors to give money to the college. The intent of his jeremiad was to persuade somebody to do something. When he complained about "mad nobodies" and "haranguers at street-corners," he was issuing no lament about a general indifference to ideas. Oakes was worried by the upsurge of unlettered exhorters who meddled with ideas without having the credentials—people who thought that they could "make themselves noted orators, and (as if by a leap) Doctors of Theology, in three days." He was worried about people who, like himself, wanted to persuade somebody to do something.[5]

Viewed as an exercise in persuasion, directed against people who were themselves preoccupied with persuasion, Oakes's commencement address provides a clue to the character of intellectual life in seventeenth-century America. The men and women who dealt with ideas in early America were not intellectuals at all, in the sense of thinkers possessed by a sheer love of abstract or critical thought or a dispassionate quest for undiscovered truth. They expounded their ideas not primarily with the intent of enriching the realm of pure truth or pushing forward the frontiers of knowledge but chiefly with the purpose of persuading.

The notion of persuasion assumes a thinker who is engaged as a partisan rather than one whose only goal is to understand and interpret. It is a practical mode of thought, aimed at forming or altering public behavior rather than merely creating pleasure or eliciting conviction, though its practical intent need not imply an absence of either sophistication or complexity. Its aim is not simply to convince people to accept an idea but to lure them into acting, to change not merely convictions but also behavior. One can hardly understand early American thought without recognizing the extent to which persuasive speech and writing permeated its forms.

European Complexity

The predominance of persuasive discourse was a mark of a colonial society. In the more complex societies of Europe, intellectual life was far more diverse. The seventeenth century was a period of singular achievement in European thought, when both speculative philosophy and the new science transformed older ways of thinking. Astronomers wrote about gravity, refraction, and planetary motion. Mathematicians expounded new ideas about notations, binomial theorems, and differential calculus. Natural philosophers published chemistry texts, botanical guides, and essays on alchemy. And physicians made new discoveries about the human body, issuing studies of plague, blood corpuscles, and body temperature.

Ventures into the natural sciences by no means constituted the full scope of European intellectual activity. Historians produced chronologies, national histories, and histories of the world. Philosophers advanced new proposals about ontology, epistemology, and cosmology. European political theorists wrote about absolute monarchy and comparative politics.

That listing only hints at the variety of seventeenth-century European intellectual life. This was a period when university teachers produced encyclopedias and etymological dictionaries; biblical scholars published polyglot editions, commentaries, and vernacular translations; theologians defended scholastic systems, Platonic revisions, and deistic innovations; political economists wrote on mercantilist theory and primitive communism; and a host of literary artists issued a proliferation of plays, tales, and poetry. In contrast, isolated colonists on the outer boundaries of European civilization had neither the resources nor the leisure to create an equally diverse culture.

European thought could flourish because it benefited from institutional wealth and complexity. Although the European universities usually languished far from the frontiers of thought, they still offered a setting in which conflicting intellectual movements could thrive. In Spain they nourished a flowering of conservative scholastic philosophical and theological speculation. In Holland they provided a foothold for advocates of René Descartes's philosophy. In England Oxford and Cambridge became primarily institutions for educating undergraduates, but they also established new professorships of Arabic, geometry, astronomy, and history; offered tutorial instruction in mathematics and cosmography; and provided a home for the revival of Platonic philosophy.

European churches too were complex institutions in which clergy with academic interests could find positions that gave them leisure and resources for scholarship. In France the Epicurean and mechanistic philosopher Pierre Gassendi retained his post as the canon of Digne even as he defended Galileo and pursued mathematical interests that had nothing to do with pastoral duties. A religious order, the Oratorians, offered a home to the clerical philosopher Nicolas Malebranche and provided him the leisure to explore the implications of Descartes's thought. The institutional complexity of the church allowed it to sustain a variety of scholarly pursuits.

More frequently intellectuals in Europe found the time and resources for reflection through the patronage of European princes, who founded libraries and laboratories and financed high culture. Johann Kepler learned astronomy at the feet of Tycho Brahe in the court of the Emperor Rudolf II in Prague; Leibniz served as a librarian for the House of Hanover. When Henry Peacham published his *Compleat Gentleman* (1622), advertising the ideal of a courtier as a scholar or patron of scholars, he voiced a trend that had already emerged in England and on the Continent. French kings and German princes, eager to display their interest in science and letters, surrounded themselves with scholars and writers; Christina of Sweden protected more than one unconventional philosopher. Catholic courts tended to patronize artists, while Protestant princes favored scholars and founded academies and universities for them. Together they determined much of the intellectual geography of Europe.

Closely related to the courts, the expansive civil service of the European governments offered a congenial living for scholars and artists. In France a large group of lawyers and magistrates found that governmental positions enabled them to carry on extensive literary and scientific work. In England the civil service gave work to John Milton, Andrew Marvell, John Dryden, Samuel Pepys, George Wither, Edmund Waller, and a host of other writers. Scholars overlooked by the courts and civil service discovered that wealthy aristocrats were ready to pay for their services. Thomas Hobbes flourished for years in the service of the Cavendish and Clifton families, who gave him access to philosophical and scientific circles on the Continent. Even in the sixteenth century more than half the translations of the classics in England contained dedications to royal and noble patrons, and during the seventeenth, wealthy nobles like Henry Percy, earl of Northumberland, collected mathematicians, astronomers, and cosmographers almost as a hobby.

Almost as important as this financial support was the intellectual support provided by groups of the learned who met for reading and discussion. These periodical gatherings in such centers as Paris, Rome, and Oxford began as informal associations of like-minded persons but sometimes transformed themselves into influential institutions of learning. In France scholars gravitated toward the homes of such patrons as Jacques-Auguste de Thou, the brothers Du Puy, or President Henri de Mesmes, men who often possessed vast private libraries. In England inauspicious gatherings at a tavern near Gresham College formed the nucleus for the formation in 1662 of the Royal Society.

Often the adherents of the informal associations were leisured gentlemen with a passion for collecting, a yearning for recognition, and an interest in classical culture, mathematics, alchemy, mechanics, or natural science. Peacham called these gentlemen "virtuosos," and their contemporaries observed, often with puzzlement, their relative lack of interest in either the usefulness or the larger implications of their scholarship. They were the true amateurs of the world of learning, pursuing knowledge for its own sake. But their independent research, too, rested on a foundation of accumulated wealth and leisure in a complex society.[6]

Such a depiction of European science and speculation should not imply that Europeans depreciated persuasion. The culture of seventeenth-century Europe was marked by a veritable flood of persuasive rhetoric. In an era of unremitting religious, dynastic, and civil warfare, appeals for allegiance and support sounded throughout England and the Continent. Protestants and Catholics, Jesuits and Puritans, Jansenists and Pietists, monarchists and republicans—these were people deeply interested in the arts of persuasion.

Persuasive discourse in Europe often reflected the force of an embedded intellectual tradition. The goal of mastering the skills of persuasion had long shaped the pedagogy of the European universities. Beginning in the thirteenth century, university students demonstrated their learning through oral disputations. At Oxford and Paris they studied grammar, rhetoric, and logic, with the aim of becoming, after about two years, "sophisters" who could take part in public disputations. On receiving the bachelor's degree, they displayed their erudition by holding open disputes with all challengers. As they advanced to the master's degree, they continued to dispute publicly, and upon attaining it, they exhibited their accomplishments through still another disputation.[7]

Humanist reformers of the fifteenth and sixteenth centuries recovered an even older rhetorical tradition. Their return to the classical sources taught them that the primary aim of learning was the pursuit of eloquence. Distrustful of abstract speculation, of purely technical or theoretical concerns, the humanists adopted a Ciceronian ideal of the orator as a heroic figure of wide learning, vast experience, and a talent for persuasion, who could guide others toward useful and worthwhile goals. They believed that knowledge should serve practical ends and that education should produce the capacity for eloquent speech and writing. Sir Thomas Eliot's *Governour* (1531) illustrated the English humanist's emphasis on the importance of rhetorical studies for gentlemen who would speak and write fluently.[8]

The humanist educational reformers of sixteenth-century England therefore argued for the elevation of rhetoric in the hierarchy of academic ideals. They returned to the classical assumption that rhetorical training should permeate academic education. At Oxford and Cambridge the humanists succeeded in reforming the study of grammar, increasing the time spent on rhetoric, and making it part of the preparation for the bachelor of arts degree. One seventeenth-century tutor at Cambridge told his students that without the knowledge of rhetoric "all the other learning, though never so eminent, is in a manner void and useless; without those [rhetorical studies] you will be baffled in your disputes, disgraced and vilified in public examinations, [and] laughed at in speeches and declamations." He instructed them to devote their afternoons to rhetorical studies throughout the four years of their arts course.[9]

By the time European colonists settled in America the religious quarrels of the Reformation had both intensified and altered the standard patterns of persuasion. During the late sixteenth century European Catholics and Protestants began to experiment with new forms of mass propaganda. Printing presses made it possible to distribute popular tracts, broadsheets, newspapers, songs, and woodcuts designed to win over the common people. Appealing to fear and suspicion, this new outpouring of words and pictures simplified complex issues by depicting ideological opponents as monstrous villains, interpreting recent events through sensational anecdotes, and using graphic visual images to shape public opinion. What had begun as a series of polemical confrontations among intellectuals and their political protectors became a sustained effort to influence popular opinions and attitudes.[10]

Nonetheless, persuasive discourse in Europe formed only one part of a far more complicated intellectual universe; in America the language of exhortation assumed greater prominence. The colonists brought European ideas with them, but the demands of settling a new world required that they select and simplify in ways appropriate to colonial institutions and societies.

On the Periphery

Americans have never since been as culturally pluralistic as they were in the seventeenth century. In the early colonial era the North American mainland contained a confusing array of distinct, though often overlapping, cultural and linguistic traditions: native American, Spanish, French, Dutch, Swedish, English, and African. And each of those large groupings comprehended a further array of cultural differences. The varying regional and local origins of both colonists and natives created subtle distinctions even among those who shared a common language and religion; religious conflicts divided even people from the same geographical background; and differing levels of literacy, social status, and economic standing also undoubtedly shaped distinctive ways of thinking.

Estimates of the native American population north of the Rio Grande when Christopher Columbus arrived in the New World in 1492 range from a million to more than ten million. Gathered sometimes in small bands, sometimes in larger confederations, they lived by hunting, trade, and farming, speaking a multiplicity of languages and dialects, and maintaining diverse and complex cultural traditions. Around forty groups had sustained contact with European societies—an encounter that introduced both the native Americans and the Europeans to an experience of cultural diversity for which neither could have been remotely prepared.[11]

The native Americans had certainly never met anyone like the Spaniards. Spanish culture in America radiated from the island of Hispaniola, where Columbus left about forty settlers when he departed after his first voyage. Through exploration and conquest the Spaniards moved quickly through the West Indies, the Aztec regions south of the Rio Grande, and the Incan empire. In 1513 Ponce de León entered Florida; in 1598 Juan de Oñate led Spanish colonists into New Mexico. The venture into Florida resulted in little more than a mission to the Indians and, eventually, an unstable settlement in St. Augustine, but the movement into New Mexico had more durable results. By 1670 about 3,500 Europeans and Africans lived there in the vicinity of the Spanish Catholic missions.[12]

In 1605 the French began to establish their main outpost in the New World as Samuel Champlain initiated the first of his colonizing efforts near the St. Lawrence River and the Great Lakes. By 1627 New France consisted of about a hundred Europeans, mostly fur traders. By 1663, when the French government took control of the colony, about 2,500 Europeans lived there as fur traders, farmers, and missionaries. France's plan was to allocate land to feudal lords called seigneurs, who could collect annual dues and require oaths of fealty from settlers. The seigneurs found it hard to impose a single pattern of social and economic relationships on the French settlers, but they did help to ensure a foothold for French culture in the New World.[13]

In the English colonies around Chesapeake Bay, economic domination proved easier to maintain, but social and religious diversity created conflicts. Within four decades after their arrival in 1607, the colonists in Virginia mastered the art of using indentured servants to work the tobacco fields. After another four decades, they were making use of close to 3,000 Africans to do most of that work. In Maryland, too, it was easier for planters to exploit the labor of indentured servants and slaves than to maintain the feudal baronies and manor courts that Lord Baltimore envisioned when the colony began in 1634. The two tobacco colonies on the mainland, like those on the Caribbean islands, soon resembled each other socially and economically, though Virginia, with a total population of around 44,000 by 1680, remained far larger than Maryland, which contained only about 18,000. The presence of a Catholic political and social elite in Maryland, moreover, caused conflict not only between that colony and Virginia but also between Catholics and Protestants within the colony.[14]

The Chesapeake region, predominantly English, was a model of uniformity compared to the middle colonies. The Dutch settled New Netherland in 1624 with some thirty families, mostly French-speaking Walloons. Within two decades the Jesuit Isaac Jogues could claim to have heard that eighteen languages were spoken there. By the time the English conquered the colony in 1664, it consisted of roughly 10,000 Dutch, Walloon, Swedish, Norwegian, German, Portuguese, Flemish, French Huguenot, African, English, and Scottish inhabitants. The founding of tiny New Sweden on the Delaware River in 1638 intensified the diversity of the region.[15]

Moving north to New England, one might have again entertained the impression of a culturally uniform region of European settlement. The New England colonies, which effectively began when the pilgrims of Plymouth arrived in 1620, were English, Protestant, and organized mainly in small farming towns with Puritan churches. But New England had its own diversity. Its settlers came from East Anglia, the North Country, and the West Country, and they brought different ideas about farming, the use of land, the choosing of leaders, and the governing of societies. They also disagreed about the fine points of religion, with the result that religious dissenters began founding their own settlements as early as 1636.[16]

The presence of Africans in the colonies added yet another dimension to the pluralism. Africans labored in New Spain as early as 1502; they arrived in the English colonies as early as 1619. By 1680 around 7,000 persons, about 4½ percent of the immigrant population on the mainland, were of African origin. They came from a number of distinctive West African regions and cultural groups, and although the slave traders tried to destroy unity by mixing cultures and languages on the slave ships, the Africans maintained even in slavery some of the traditions of their homelands and thus complicated the mosaic of culture in early America.[17]

Unlike the native American societies, the colonies, however diverse, shared one feature in common: all stood on the periphery of the core cultures from which they originated. The British colonies in North America were part of a ring of territories extending from Wales through Ireland to the Caribbean, each linked in a different way to the culture of England, especially of London. The Dutch in New Netherland, the Spanish in New Spain, the French settlers in New France, and the Swedes along the Delaware River also stood on the periphery of central cultures, geographically distant from them yet linked by ties of language, commerce, political allegiance, and memory. In those peripheral settings, institutions and ideas transported from the core cultures took on different forms. Spatial diffusion altered the older cultural patterns in unpredictable ways.[18]

Some colonists living on the periphery experienced a profound sense of isolation from the metropolitan centers. John Pory, the first secretary of the Virginia Company, the joint-stock company that controlled the colony, complained in 1619 about "the solitary uncouthnes of this place." His being "sequestred from all occurrents and passages which are so rife" in Europe, he said, "did not a little vexe me." Even ships from England seemed "fraighted more with ignorance, than with any other merchandize." He became reconciled to the isolation: "At length being hardned to this custome of abstinence from curiosity, I am resolved wholly to minde my busines here, and nexte after my penne, to have some good book alwayes in store, being in solitude the best and choicest company." But that resolve had its limits, and he begged for pamphlets and reports of current happenings. In England Pory might have frequented an informal association of curious virtuosos. In America it took a long time to build the institutions, formal and informal, that created and nurtured virtuosity.[19]

Educated colonists, even those for whom America represented a religious utopia, complained about the isolation. The New England preacher Thomas Hooker explained that his writing wore a "homely dresse and coarse habit" because it came "out of the wildernesse, where curiosity is not studied." Even in 1664 John Winthrop, Jr., the governor of Connecticut, could lament "the unhappinesse of the condition of a wilderness life so remote from the fountains of learning and noble sciences." The minister Thomas Shepard, Jr., born and educated in New England, recognized that "it is no small part of our great unhappinesse who dwell in these out-skirts of the earth that we are so little acquainted with those Excellent things that are done, and found out in the world and discoursed of by those learned and worthy personages" in the Royal Society in England.[20]

For all of the colonists, living on the periphery meant having to adjust to a radical simplification of European culture. From one perspective the simplifying began even in Europe, when small fragments of the larger society detached themselves from its restraints. The Puritan preachers who journeyed to New England, for example, could concentrate on working out the implications of their own fragmentary vision of Christianity, unchecked by competing visions. From another perspective the simplification resulted from the encounter with a wilderness, from the access to new land and new space and the absence of some of the traditional constraints that remained vigorous in the homelands.[21]

Colonial societies had, of course, their own forms of complexity: political machinations, uncertainty about criteria for distributing land and honor, confusion in the organizing of new governments, insecurity created by the exploitation of indentured servants and chattel slaves, and resentments caused by the uneven power of winners and losers. Such social tensions could exist alongside covenantal commitments to mutual care, deferential obeisance to superiors, or a high appreciation of family-centered and communal values.[22]

For understanding the articulation of ideas in early America, however, the crucial feature of simplification was the absence of the institutional complexity that undergirded intellectual diversity in Europe. The colonies lacked the complex institutions of the European homelands: the ancient universities, royal courts, wealthy patrons, scholarly academies, and vast libraries. They had churches but no positions of leisure for scholarly clergy who preferred speculation to pastoral duties. They had governments but no established civil service that provided routine jobs for scholars who wanted to devote their attention to other matters.[23]

The colonies did have a literate and educated elite, and some colonists joined the conversations of the learned in the mother country. A few Virginians wrote letters to the Royal Society on topics ranging from silk production to colonial geography, and they served as agents for English natural philosophers who sought relics, information, and curiosities from the New World. In Connecticut, John Winthrop, Jr., the first colonial fellow of the Royal Society, prepared technical papers on maize, pitch, and tar, and his telescope permitted him after 1663 to join in erudite English discussions of astronomy.[24]

A few others tried to remain abreast of trends in European scientific thought. The students and tutors at Harvard college, for example, developed during the 1650s an interest in Copernican astronomy, and they used the colony's annual almanacs—practical publications that provided information about the calendar and the weather, colonial and world history, and poetry and morality—to popularize their scientific views. Sometimes referring to themselves as "lovers of mathematics," they began in 1656 to expound their astronomical theory. The initial essay assumed a Ptolemaic notion of a geocentric universe; it reflected the traditional cosmogony taught at Harvard in the early 1640s, depicting the earth located at the center of nine concentric spheres that moved in melodious time within the immutable empyrean, the highest heaven, of God the prime mover.

In 1659, however, Zechariah Brigden, fresh from Harvard, explained to New England's merchants and farmers that the Copernican theory was "the true and genuine Systeme of the world." Brigden argued that the Copernican scheme squared with the phenomenon of planetary motion and eliminated the "farrago of concentrical, eccentrical and epicyclical, whimsyes, which pester the other Hypothesis." If Copernicus seemed to conflict with the Bible, he added, that was only because Scripture, fitted to "the rudest mechanick," did not intend scientific exactness: "In Philosophicall truths therein contained, the proper literal sense is always subservient to the casting vote of reason." The authors of subsequent almanacs usually cast their vote for Copernicus, publishing essays on planetary spheres, celestial movement, and the attraction between the planets and the sun. Brigden and his successors shared an obvious sense of pride in their ability to interpret recent European science to the men and women of Massachusetts Bay.[25]

That the literate often derived a sense of sheer delight from their literacy was evidenced by their remarkable inclination to write poetry. If everyone who wrote poetry can be designated a poet, the colonies can be said to have overflowed with them. The seventeenth century gave rise to more poetry, proportionately, than any other period in American history. Colonists inserted poetry into polemical treatises, promotional tracts, histories, and almanacs; they distributed elegies as tokens at funerals; they read poetry at college commencements and used it to dedicate their books. The best-selling publication in New England—Michael Wigglesworth's *Day of Doom* (1662)—was a poem.[26]

Colonial verse encompassed a panoply of forms and topics. George Sandys, the treasurer at Jamestown, labored during the early 1620s on his translation of Ovid's *Metamorphoses*. John Cotton of Queen's Creek in Virginia and Benjamin Tompson of Boston captured in verse the political and military turmoil of the 1670s. Roger Williams in Rhode Island included didactic poetry in his study of Indian language. William Wood used verse to describe for English readers the vegetation and wildlife of New England. John Saffin wrote love lyrics; the minister John Fiske prepared funeral elegies, the Quaker Peter Folger excoriated Bay Colony Puritans in verse. Anne Bradstreet in Massachusetts Bay, the best of the early colonial poets, wrote her poems for herself and for the glory of God. Her verse might not even have been published if her brother-in-law had not spirited it away to London to be "expos'd to publick view." Especially in her later private poetry about her husband, children, and friends and her natural surroundings, she wrote to satisfy her own quest for unity and harmony.[27]

One can also glimpse the self-consciousness of the literate by perusing colonial letters, which often revealed a careful attentiveness to rhetorical rules. Medieval schools for notaries and curial officials had long taught the *ars dictaminis*, the diplomatic art of composing official letters. After sixteenth-century humanists adapted the older guidelines to their pedagogical aims, instruction in letter writing became a standard part of the curriculum in European grammar schools. In his study of letters in seventeenth-century Virginia, Richard Beale Davis discovered that the traditions of epistolary rhetoric taught in those schools remained alive even in purely personal letters. More than a few private libraries contained popular books for letter writers and orators, filled with long lists of elegant similes, tropes, aphorisms, examples, and adages.[28]

The colonists tried, furthermore, to build institutions that could maintain the traditions of a literate elite. In 1647 Massachusetts required every town of a hundred families to establish a grammar school as a defense against "that old deluder, Satan," and Connecticut passed similar legislation in 1650. They did this with the confidence that a grammar school education would, in the words of a Northampton town meeting, "fit them for the college, that so they may be fit for the service of God in the church or otherwise in the public." The purpose was to train leaders through the reading of authors like Erasmus, Ovid, and Cicero; the writing of Latin themes, letters, and orations according to set rhetorical patterns; and the constant drudgery of oral recitation.[29]

A similar desire to maintain older European values found expression in the founding of colonial colleges. The first university in the New World, the Royal University of Mexico, founded in 1551, boasted professors of law, medicine, and theology, in addition to those in the arts. When the Jesuits in New France built a college in Quebec in 1632, they modeled their institution after European Jesuit schools that concentrated on rhetorical studies designed to teach students to write and speak "purely, properly, abundantly, and elegantly."[30]

English settlers founded Harvard College in 1636. The course of study was as diverse as President Henry Dunster and his assistants could make it: logic, physics, ethics, politics, arithmetic, geometry, and astronomy. The chief clue to the cultural function of the college came in the requirement that students spend every Friday for three or four years studying rhetoric and oratory, learning how to argue with eloquence. They improved their Latin by studying grammar and reading classical poetry and prose; they mastered the grammar and syntax of Greek and Hebrew; they delivered monthly public declamations in Latin and Greek; and they prepared disputations on logical and philosophical topics.[31]

The disputations were the heart of a Harvard education. In addition to preparing weekly disputations in the college hall, the students demonstrated their learning through disputations held monthly before the magistrates, ministers, and other students. The first degree, the bachelor of arts, signified that they had excelled for four years at such "publick Acts," and the second degree, the master of arts, signified that they had written a treatise on one of the arts and defended it in yet another public exercise. The commencement festivities consisted mainly of such public defenses. They continued an ancient rhetorical tradition that conceived of thought and expression as agonistic, a mental combat designed to overcome opposition. Harvard did not teach its students to excel in objective description or creative inquiry; it taught them to take a stand, defend it, and attack the views of others.[32]

Such efforts to import educational institutions had only limited success in colonial cultures, however. The influence of even Harvard was modest; from its founding to the end of the century, fewer than 600 students attended the college, and only 465 graduated, an average of around seven a year. It took a group of Virginians almost a century to build a college. Only ten New England towns had grammar schools for any length of time in the seventeenth century. The two grammar schools in New Netherland had only a brief existence, and settlers in the Chesapeake colonies, though they made plans for several such schools, failed through the seventeenth century to build any that lasted. The colonies lacked the resources to maintain the complex of institutions that undergirded formal education in Europe.[33]

A considerable percentage of the colonists could neither write nor read. Conclusions about colonial literacy remain tentative because the usual method of determining literacy rates—counting marks and signatures on wills, deeds, and similar records—can be misleading if it is true, as some scholars argue, that more people could read than could write. But several studies suggest that in the mid-seventeenth century, only slightly more than half the adult males and fewer than half the women in the colonies could sign their names. Colonial Americans admired literacy and learning, however. In New England university graduates were addressed with the honorific designation of "master," and not only the laws passed by the elite but also the numerous parental bequests leaving money and goods for educating their children bespoke a high evaluation of literacy.[34]

The evidence thus far might suggest a sharp distinction between a tiny learned elite, clinging self-consciously to the values of the core cultures, and the illiterate, barely literate, and benighted masses. But that conclusion too is misleading. It is useful to recall the extent to which the learned and the unlearned shared the same assumptions about the world. American colonists, like other Europeans, lived in a world of wonders—an enchanted universe in which the lines between science and magic often blurred. They read nature as a book of signs and symbols revealing the intentions of supernatural beings; meteors, comets, and eclipses were messages from God, requiring obedience rather than simply observation. John Winthrop, Jr., devoted as much time to alchemy—the effort to transmute base metals into gold—as he did to astronomy. The collegiate astronomers who displayed their learning in the almanacs also imparted astrological wisdom and read natural occurrences as clues to the will of God or the intentions of Satan. Even a learned minister like Samuel Danforth in Roxbury appended to his *Astronomic Description of the Late Comet or Blazing Star* (1665) a "brief theological application" arguing that while comets proceeded from natural causes and remained subject to natural laws, they also served as divine portents. Recourse to charms and occult cures appears to have been widespread. Both the learned and the unlearned shared a fascination with accounts of apparitions, portents, astrology, and prodigies.[35]

Most of the people of seventeenth-century America who left traces of their thought for historians to interpret seem to have spent a considerable amount of mental energy in efforts at persuasion. They directed those efforts not simply at other members of an elite but also at larger groups: congregations, investors, freemen, native Americans, even the general public. They might not have influenced listeners and readers as much as they hoped, but their audience consisted mainly of ordinary men and women.

Institutions

The three main institutional settings for the formulation of ideas were commerce, religion, and governance. All the colonies, even those founded partly as religious utopias, advertised their commercial promise, and the literature of commerce included not only promotional treatises but also exploration narratives, discovery accounts, and appeals for support by European sponsors. Religious institutions, ranging from Catholic missions to Puritan churches, accounted for a disproportionate amount of public discourse throughout the century. Conflicts over government generated the next significant body of reflection, not in abstract treatises on political theory but in arguments and distinctions designed to accomplish immediate political ends.

The first outpouring of ideas came from explorers and colonizers who tried to make other Europeans take note of the New World. From New England to New Spain colonists and conquistadors discovered soon enough that patrons and sponsors back home required an array of letters and treatises to promote colonization and shape court policy. Promoters were everywhere, arguing, defining, and describing in an unending effort to influence decisions in Europe: Antonio Espejo urging the Spanish court to entrust to him "the exploration and pacification" of New Mexico; Thomas West, the third Lord De la Warr, writing for the Virginia Company to dissuade skeptical investors from withdrawing "those paiments, which they have subscribed towards the Charge of the Plantation" at Jamestown; Captain John Smith describing commodities and natives ripe for exploitation and trying to convince the council of the Virginia Company that he was the best person to subject "the Savages to our desired obedience."[36]

Between 1492 and 1680 at least 120 explorers and promoters published accounts of North America, and if everything printed had survived, the list would undoubtedly be far longer. The earliest reports of discovery, written in the late fifteenth century, seemed of little interest to European printers, who believed that their customers preferred imaginative geographical books about gold-digging ants and dog-headed tribes or pilgrimage books cataloging holy places and relics. The first accounts were little more than captains' logs. Not until the early sixteenth century did they develop into exploratory narratives designed to appeal to a public demand for reports on exotic lands. Once established, however, they became a means for soliciting financial support and luring colonists.[37]

The next great body of colonial writing came from missionaries, preachers, and religious dissenters. No one knows how many priests and preachers labored in America prior to 1680, but at least 270 ministers, mostly Puritans, preached in New England, and 119 more, mostly clergy comfortable with the rites of the Church of England, worked in Virginia. Maryland provided a place for at least forty-five clerics, most of them Catholic missionaries. The Delaware valley served as home for at least twelve, half of them Swedish Lutherans. A glance at New Netherland and New York produces a list of forty-six Protestants, mostly Dutch Reformed and Presbyterian, and fifteen French Catholic missionaries. At least 142 additional Catholic missionaries, including 116 Jesuits, worked elsewhere in the settlements of New France.

Because records have disappeared, no one knows how many Franciscans, Dominicans, and Jesuits spent their energies in Florida and New Mexico. At least 218 Franciscans labored in Florida. In 1634 around thirty-five of them maintained the forty-four missions there; in 1630 fifty Franciscan priests worked in the twenty-five missions of New Mexico.[38]

The missionaries in the Catholic religious orders wrote and preached with the aim of converting Native Americans to Catholicism and soliciting support from pious Europeans. In either case, their evangelistic aims shaped the public expression of their thought. The *Relations des Jésuites* that fifty-four priests and two Ursuline nuns sent to France between 1632 and 1673 constituted one of the remarkable intellectual achievements of colonial America; they remain a treasury of primitive ethnographic description. But they represented primarily an effort to secure support and contributions for the Jesuit order in New France. Like most other literary productions of the Catholic mission, they were exercises in persuasion.

As the missionaries soon discovered, no one admired persuasive rhetoric more than the Indians whom they hoped to convert. The Jesuits in New France marveled that "there is no place in the world where Rhetoric is more powerful" and that the native Americans whom they encountered were Ciceros in the wilderness. They reported that the Indians chose eloquent leaders and obeyed them solely because of this quality. A chief became "powerful in so far as he is eloquent." In the oral cultures of the native Americans, "eloquence alone" could exert enormous power over behavior. The Narraganset in New England so admired "eloquent" speakers, said Roger Williams, that they "esteeme them Gods."[39]

Most religious persuasion occurred not in missions but in churches. By 1650 American colonists created at least 112 congregations in addition to the mission churches; by 1660 the number grew to at least 154, supplemented by missions and Quaker meetings. In those churches people gathered to hear the most frequent public form of persuasive speech, the sermon. In New England the sermon stood alone as the society's regular weekly means of public communication. With no competing speakers of comparable influence offering alternative messages, the preachers provided, week after week, images and information that permeated large segments of the culture. The clergy of Massachusetts Bay preached a two-hour sermon on the Sabbath morning, a lengthy sermon that afternoon, and another on Thursdays. A single minister, Joshua Moody of Portsmouth, New Hampshire, left behind 4,070 sermon manuscripts when he died. A pious resident of the Bay Colony could have heard more than 8,000 sermons in a lifetime.[40]

Ministers could write theological tomes without immediate hortatory intent. In 1656, for example, Samuel Stone at Hartford completed—but never published—a "Whole Body of Divinity" covering every standard topic in Reformed scholastic theology. But few other ministers attempted such technical works prior to 1680. Most concentrated on sermons and polemical writings.[41]

Not every preacher wrote for publication. Almost all the extant printed seventeenth-century colonial sermons originated in New England, but even there 66 percent of the clergy never published anything; only 5 percent managed to publish ten or more tracts or treatises. The prolific publishers were usually the ministers who held pulpits in or near Boston, the only city in seventeenth-century America that maintained a printing press. They had access to the press, the means to send manuscripts to printers in London, and wealthy congregations to subsidize the printing. When the New England clergy did publish their thoughts, they rarely indulged in highly technical or systematic speculation. They shied away from speculative divinity, with the result that only 8 percent of their published works exceeded 100 pages. Most were shorter pieces designed for polemical or devotional purposes. Sixty-nine percent were sermons. They often explored difficult theological topics, but their intention was to nurture piety and promote ethical behavior. The preacher opened the biblical text, explicated its doctrine, and outlined the reasons supporting the doctrine, but the conclusion consisted always of the "uses," the practical exhortation designed to persuade the faithful or the faithless.[42]

In the backwoods of both Maryland and Massachusetts Bay, a pious but isolated colonist might have gone for years without hearing a single sermon. But sermons were in demand wherever people congregated. A Dutch group protested in 1657 when Dominie Johannes Polhemus offered them no sermon but only a prayer, from which, they protested, "we learn and understand little." Although Catholic missionaries elevated sacramental service over didactic sermons, they did not neglect preaching. Jesuits in Maryland in the 1630s preached sermons only on feast days, but they delivered catechetical lectures to "more advanced [Christians] every Sunday." In the Catholic missions simple sermons became a fixture of missionary strategy. And sermons, Protestant or Catholic, were designed not for speculative flight or aesthetic grandeur but for guiding behavior and altering dispositions.[43]

Colonists who disdained to listen to the preachers sometimes found themselves at odds with the magistrates. In 1619 the first legislative assembly in Virginia required "all persons" to "frequente divine service and sermons both forenoon and afternoon" every "Sabaoth daye," and subsequent assemblies tried to make certain that ministers preached in their parishes every Sunday even though the *Book of Common Prayer* required a sermon only once every quarter. In 1624 Plymouth made church attendance mandatory; in 1635 Massachusetts did the same; New Haven and Connecticut soon followed its example; even the Dutch in New Netherland made sporadic efforts, beginning in 1648, to compel everyone to hear sermons. The laws do not mean that everyone attended church, but they do reveal the conviction of colonial rulers that their societies would work better if everyone were subjected to regular sermonic persuasion.[44]

The third institutional setting for the formulation of ideas was colonial government. A few colonists formulated reasoned treatises on the character of a good ruler. In Boston selected Puritan preachers delivered an election sermon each year to the magistrates and freemen assembled for the annual elections, and those sermons often delved into political theory. But political thought usually found expression in struggles and controversies, with magistrates defending their policies and dissenters arguing against them. Colonists called upon the vocabulary of governance to accomplish concrete political ends. And this usually meant that the language of politics served also as a discourse for persuasion.

The Maryland promoter George Alsop once remarked whimsically that in order to win wives, men in America had to be "good Rhetoricians, and well vers'd in the Art of perswasion." He intended the comment as a joke, but it suggested a larger truth. To win their way in colonial societies, men and women did have to be adept in persuasive skills. Most had neither the leisure nor the resources to pursue intellectual interests for their own sake. Few enjoyed the formal rhetorical training of the schools. But in the academic culture represented by the curriculum at Harvard and in the forms of literary expression produced by unschooled explorers and promoters, the aim to persuade usually established the agenda.[45]

two

_____

Promoters

In 1609 an Englishman named Robert Johnson published a narrative of a conversion. Like most other conversions in seventeenth-century England, it occurred in the midst of a small group exhorting one another about Christian duty, missionary zeal, public good, and the Kingdom of God. The convert, who had suffered doubt, discovered in the group's testimonies "sufficient reasons answering all objections." He found himself compelled, he said, to confess his errors and yield his money and endeavor to "advance the kingdome of God." This conversion, however, took place in no church. It happened at a meeting of adventurers gathered to discuss their "plantation in *Virginia*." The exhorter was no Puritan preacher but an investor in the enterprise. His speech converted a doubter to the cause of colonization, and Johnson, publishing the news, tried to convert other doubters to the same cause.[1]

The hope of eliciting such conversions produced the initial outburst of literary endeavor in America. America's first intellectuals were promoters intent on attracting money and endeavors for the noble cause, zealous for conversions. Yet they discovered that their promotional zeal could cloud the truth—or create the impression that it had been clouded—and they had constantly to convince their readers that truth and persuasion were compatible. In trying to persuade investors and settlers to cast their lots in America, they discovered persistent questions about promises and realities, simplicity and complexity, persuasion and truth.

Promotional writings appeared shortly after the Spanish in 1513 and the French in 1524 began to explore and colonize the eastern coast. Questions about their credibility surfaced in New Spain as early as 1540 and bedeviled later English promoters, who complained frequently that no one believed

18

them. Indeed it was not easy to explain away the failure of Raleigh's 1584 colony on Roanoke Island and the turmoil that beset the Virginia Company throughout almost two decades following the settlement of Virginia in 1607. Promoters of Virginia—as well as of Plymouth (1620), New Amsterdam (1624), Massachusetts Bay (1628), and Maryland (1634)—therefore developed ingenious strategies designed to overcome resistance to promotional persuasion.

Beginnings

The question of credibility first emerged among the people the English most despised: the priests and soldiers of New Spain. It may be said to have surfaced—though the dating is arbitrary—when Juan Ponce de León assured King Charles I of Spain in 1521 that he was settling "the island of Florida" so that his majesty could gain its bounty and the Indians could obtain salvation. His hope that the land contained the "sacred fountain . . . whose waters rejuvenated the aged" anticipated a thousand similar hopes that would shape a literature of promises and optimism. His violent death prefigured a thousand and more similar deaths, prompting the Spanish historian Gonzalo Fernández de Oviedo to expound a recurring theme: "Oh Captains, you who [make] . . . promises that come home to roost on the unfortunate souls who believe you when they hear you. . . . May God forgive you!" But such admonitions hardly sufficed to stifle the flow of promises.[2]

The first great American treatise in the literature of promises resulted from a disaster. In 1527 Alvar Núñez Cabeza de Vaca, a soldier from a wealthy family of gentry in southern Spain, joined the expedition of Pánfilo de Narváez to conquer and colonize the territory between Mexico and Florida. Storms, shipwrecks, and desertions reduced the six hundred colonists and soldiers to four men, who endured eight years of hardship, servitude, and isolation on a journey across the continent from the gulf to western Mexico.

Cabeza de Vaca wrote his *Relation* of the journey to encourage fellow Spaniards "to subdue those countries and bring them to a knowledge of the true faith and true Lord." His experiences left him with mixed judgments about the new world; travel was difficult and dangerous, food hard to find, and the natives warlike, yet he was impressed by what he saw. He grew to admire the Indians, who looked upon him as a healer, and he described their customs with wonder. If the Spanish treated them with kindness, he said, their conversion to Christianity would be "not difficult to accomplish," for he had seen neither sacrifices nor idolatry. The land revealed clear traces of gold and other precious metals, and he knew that it also offered "pearls and great riches," for the Indians had assured him of it.[3]

Compared to what came later, Cabeza de Vaca's *Relation* was a model of restraint. Excited by his accounts, however, the viceroy in Mexico City, Antonio de Mendoza, commissioned Don Francisco Vásquez de Coronado to find the riches and bring them back. An advance party led by the imaginative Franciscan Marcos de Niza assured everyone that the wealth lay within Spanish reach, and his *Relation* of his journey north of Mexico expanded the limits of promotional hyperbole. Fray Marcos believed that he had found the legendary Seven Cities of Cibola, where the temples had walls of gold and the houses had doors of turquoise; he claimed to have seen from afar a city larger than Mexico City, filled with emeralds, turquoise, and vessels of gold and silver.[4]

Marcos's report created both enthusiasm and skepticism. The viceroy sent Melchior Diaz in 1540 to "see if what he might discover conformed to the report of Father Marcos." His report was mixed: Cibola was really there, and the people did have "turquoises in quantity." But some questions remained. They did not have quite as many turquoises "as the father provincial says." Not everything conformed exactly to the friar's report.[5]

Vásquez de Coronado learned the extent of Marcos's exaggerations when he made his own expedition beyond the Rio Grande. Cibola turned out to be "a small, rocky pueblo, all crumpled up." The seven cities were "seven little villages." The soldiers felt devastated: "The curses that some hurled at Fray Marcos were such that God forbid they may befall him." Vásquez offered a sober judgment. "I can assure you," he told the viceroy, "that he has not told the truth in a single thing that he said, but everything is the opposite of what he related."[6]

The disappointment led to some reflection on the elusiveness of truth about America. Writing years after the expedition, a colonist at San Miguel Culiacan, the soldier Pedro de Castañeda, completed a *Narrative of the Expedition to Cibola*. It combined description and promotion with an essay on the difficulty of reporting the truth about either the journey or land. The adventure, he said, offered the writer "plenty of substance with which to test his mind." Misleading, exaggerated reports had created confusion about the geography, the dress and customs of the natives, and even the strange animals. This was because people often magnified or belittled second-hand reports. But the truth was hard to convey. Even when "presented truthfully," the expedition was "so marvelous as to seem incredible." He could speak the truth plainly: "I have seen with my own eyes." Yet his truth would remain inadequate, he said, for he was a man of limited understanding; he had no polished style; he was no writer; he was no rhetorician.[7]

More than one writer of polished style, however, suggested that credibility also required some honesty about the suffering and harshness in the clash of Spanish and American cultures. In 1539 Hernando de Soto set out to conquer and rule the territory between Mexico and Florida. After landing on the western shore of Florida, he moved inland in a journey that ended for him three years later on the banks of the Mississippi River, where he died without gold or dominion. The chief narrator of the journey, an unnamed Portuguese "Gentleman of Elvas," possibly Alvaro Fernandez, published in 1557 his *Narrative of the Expedition of Hernando de Soto.* His printer avouched his confidence in its accuracy: "What he has written I undoubtingly credit: he tells no tales, nor speaks of fabulous things."[8]

Certainly he told few enticing tales. He interpreted de Soto's journey as an episode of vicissitude and toil. Writing from memory years after the expedition, he recalled the heroism but also the gloom and death of the futile quest for silver and gold. He told of Indian slaves in Cuba who "destroyed themselves because of the hard usage they receive from the Christians in the mines." He remembered the Indians of Florida, so quick that they could avoid the flight of an arrow and fall upon the Spanish in a second. His America was a place of privation and hunger, treachery and enslavement. It was also a land of good fields, fruits in abundance, and gold. To the printer, the ambiguity of the vision lent credibility to the report, but the somber tale also helped discourage further exploration of the region.[9]

In the long run, grim reports had no chance against the tales of wealth and wonders. In 1581 Father Augustín Rodríguez led an expedition up the Rio Grande. The resulting "Brief and True Account of the Exploration of New Mexico" announced "eleven mine prospects, all having great veins of silver." In 1582 Antonio de Espejo led a rescue mission into the same provinces. His subsequent narrative reported "large settlements, very fertile lands, silver mines, gold." The report of Sebastián Vizcaino's exploration of the Gulf of California in 1602, written by Antonio de la Ascensión, told of a region rich in pearls, silver, and gold and filled with natives eager for conversion.[10]

Father Francisco Escobar departed in 1605 on still another expedition to California. The Indians told him of wealthy nations bedecked with gold ornaments, and they noted other marvels as well: of people with ears so large that four or five persons could stand under them; of a nation consisting of people with only one foot; and of still another whose people slept underwater. He entertained some doubts but could not ignore the possibility that the tales might be true: "It seemed to be wrong in not telling of things which, if discovered, would, I believe, redound to the glory of God and the service of the king our Lord." God was able to create marvels, and a multitude of witnesses had corroborated the reports so they had to have some basis. With fewer than a hundred men, he added, the Spanish could verify the reports of precious metals. Escobar's America had little in common with that of the Gentleman of Elvas.[11]

Such conflicting depictions intensified the problem of credibility, and the Spanish narratives returned to the issue repeatedly. Antonio de Espejo appended to his account a customary assurance: "Everything narrated herein I saw with my own eyes, and is true, for I was present at everything." To other Spanish writers, a simple assurance was insufficient. Father Escobar included more elaborate testimonies. He appeared before the viceroy and swore "*in verbo sacerdotis*, placing his hand on his breast, that what he has recorded in this memorial is the truth." All the soldiers with him "swore in the name of God, holy Mary, and by the sign of the cross in due and legal manner and promised to tell the truth."[12]

Juan de Oñate, the governor and captain-general of New Mexico, went to similar lengths to bolster his credibility. When he prepared a narrative of a journey in 1601, he let it be known that he had entrusted the writing to "a person of much fidelity and trustworthiness." He had the clergy testify under oath that the narration was true and asked all the captains and soldiers to swear publicly to its truthfulness. The reader of Oñate's narrative could rest assured, therefore, that "it contains no exaggerations, as everything occurred as stated therein."[13]

By no means did the Spanish have a monopoly on optimism and exaggeration. The Frenchman Jacques Cartier sailed in 1534 to New France, and soon he and King Francis I were scheming together about how to find the riches in a city called Saguenay. The narratives of his voyages contained all the familiar intimations of gold, silver, and natural abundance. Jean Ribault returned in 1562 from "Terra Florida"—Port Royal Island off South Carolina—reporting that the country was "the fairest, frutefullest, and pleasantest of all the worlde" and writing that the legendary Cibola was only twenty days distant from the French settlement. René de Laudonniére, commander of a French colony in Florida, published narratives telling of "a very faire city" where the inhabitants "made none account of gold, or silver, nor of pearles, seeing they had thereof in abundance."[14]

The modest Samuel de Champlain, whose narratives of his voyages to New France between 1604 and 1620 stand out for sobriety and realism, had little to say about silver and gold, and he was even restrained when he wrote about his cherished plans for converting the Indians to Catholicism. But rare indeed was the explorer who could resist the temptation of exaggerated promises.[15]

So it went, well into the seventeenth century: the Kingdom of Copola, filled with gold, or the Kingdom of Teguayo, rich with wealth, or some similar, unreachable, unimaginable kingdom beckoned always from afar. Or the Indians seemed always ripe for conversion. The explorers, conquerors, and missionaries needed invariably to persuade someone, king or governor, patron or investor, to make possible one final search or one more evangelistic foray. Increasingly they explored the boundaries of persuasion and truth and tested the limits of a literature of promises.

Virginia and Beyond

The English knew the French and Spanish stories. When English propagandists began in the mid-sixteenth century to advertise the benefits of exploration, they translated the writings of foreign authors and marveled at the accounts of "fayre and frutefull regions, hygh mountaynes, and fayre rivers, with abundance of golde." They emphasized the promises and downplayed the hardships in the Spanish and French accounts. The narrative of Laudon-niére's voyages to Florida became, according to the translator, a revelation of "the great riches and fruitefulnes of the countrey." Even the somber narrative of de Soto's journey, translated into English as *Virginia Richly Valued*, became an account of "the riches and fertilitie of those parts" and their "divers excellent and rich Mynes, of Golde, Silver, and other Mettals."[16]

Elizabethan adventurers embarked with hopes of finding the riches. Thomas Stukeley sailed for Florida in 1563 after hearing Ribault's stories about Cibola; Sir Humphrey Gilbert, in search of a northwest passage to China, kept an eye open for the gold that French writers had located in legendary Indian cities; Sir Walter Raleigh believed Spanish legends about a fabulous golden city of El Dorado and hoped to find it in Guiana. English gentlemen explorers accepted the promises at face value.[17]

The gold proved elusive, but discovery narratives resulting from the English voyages escalated the promises. Elizabethan adventurers continued to babble about gold and conquest. Raleigh returned from Guiana writing about "that great and Golden Citie, which the Spanyards call El Dorado," and swearing that he told nothing but the truth because "the way of deceipt, is not the way of honor or good opinion." A few English visionaries, like Richard Hakluyt, insisted that the bounty of exploration far exceeded the narrow aims of the gold hunters. To Hakluyt America also meant colonies, imperial power, a victory over Spain, a northwest passage to China, an array of commodities, a market for wool, conversion of the Indians, a home for the poor and idle, a dumping ground for criminals, an excuse for enlarging the navy, riches for fishing captains, and game for hunters. But the more loudly they announced the benefits of colonial enterprise, the more difficulty they had convincing people they were telling the truth.[18]

The wiser explorers recognized that part of the problem of credibility was the elusiveness of the truth about the New World. When the mathematician Thomas Hariot returned from a year-long sojourn on Roanoke Island and published in 1588 *A Briefe and True Report of the New Found Land of Virginia*, he described the abundance of commodities: grass silk and worm silk, flax and hemp, sassafras and wine, copper and pearl. The abundance overflowed the boundaries of English diction, but because Hariot had learned, probably before the voyage, to speak Algonkian, he could allure the English with descriptions of a culinary bounty that exceeded their imaginative and linguistic capacities: pagatowr and okindgir, wickonzowr and macocquer, Openauk and Okeepenauk. And he also described, with as much sympathetic insight as an Elizabethan Englishman could muster, how the native Roanokes worked and worshipped, fought and played, lived and died.[19]

Later historians have seen Hariot's tract as "almost the only original English contribution to the advance of natural history." A mathematician whose taste for exploration came partly from his association with Hakluyt at Oxford, Hariot entered Raleigh's household around 1582 to teach mathematics to navigators. Raleigh sent him to America with instructions to provide navigational guidance, map the new territories, and study the native Indians. Traveling with the artist John White, he spent a year recording the wonders of American natural history and Algonkian culture. Theodor de Bry in Frankfort would in 1590 reissue Hariot's text, accompanied by engravings made from White's watercolors, in a magnificent folio that, more than any other book, introduced America to Europe.[20]

Whatever its merits as a treatise in natural history, Hariot's *Briefe and True Report*, the first book by a resident of America written in English about the New World, was chiefly a promotional treatise to persuade English readers— "you which are and shall bee the planters and inhabitants" of Raleigh's colony—to ignore the "divers and variable reports" of critics and skeptics. It was an effort to counter "slaunderous and shamefull speeches bruited abroode" by disgruntled colonists and to persuade "adventurers, favourers, & welwillers" not to withdraw support.[21]

The critics, Hariot wrote, slandered the country without understanding it, having never ventured beyond the island settlement or cast their ambitions beyond the pursuit of gold. They were delicate souls, products "of a nice bringing up, only in cities or townes," unable to adjust to a land where bolder spirits would flourish. With some effort they could have seen a different America. The farther inland we went, Hariot wrote, "we found the soyle to be fatter; the trees greater and to grow thinner; the grounde more firme and deeper mould." To tell the truth about America, he said, one had to venture into its frontiers. He failed, however, to mention the hardships of those frontiers; he glimpsed the complexity, but his report remained within the limits of promotional simplicity.[22]

Raleigh's colony on Roanoke Island—"the goodliest and most pleasing territorie of the world"—disappeared. But its demise failed to temper the propensity for promotional exaggeration. When the Anglican rector John Brereton returned from a 1602 voyage to what would later be called New England and published *A Brief and True Relation of the Discoverie of the North Part of Virginia*, he praised the climate and the commodities, but his sponsors, dissatisfied with straightforward description, appended to the second edition misleading lists of commodities and minerals drawn from the older accounts by Laudonniére and the Gentleman of Elvas. And when James Rosier returned from his 1605 voyage with George Waymouth to the same region, he included in his *True Relation of the Most Prosperous Voyage* expansive lists of commodities that would yield profit, along with a description that serves as a metaphor of the whole promotional effort. They discovered, he said, a river that "did so ravish us all with variety of pleasantnesse, as we could not tell what to commend, but only admired. . . . For the further we went, the more pleasing it was to every man, alluring us still with expectation of better."[23]

The promoters of Virginia therefore, inherited the journalistic conventions—and problems—of a well-established literature of promises. Even before the first ships set sail, London playwrights had begun to make jokes about the hyperbole. Captain Seagull, a character in a 1605 play called *Eastward Ho*, exclaimed that "golde is more plentiful there than copper is with us": "Why, man, all their dripping pans and their chamberpotts are pure gold." Undeterred by sarcasm, the Virginia colonists hastened to confirm the enthusiasm. The council in Virginia sent back a report about the fruitful soil and the "gold showing mountaines." One impressionable colonist confided that the soil, sweet and rich, was "more fertill than can be wel exprest." And though the native Americans had a reputation for treachery, he added, the English had found them loving.[24]

The rejoicing was premature. The colony collapsed into chaos—the gentlemen refusing to work, the commoners refusing to obey, the leaders quarreling among themselves, and the Indians disdaining to meet English expectations. George Perry saw the food run out and the colonists begin to die, and he concluded that "there were never Englishmen left in a forreigne Countrey in such miserie as wee were in this new discovered Virginia." He said that the whole colony would have died had not the Indians—the "mortall enemies" of the English—provided bread, corn, fish, and meat.[25]

Such was the setting in which Captain John Smith wrote his first account of America, a book that began a continuing debate about the truthfulness of Smith's own efforts at persuasion. His enemies in Virginia charged that he was a liar who spread malicious rumors; his critics among later historians charged that he was a liar who peddled harmless exaggerations. It was hard to know what to make of the man who told the tales. He had set out for Hungary to fight the Turks. Religious zealots threw him overboard, but he swam to safety. The ship that rescued him fell into battle with Venetians, but he fought his way out of danger. Arriving in Hungary, he served nobly in three armies of Emperor Rudolph II and beheaded three Turks in single combat but ended up as a slave, an iron ring around his neck. All agreed that escape was impossible, but he escaped, rode his owner's horse to Russia, and made his way back to England, partly by selling his services to a pirate off the coast of Africa. He would one day recount the adventures in a book called *True Travels*. The recent consensus seems to be that most of what he wrote in the book was indeed true.[26]

Boosters in the Virginia Company would doubtless have preferred slightly less truth from Smith. His *True Relation of Such Occurences and Accidents of Noate, as Hath Hapned in Virginia* reached the English public in 1608 as a promotional treatise published at the behest of Virginia's "well willers." But the editor felt obliged to excise some "private" sections of the manuscript and to insert an introduction assuring the reader that "the Country is excellent and pleasant" and its troubles past. Smith included some standard promotional paragraphs. He avowed himself eager to see the English "enjoy a Country, not onely exceeding pleasant for habitation, but also very profitable for commerce in generall." Yet he also told about the disorder and discontent, complained about colonists who would "rather starve and rot with idleness" than work, and wrote candidly about conflicts with the Indians.[27]

He said nothing about converting Indians to Christianity, so his editor used the introduction to correct the omission. The real end of colonization in Virginia, he wrote, was "the erecting of true religion among Infidells, to the overthrow of superstition and idolatrie, to the winning of many thousands of wandring sheepe, unto Christs fold." Such a call for conversion was not new, but the campaign to promote Virginia in 1609 resulted in an unprecedented outpouring of missionary appeals. The company mobilized the preachers of London to convince critics and potential investors that the English sailed to Virginia not to gain private ends but to "advance the kingdome of God." The preachers outlined a host of arguments for colonization, all subsumed, however, under the theme of evangelistic zeal.[28]

When Smith and several other colonists published in 1612 their *Map of Virginia*, he too claimed that the English were intent most of all on bringing "poore infidels to the true knowledge of God and his holy Gospell." On one level, the book was yet another promotion, written to answer "bad natures" who would "not sticke to slander the countrey." They had lied, and their lies—"the clamor and ignorance of false informers"—had led to some of the disasters that befell the colony. Smith and his allies would now present the truth.[29]

They almost did. As a promotional treatise, the *Map of Virginia* was unusually careful and candid, countering the deceptive propaganda the company was issuing. It is still read for its ethnological information on the Indians of Tidewater Virginia; it displayed acute powers of observation; and the map itself was a remarkable accomplishment. Smith could lapse into the old clichés: "The mildnesses of the aire, the fertilitie of the soile, and the situation of the rivers are so propitious to the nature and use of man as no place is so convenient for pleasure, profit, and mans sustenance." But the book also acknowledged that Virginia seemed to all the world a miserable "defailement," and it confessed that many of the problems came from bungling and greed: "There was not talke, no hope, nor worke, but dig gold, wash gold, refine gold, load gold."[30]

The book came close to transcending the genre of promotional literature, but it finally failed, for having turned away from a simplistic promotion of the colony, it turned to a simplistic promotion of Smith as the man who could save the colony. The message was clear: Smith had overcome scoundrels; Smith had made people work; Smith had "lost but 7 or 8 men: yet subjected the Savages to our desired obedience." The truth about Virginia turned out, once again, to be a simple proposition.[31]

It was not as simple as the truth about New England. In 1614 Smith sailed to the northern part of Virginia, which he renamed "New England," a region that corresponds to the area known as New England today. His *Description of New England* (1616) resumed promotion in the grand style as a secular sermon, directed to the idle sons of English nobles and the idle poor of English cities. To the nobles the region offered "imployments for gentlemen," from fowling and fishing to hunting and hawking, and to the laboring poor it offered a chance to grow rich, free of landlords and lawyers. To the pious it offered the grandest opportunity of all: "to shewe our faith by our workes; in converting those poor salvages, to the knowledge of God, seeing what paines the *Spanyards* take to bring them to their adulterated faith."[32]

Smith could never get the Spaniards off his mind. They had marched forth with "incomparable honour and constant resolution," their achievements "beyond beleefe." The problem now was that the English no longer believed tales of heroism and adventure that were beyond belief. The rhetoric of the promoters fell on deaf ears and scornful hearts: we "ignorantly beleeve nothing." Perhaps for that reason Smith made no outlandish claims about gold and silver in his New England. The wealth of New England lay in the oceans; fishing would be the way to riches. It would be an easy way, inasmuch as a man in New England could work only three days a week and earn more than he could spend. But Smith purveyed no incredible stories about golden cities, for as he himself said, no one believed them anymore.[33]

He never returned to America. His ship foundered the first time he tried, pirates stopped him on the second try, and financial backers ignored him thereafter. He also failed to gain the credibility he wanted. When he published his *New Englands Trials* in 1620, he complained in his dedicatory epistle to Prince Charles that "scarce any would beleeve mee." His new book was a panegyric on behalf of fishing, and Smith had no hesitation in comparing the fishing fields of New England to the gold mines of El Dorado: "Let not the meannesse of the word *Fish* distaste you, for it will afford as good gold as the mines of *Guiana* or *Tumbatu*, with lesse hazard and charge, and more certaintie and facilitie; and so I humbly rest." But by 1620 loose comparisons of fish and gold attracted little assent.[34]

Smith never gained the backing to found his colony. Instead of building a city in the New World, he wrote another book in the old. His *Generall Historie of Virginia, New England, & The Summer Isles*, printed in London in 1624, continued to promote colonization. It was a compilation of his earlier writings, supplemented by other narratives and stitched together with editorial comments. Because he had "lived in the midst of those parts," he said, he had been able to collect "the substantiall truth" from his collection of sources. But once again he worried too much about making the case for himself.

27

Smith knew as much about America as anyone else, but the demands of his ego made it hard for him to tell the story in all its complexity.[35]

Smith's departure from Virginia in 1609 had not stopped the colonists from promoting their own causes. The hapless Edward Maria Wingfield wrote but never published a "Discourse of Virginia" denying that he had gorged on roasted chickens and sequestered brandy during the starving time. In his *Newes from Virginia* Richard Rich sought credibility through poetry: "I am a Soldier, blunt and plaine, and so is the phrase of my news: and I protest it is true." In 1613 the Anglican priest Alexander Whitaker harkened back to an earlier strategy of promoting conversions among the Indians; his *Good Newes from Virginia* (1613) urged the English to "let the miserable condition of those naked slaves of the divell move you to compassion toward them." Compared to what other Virginians were writing, in other words, Smith's promotions seemed both realistic and candid.[36]

"Those naked slaves of the devil" proved to be a problem for both colonists and promoters, however. In Virginia the Powhatans became increasingly angry about English rapacity. In England critics said openly that the English had no legal right to the land and no moral right to injure the Indians. William Strachey, the secretary and lieutenant governor of the colony, therefore decided to counter such "ignorance and slander" by offering "a true narration or historie of the countrie." Because his scenes of Virginia would be "scaenes of truith," they would "suffice to begett a settled opinion of goodnes, and of the right of this busines, in any who hath heretofore doubted."[37]

Strachey's *Historie of Travaile into Virginia Britannia* traced the history of exploration in the region and described its geography and native people. He hoped that readers would come away convinced that the English sailed to Virginia "principally to endeavour the conversion of the natives to the knowledge and worship of the true God, and the world's redeemer, Christ Jesus." His scenes of truth would demonstrate that Spain had no title to Virginia and that the English took no land from Indians; we "prepare and breake up newe groundes, and thereby open unto them likewise a newe waye of thrift or husbandry." How could it injure them, he asked, to offer them trade and Christianity?[38]

Strachey incorporated large chunks of Smith's *Map of Virginia*, possibly not knowing that Smith was the author. His account, however, marked no improvement over Smith's, for although Strachey refrained from self-promotion, he presented such a simplistic account of English motives that his history remained, despite its useful descriptions of Indian culture, within the limits of promotional innocence. In any case he could stir up little interest. No one would help him publish it, and while he waited for patronage, Smith's book appeared in print. Strachey's scenes of truth went largely unread, except in a small number of manuscript copies presented to Francis Bacon and other notables.[39]

When Ralph Hamor, a member of the governing council in Virginia, decided to try still another promotional treatise in 1615, he complained in advance that he expected few readers to believe him or support his cause. "Incredulity of every thing" had become so common that people would believe nothing "save what their eies tell them to be true." Perversity had become so deep-seated that they refused to pursue honorable enterprises. Yet he still hoped to move his reader "to become a hasty and devoted furtherer of an action so noble" as Virginia.[40]

Hamor argued that the colony now thrived under the firm hands of Sir Thomas Gates and Thomas Dale, that the colonists still sought chiefly "the glory of God in the conversion of those Infidels, and the honour of our King and country," and that after five years of conflict, the Indians had become peaceful, "even that subtill old revengeful Powhatan." Pocahontas, despite her "rude education, [and] manners barbarous," made a good wife for John Rolfe, and her father had told Hamor that he had no fight left: "I am now olde, and would gladly end my daies in peace. . . . My country is large enough. I will remove my selfe farther from you." To Hamor the conversation offered proof that peace was assured. Dale, moreover, had abolished the rule that colonists devote their labor to a common store. He had allotted each man "three English acres of cleere Corne ground," and everyone had learned how to cure tobacco. Virginia had become altogether congenial.[41]

If any Englishmen read Hamor's treatise and rushed to Virginia, they learned some hard truths about promotional treatises. Between 1614 and 1620 some three thousand to four thousand Virginians died. The company in England, under Edwin Sandys, crammed colonists aboard ships with inadequate stores; the Virginians, under Governor George Yeardley, planted tobacco instead of corn. Just when the propagandists stopped making extravagant promises, the colony boomed, bringing men—and a few women—on the prowl for a fast killing, and they had no time for drab crops of food. They planted tobacco in the streets, exploited servants, and scrambled over each other. Then the Indians rebelled; during one month in 1622 they killed over three hundred colonists. So much for the promises in Hamor's true discourse.[42] King James decided that the company had irreparably bungled, and Virginia became a royal colony. The promoters fell silent.

Strategies of Credibility

No one, it seemed, would believe Virginia promoters. William Bullock, an Englishman, bemoaned in 1649 the "slight esteem this place hath amongst the generality of the people." William Berkeley, a Virginian, complained that after 1622 "the danger and scarcity of the Inhabitants was so famed thorough England, that none but such as were forced could be induced to plant or defend the place." In 1651 a promoter named Edward Bland published *The Discovery of New Brittaine,* trying to persuade able-bodied men to settle below the James River. He talked about advancing God's glory by converting Indians; he depicted a glorious extension of the English commonwealth; he described the "rich, red, fat, marle Land"; and he even observed that the region stood in the latitude in which Raleigh placed the garden of Eden. But he failed to attract settlers.[43]

By no means did the debacle in Virginia end the promises. Throughout the half-century following the Indian uprising of 1622, promoters adopted a variety of strategies to persuade their readers to emigrate—and convince them they were telling the truth. Each new batch of treatises focused attention anew on the problem of credibility. By the 1620s, as John Smith recognized, simplistic accounts of gold no longer sufficed. The promoters needed to become more complex and subtle. But too much complexity, too ambiguous a vision, could dissuade the settlers and investors whom they hoped to reach. Promotion had to be simple without being simpleminded.

One strategy was for promoters to advertise their own caution and sometimes even to hazard critical judgments. When the Jesuit Andrew White sent promotional letters from Maryland in 1634, he appended the customary signatures of colonists attesting to the truth of his account, but he also adopted a tone of reserve: "We have been upon it but one month," he said, "and therefore can make no large relation of it." In 1649 a series of letters from Virginia became the basis for still another account of that colony's "health, peace, and plenty." Its opening lines had a familiar ring. "Let no man," the author wrote, "doubt the truth of it," for many in England could "beare witnesse" to its truthfulness. This *Perfect Description of Virginia* did have a more credible tone than the earlier tracts. It promised a fruitful country, hinted at a river passageway to China, and claimed, with brutal self-satisfaction, that the English no longer worried about Indians, who had been "driven far away," their towns and houses ruined and "their clear grounds possessed by the English to sow wheat in." But the writer also admitted that tobacco had crowded out every other crop and that Virginians lived for the moment: "Men have had no heart to Plant for Posterity, but every man for the present, plantest tobacco to get a livelyhood by it."[44]

A similar reserve permeated John Hammond's *Leah and Rachel,* which likened Virginia and Maryland to the two wives of the biblical Jacob. Hammond knew what it was like to have people doubt his word. A shadowy figure who lived in Virginia twenty-one years, he had won election to the House of Burgesses only to have his fellow burgesses declare that his scandalous reputation rendered him unfit. Embarrassed by their rebuff, he bought a plantation in Maryland, where he farmed and practiced law. After Protestants overthrew Lord Baltimore's government, Hammond fled to England, where in 1656 he wrote his treatise to the poor and dispossessed.[45]

He assured them that his was a different kind of promotion. He said he would not "over extoll the places, as if they were rather Paradises, than earthly habitations; but truly let ye know . . . how the people there live." Virginia was not a utopia, but it was no longer "an unhealthy place, a nest of Rogues, whores, desolute and rooking persons; a place of intolerable labour, bad usage and hard Diet, &c." The planters there relied too much on tobacco, but the colony was pleasant and profitable, and anyone who chose to beg and steal in England when they could flourish in Virginia suffered from stupidity. Hammond believed that a "blunt" relation, giving the "true state" of the colony, could overcome the "infamous lyars" who slandered Virginia. "If I should deviate from the truth," he added, "I have at this present carping enemies in London enough" to expose the deviation.[46]

Francis Higginson in New England proclaimed himself willing to present both the good and the bad. He was a Puritan minister who in 1630 assured the readers of his *New-Englands Plantation* that his clerical vocation confirmed his veracity: "It becommeth not a Preacher of Truth to be a Writer of Falshod in any degree." But his primary strategy—apart from insisting that he reported "nothing of *New-England* but what I have partly seene with mine owne Eyes, and partly heard and inquired from the mouths of verie honest and religious persons"—was to announce, even in the subtitle of his tract, that he intended to reveal both "the Commodities and the Discommodities of that Country."[47]

It turned out that the commodities were a "wonderment." They included fertile soil, fresh air that could heal illnesses, springs and rivers flowing into an ocean filled with fish, and plentiful timber. The discommodities seemed limited to mosquitoes in summer, snow in winter, snakes in their season, and a paucity of settlers.

Despite Higginson's resolve to admit the difficulties, at least one of his readers charged later that the honest Puritan minister had not been sufficiently forthcoming about discommodities. Thomas Dudley, the deputy governor of the Bay Colony, in his own sober promotional letter of 1631, complained about publicists who had indulged in "too large commendations of the country and the commodities thereof." He resolved to be "open and plain" so that others would not "fall short of their expectations when they come hither" by trusting promoters who "wrote somewhat hyperbolically of many things here."[48]

He was not alone in his discontent. One colonist wrote back home in 1631 that "the cuntry is not so [good] as we did expect it." Another found himself in trouble with the magistrates for writing an "ill report" to correct earlier accounts that "hadd made larger reports into England of the country than I had found to be true." Still another complained in 1637 that reports of rich soil had reflected "affection, not judgment." and a few letter writers took pains to refute the promotional rhetoric. "The air of the country," wrote one

New Englander, "is sharp, the rocks many, the trees innumerable, the grass little, the winter cold, the summer hot, the gnats in summer biting, the wolves at midnight howling." The letter conceded that New England had some religious virtues: "Look upon it, as it hath the means of grace, and, if you please, you may call it a Canaan." But to believe the promoters, it implied, was to court disappointment.[49]

Dudley tried a different kind of promotion. He acknowledged, even emphasized, the difficulties—the sickness and mortality. New England was no place for worldly entrepreneurs. The colony's chief commodity was, rather, its piety. But colonists who came for spiritual ends, he said, could find in America "what [might] well content" them, including ample ground to plant. Dudley adopted Higginson's strategy of revealing both the good and the bad; he simply redefined the commodities and discommodities.[50]

Some promoters insisted that they were plain and simple people and that their rude manner of writing was witness to their honesty. Higginson's editor in England noted the absence of "frothy bumbasting words" in *New-Englands Plantation*. Edward Winslow, writing his *Good Newes from New England*, drew attention to his plainness, and Robert Cushman, introducing narratives that Winslow and William Bradford sent from Plymouth, contended that their "plaine and rude manner" should convince readers to "doubt nothing of the truth thereof." John Hammond argued that his awkward prose conveyed the truth far better than did elegant phrases; since "truth knows little of eloquence," the absence of eloquence signaled the presence of truth. Even in a culture that extolled rhetoric, too much of it could arouse suspicion.[51]

The main strategy remained the appeal to "experimental" authority. To be an eyewitness, or to convey the testimony of eyewitnesses, entailed an immediate claim on belief, which the promoters pushed for all it was worth. Thomas Morton in New England wrote his *New English Canaan*, he said, from "mine owne observation." Edward Winslow promised that he conveyed "the truth of things as nere as I could experimentally take knowledge of" them. William Wood's *New England's Prospect* offered an "experimentall description" of the land. George Alsop in Maryland explained that he wrote "from an experimental knowledge of the Country, and not from any imaginary supposition." No globe, he added, could substitute for "the ocular and experimental view of a Countrey."[52]

For Alsop, however, the matter of credibility finally became a joke. In his *Character of the Province of Maryland* (1666), he assured his readers that if he were found to be exaggerating, he would never write again. But if he had written anything "wilde or confused," he should be pardoned: "I am so my self, and the world, as far as I can perceive, is not much out of the same trim." If brought before the bar of common law, he would plead *non compos mentis*. Having served four years as a servant in Maryland, however, Alsop felt sure, he said, that the colony provided an ideal home for those whom "Providence hath ordained to live as Servants," and he tried to convince

England's providential servants to ignore scandalous reports that in Maryland they would be "sold in open Market for Slaves." To the poor and dispossessed, Maryland offered a new chance: "Dwell here, live plentifully, and be rich." He had been there, so he could be believed even if he was a little crazy.[53]

William Wood acknowledged, however, that even "experimental" authority elicited skepticism. He observed the "unjust aspersion" often laid on travelers: "They may lie by authority because none can control them." He knew of no solution, tending rather to believe that no one could convince the "home-bred dormouse" who comprehended "not either the rarity or possibility of those things he sees not." The promoter had to give up on "thick-witted readers" and try only to reach "more credulous, ingenious, and less censorious countrymen," who would believe him when he vowed that "my conscience is to me a thousand witnesses that what I speak is the very truth."[54]

Alsop could laugh about the stigma attached to promotional writings, and Wood could treat it with resignation, but John Josselyn, writing in the 1670s, could not hide his frustration. After two voyages and eight years of residence in New England, he wrote two treatises to display the natural "rarities" of the country. They constituted "the most complete natural history of New England produced during the Old Colonial Era," but they were nonetheless promotional treatises, and Josselyn complained about the reception he anticipated from readers. Trained as a physician, he attended to the therapeutic properties of New England's wildlife, but he knew no cure for the skepticism of the "stagnant stinking spirits" who would scoff at his book. He had to contend with critics marked by both "ignorance and want of discretion," and after writing almost 200 pages, he betrayed the frustration: "Methinks I hear my sceptick Readers muttering out of their scuttle mouths. . . . Oh I see the pad, you never heard nor saw the like, therefore you do not believe me; well Sirs, I will not straine your belief any further."[55]

Josselyn's skeptical readers had some reason for incredulity. He provided a copious listing of plants and wildlife, but his claims for their curative properties often stretched belief, and he could not resist repeating wondrous tales he had heard from the Indians. For all their descriptive complexity, Josselyn's treatises betrayed the promoter's inclination to simplify, to aim for assent by skipping lightly over the ambiguities.

The promoters might acknowledge difficulties, but the genre almost demanded hasty reassurances that solutions waited around the next corner. Three subjects permeated the colonial promotional writings—nature, the Indians, and colonial society—and each aroused the urge to oversimplify. It seemed hardly fitting to linger over the ambiguities if the intention was to persuade. The problem, as some colonists pointed out, was that the simplicity sometimes encouraged simpleminded actions.

In their depiction of the landscape the promoters could be exultant, as when Adriaen van der Donck, writing his *Description of the New Netherlands* (1655), insisted that he was "incompetent to describe the beauties, the grand and sublime works, wherewith Providence has diversified this land"; or Francis Higginson, recalling his arrival in New England, depicted "every island" as "full of gay woods and high trees"; or Thomas Morton described an American landscape that was "Natures Masterpeece."[56]

They could be soberly restrained, as when Andrew White described Maryland as "a plaine ground, growne over with trees and undershrubs without passage, except where the planters have cleared"; or encyclopedic, as when William Wood and John Josselyn sent back long lists of American birds, beasts, fish, serpents, insects, plants, herbs, trees, stones, and minerals; or picturesque, as when John Smith described Virginia's "pleasant plaine hils and fertile valleyes, one prettily crossing an other, and watered so conveniently with their sweet brookes and christall springs, as if art itself had devised them."[57]

Nature could serve as a vast repository of types and symbols pointing to truths beyond themselves. It could recall a golden age of virtue and innocence; it could symbolize, in its violence, the wrathful scourging of a medieval God; it could be valued as a clue to the divine will. Alsop described the plants of Maryland as "Emblems or Hieroglyphicks of our Adamitical or Primitive situation"; Higginson saw the ocean overflowing with "wonderful workes of Almighty God," the contrary winds signifying God's wrath and the calm seas signifying divine mercy.[58]

As a group the promotional writers drew a complex landscape, but every depiction had one underlying thesis: nature in America was tractable, manageable, useful. The doctrine of utility prevailed over every other; the promotional treatises almost always carried the statement or implication of useful plenitude. Daniel Denton, whose *Brief Description of New York* (1670) promised a "true Relation" and gently chided earlier exaggerated promotional accounts, insisted that New Yorkers never heard "the least complaint for want": "If there be any terrestrial Canaan, 'tis surely here, where the Land floweth with milk and honey."[59] He repeated a theme that had permeated the promotional literature for over half a century.

No one became ill in America, some of the treatises implied. Higginson swore that he had been sickly in England but that America had brought him perfect health. American air was itself medicinal for "all such as are a Cold, Melancholy, Flegmatick, Rheumatick temper of Body." Other promoters agreed; no one suffered from colds in New England; many in New York went twenty years without being sick; the "maine blessing of God" in America was that "few or none doe here fal sicke." Josselyn acknowledged that diseases in America were like diseases in England, but even he pointed out that American game and plants contained unusual healing powers.[60]

The English were remarkably confident of their ability to exploit the landscape, even to re-form it. The point of their treatises was not that the natural abundance made labor unnecessary but that nature in America would prove to be unusually responsive to improvement. Even a child, said Higginson, could make the soil yield its treasure. By improving the land, the colonists would confirm their right to possess it; they would also transform it. English colonists believed that by felling trees and plowing fields, they could alter even the climate. New England was cold, but the English could soon make it warm.[61]

The abundance was real, as was the land's promise, but a disillusioned John Smith, writing in 1631, revealed why the promotion was dangerously simplistic: America abounded in deer, fish, and fowl, he said, but colonists starved because they were "too unskillful to catch them." Edward Winslow's *Good Newes from New England*, written in 1624 after English settlers had starved in Plymouth, posed a troubling question: "If the country abound with fish and fowl in such measure as is reported, how could men undergo such measure of hardness, except through their own negligence?" The oceans overflowed with fish, but the settlers lacked "fit and strong seines and other netting"; they had "neither tackling nor hawsers" for their boats. Natural abundance did not necessarily bring comfort, for colonies often lacked the means to exploit nature. But few promoters were as candid as Winslow. Most gave a simpler account of America's natural bounty.[62]

They gave an equally simple account of America's native peoples. True, they sent back conflicting depictions of the Indians. Someone who read all the reports would have learned that all Indians were "noble and Heroick" and all Indians were crafty and cowardly; that Indians shared their food with Europeans and that Indians used Europeans as food. They loved children inordinately; they sacrificed children. They were a large and healthy people who lived to a great age; they were a sickly people who perished in plagues that hardly affected Europeans. They were people of wit, quick of apprehension; they were "stupid as garden poles." They acknowledged "a God who is the giver of all good things"; they acknowledged only the devil. They eagerly heard the Christian gospel and sought "fit men to instruct the inhabitants in saving doctrine"; they responded to the gospel by shaking their heads "as if it were a silly fable."[63]

The depictions differed partly because the promoters met different Indians. They also differed because promoters followed fashion. Many of the earliest promotional narratives repeated Spanish reports and concluded that the Indians could not be trusted; only a few, like Thomas Hariot's relation, exhibited much sympathy for the Indians. After 1590 promotional writers presented more favorable views of the Indian, partly because the aims of promotion began to shift from imperial expansion to colonization, and frightening views of native Americans seemed unlikely to attract settlers. In those later accounts the writers seemed markedly enthusiastic about converting the

Indians to Christianity. After the uprising of 1622, however, promoters of the southern colonies dropped the evangelistic appeals. Only Puritan writers in New England and Jesuit missionaries in Maryland and New France continued to offer optimistic predictions of impending conversions.[64]

Despite the differences, the accounts advanced one consistent—and simplistic—theme: the Indians could be managed. Like nature, they would prove to be tractable. Either they would seek Christianity—and European civility—or they would fall before the military might of European Christians. Most promoters emphasized the Indians' friendliness, but they also made it clear that colonial security rested on more than trust. "We neither feare nor trust them" wrote Francis Higginson, though it hardly mattered, he added, for forty English musketeers could drive 500 Indian warriors from the field. "What need we now fear them," asked William Wood, "being grown into thousands and having knowledge of martial discipline?" Some say they are warlike, some say friendly, wrote Andrew White in Maryland, though again it mattered little, for "the oddes wee have of them in our weapons, keepes them in awe." Many were aware that the English and the Powhatan Confederacy fought each other in Virginia for years after 1622, but eventually promoters reassured their readers that in Virginia, too, the Indians languished in subjection.[65]

Even providence seemed to ensure that the Indians would be manageable. Writers marveled at the plagues that reduced the Indian population, assuming that they illustrated God's care for Europeans. New Englanders announced in 1630 that "a great and grievous Plague" had emptied their region; Thomas Morton saw the plagues as a display of the wisdom and love of God. Forty years later Daniel Denton in New York could still offer the same explanation. "It is to be admired," he wrote, "how strangely they have decreast by the Hand of God, since the English first settling of these parts. . . . Where the English come to settle, a Divine Hand makes way for them, by removing or cutting off the Indians, either by Wars one with the other or by some raging mortal Disease."[66]

Any decline in the native population strengthened the argument that the European colonists, far from stealing Indian lands, merely wished to help the Indians cultivate empty grounds. Higginson insisted that the New England tribes "generally professed to like well of our coming and planting here" because they were "not able to make use of the one fourth part of the Land." In English eyes the nomadic habits of the Indians suggested that the land had no owners.[67]

Indians made good reading, and the promoters filled their accounts with descriptions. Some exhibited curiosity about Indian governance and religion, marriages and burials, wars and games, languages and sports. William Wood and John Smith made detailed ethnographic observations. But even the most detailed accounts oversimplified Indian society because promotion required simplicity. The issue was always utility, defined from the promoter's point of view. The genre defined its own conclusions: the overriding aim was to show that the Indians, sooner or later, would prove themselves serviceable, or at least "no ways hurtful," to the Europeans.[68]

The impulse toward optimistic simplicity also shaped the ways promoters depicted colonial societies. The Virginians had to confess to some problems, but the hallmark of promotional analysis in Virginia was always the assurance that the colony was turning the corner, and when Hammond wrote *Leah and Rachel* in 1656, the notion was circulating in promotional writings that colonists even in Virginia had succeeded in creating closely knit communities marked by "extraordinary good neighbour-hood and loving conversation." Hammond claimed that piety and natural abundance made the inhabitants "affable, courteous, and very assistant to strangers."[69]

Virginians were industrious; even colonists who in England had been lewd and idle grew ashamed of laziness in America. Virginians were generous and always ready to lend a helping hand: they worked the fields of sick neighbors with no expectation of reward; they provided hospitality for travelers at no charge; and they gave food to each other. Virginians were pious: some of the early ministers had been men who "could babble in a Pulpet, roare in a Tavern, exact from their Parishoners," but the people silenced these "Wolves in sheeps cloathing" and "then began the Gospel to flourish." Virginians were honest: "Doores are nightly left open. . . . Hedges hanging full of Cloathes; Plate frequently used amongst all comers and goers. . . . Yet I never heard of any losse ever received either in Plate, Linnen, or any thing else out of their Houses." And if a Virginian did stray from the narrow path, justice was certain and easy: everyone could find a judge within two miles, and the courts met every two months. Hammond conceded that Virginia was no utopia, but his descriptions bore a decidedly utopian aura.[70]

Like Hammond, other promoters depicted the colonies as communities marked by mutuality, peaceable deference, industrious labor, and sober piety. In the America of the promoters, Maryland could boast a well-ordered government overseeing a vigilant, industrious people who, despite their religious differences, had agreed to "concur in an unanimous parallel of friendship, and inseparable love intayled unto one another." New York contained a people "free from pride and oppression," whose door always stood open to symbolize their continual willingness "to assist each other, or relieve a stranger." Plymouth Colony consisted of freeholders who had covenanted to live in "love, peace, and holiness." The Massachusetts Bay settlers lived in "fair and handsome" towns and took comfort in knowing that they had "the true Religion and holy Ordinances of Almightie God." A few promoters qualified such idyllic descriptions with cranky complaints; Thomas Morton and John Josselyn in New England groused about hypocritical Puritans. But most vastly oversimplified colonial realities.[71]

Virginia, far from being a gathering of industrious, hospitable, pious souls, was in the 1650s still a volatile society of exploiting landholders and the discontented landless, of wealthy planters and resentful slaves and servants, of a few big winners and a multitude of angry losers. Most Virginians lived on modest farms, "placed straglingly and scatteringly, as a choice veine of rich ground invited them, and further from neighbours the better." They ordered themselves in families and scattered neighborhoods, thus establishing their own forms of community, but Virginia communities bore little relation to Hammond's descriptions of a peaceful, consensual society.[72]

Maryland, far from being an assemblage of friends and lovers, collapsed into virtual anarchy during the 1640s; its Catholics and Protestants contended during the 1650s; and even in the 1660s, when George Alsop wrote his promotional paean, a high death rate continued to plague the settlers, who lived, for the most part, in small, dark, drafty, overcrowded cabins with earth floors and crude furnishings. New Yorkers might have been willing to assist each other and aid strangers, but during the 1640s and 1650s their critics considered them a "rough and dissolute people," and the English conquest in 1664 resulted in continuing hostility between Dutch and English settlers. Plymouth Colony suffered when its settlers began to move away in the 1640s, and Massachusetts Bay endured conflicts over religion and tensions about the dispersal of settlers and the distribution of land.[73]

The promoters had little to say about tensions, brutalities, and death rates. Their writing forced them into simplicities that accentuated the old problem of credibility. The promoters claimed that they could be believed because they had seen with their own eyes. America's first treatises celebrated first-hand experience as both a source and a criterion of truth about the New World. But just as seventeenth-century philosophers were finding that they could not always trust their senses, so the promoters—and their readers—found that first-hand experience of new worlds could be equally deceptive. Even as late as the 1670s, promoters still complained about skepticism.

In a wider European culture that admired rhetorical elegance, the promoters insisted that they were credible because they spoke plainly and rudely. Yet their labored apologetics suggest that they worried about rhetorical effectiveness quite as much as any Jacobean actor or preacher. And the promotional treatises tell us as much about seventeenth-century rhetoric as the Aristotelian rhetorical treatises studied in the universities. The new England Puritans who strove for a plain style of sermonic exhortation had their commercial counterparts in the colonial promoters who boasted of their own straightforward simplicity. Their struggles to persuade, in any case, allied them with most of the other men and women who dealt with ideas in a colonial setting. In seventeenth-century America, most intellectuals were promoters of one kind or another.

three

The Persuasive Past

In 1676 Increase Mather, teacher of the Second Church in Boston, explained that "the part of an *Historian*" was "to relate things truly and impartially." Other colonists who wrote historical narratives pledged themselves in a similar manner to the "simple truth." Yet Mather, like the other writers, also gave the historian the task of "exhortation." From New England to New Mexico, people who wrote about the past assumed that their labors miscarried if they neglected to exhort their readers; none thought that truth and exhortation stood in tension.[1]

No sharp line, then, divided historians from promoters. The promoters often made their pitch through historical narration; historians often wrote their chronicles with promotional intent, and like the promoters, they simplified complex stories. Yet a rough distinction between promoters and historians illumines the themes of truthfulness and persuasion: the latter had a greater willingness to acknowledge complexity and ambiguity. Promoters wrote for Europeans who had never seen America; most historians wrote also for Americans who knew that the land and its people were more complicated than the promoters implied.

The colonists thought most about the past when they had to interpret, or justify, the cultural and social transitions that affected their lives in the present. The Puritan reform in England, especially during the reign of Elizabeth I from 1558 to 1603, stimulated a preoccupation with ancient biblical events that would indelibly mark the historical consciousness of New Englanders. The English civil wars, beginning in 1642 and reaching a climax in the execution of Charles I in 1649, created in New England an interest in a millennialist historiography that charted the way to a glorious transformation of history at the end of time. But events closer to home also evoked a curiosity about the past. The intense debate over baptism in New England during the early 1660s gave rise to conflicting interpretations of the region's history; the outbreak of King Philip's War in 1675 produced a flurry of historical narratives; and Nathaniel Bacon's rebellion in Virginia the following year prompted some historical interest among writers in the Chesapeake colonies.

In all the colonies history was a popular guide. Inventories of private libraries suggest that books of history ranked second in number only to religious treatises. Substantial numbers of literate colonists, from New England to Virginia, read or at least owned histories of Greece and Rome, England and France, Turkey and Normandy, Florence and London. Sir Walter Raleigh's *History of the World* appeared repeatedly in private collections, as did Matthias Prideaux's *Introduction for Reading All Sorts of Histories*. A few educated colonists read Eusebius's history of the church, Josephus's history of the Jews, and Plutarch's *Lives*. Schoolboys read history too. Works of classical history appeared in the reading lists of the grammar schools, and at Harvard the students read ancient history every Saturday afternoon during the winter term. Undoubtedly more colonists read the popular historical romances that filtered exhortation through tales of heroism and enchantment; such books sold steadily in New England bookshops. When New Englanders began printing books in 1639 they included works of history almost from the outset.[2]

In all the colonies appeals to historical precedent carried persuasive authority. Promoters clinched their arguments and reassured themselves by recalling precedents. Edward Maria Wingfield in Virginia sought comfort by remembering "the hard beginninges, which, in former ages, betided those worthy spirites that planted the greatest monarchies in Asia and Europe." John Smith promoted the colonizing of New England by recalling the example of Rome. Morgan Godwin on Barbados defended appeals to the mother country by pointing out that the Greek Epidamnians had appealed "to Corcyca, their Mother-Country." Polemicists regularly made their case by appealing to historical precedent. Nathaniel Ward of Ipswich and John Cotton of Boston argued against religious toleration, for example, by recalling intolerant Christian emperors.[3]

Colonists far from New England could share Increase Mather's confidence in the compatibility of truth and exhortation. In New Spain, for example, the soldier Gaspar Perez de Villagra published in 1610 *The History of New Mexico*, a historical ballad designed to recall "the many sacrifices and heroic deeds of those who conquered and converted the many tribes and people of New Mexico." He wrote his story partly to preserve a true account of the past, but he also wrote with a more immediate practical intention: to secure the favor of Philip III toward "those few Spaniards who have remained in these lands." He fully accepted the assumption that the historian's task was to combine truth and exhortation.[4]

Like Increase Mather historians in Virginia never hesitated to advance theological explanations for historical change. The Virginians who wrote the narratives that John Smith would use in compiling his *General History* assumed that "God's infinite providence" caused "all casuall events to worke the necessary helpe of his saints." And Smith's descriptions of English venality might well have served, in Puritan hands, as a sermon on human sinfulness.[5]

But both Smith and his sources remained indifferent to the questions about ancient origins that marked intellectual life in New England, and later Virginians seemed often to lack any inclination whatsoever to look back. John Hammond's *Leah and Rachel* bemoaned the colony's sordid beginnings, but Hammond accorded them only a few scattered references before turning his attention to the future. William Berkeley proposed in 1663 in his *Discourse and View of Virginia* that the early history of the colony simply be forgotten. Only the progress since 1622 should count: "from that time we must begin the account of the Plantation." Not until the eighteenth century did any Virginian write an account devoted solely to the colony's past. Throughout the seventeenth, writers in Virginia looked always to the present and the future.[6]

Bacon's Rebellion, the 1676 uprising of discontented settlers against William Berkeley's government, did stimulate a few historical narratives. The lawyer William Sherwood provided an unpublished history of "Virginias Deploured Condition" that placed all the blame for the revolt on Nathaniel Bacon's rebellious "outrages." An anonymous Virginian—probably the poet John Cotton of Queen's Creek—wrote another unpublished, untitled account depicting Bacon as a master of "sophistical dixterity," the governor's counselors as men who went about framing "specious pretences" to preserve their own position, and the people as the victims of their own "ill disarneing judgments." But the only other contemporary history of the rebellion came from royal commissioners sent from England.[7]

The colonists who most often wrote history were usually New England Puritans, trying to make sense of the past as a way to preserve pure churches and pious communities. Like other historians of the time they drew on the theme of divine providence to assert that historical events occurred because God used them to accomplish his own ends. Unlike most other historians, however, the Puritan writers also measured their society by comparing it to the standard of "Scripture Antiquitie." Intellectual life in the New England colonies embodied a profound sensitivity to the past—especially to the primitive past recorded by the biblical writers. The appeal to that past bore unusual power to persuade. It is to New England that we must turn to chart in any detail the patterns of historical reflection in early America.[8]

Sacred and Hortatory Histories

Most literate New Englanders would have assumed that the archetypal historical narrative, from which all others derived their meaning, was the Bible. Europeans commonly viewed the Bible as an authoritative history. When Sir Walter Raleigh wrote *History of the World,* he observed that sacred history had a "singular prerogative" over any history written by merely human authors because "it setteth down expressly the true and first causes of all that happened." In a further commonplace, Degory Wheare at Oxford told the undergraduates to rely without hesitation on the biblical history: "It is the Sacred History onely which discovers the secrets of the most remote Antiquity, and never lies."[9]

In New England the Puritan clergy viewed the Bible as an inspired historical narrative that established binding precedents for all subsequent history. They stood within a tradition that read the Bible preeminently as sacred history. In medieval exegesis, the historical or literal reading—"historia"—competed with three other exegetical principles. To medieval exegetes, the historical reading was no more compelling—often less so—than the tropological, which pursued moral implications; the allegorical, which sought hidden spiritual meanings; and the anagogical, which referred to heaven and eternal life. But to the Protestant reformers historia assumed primacy. Martin Luther insisted that "the historical meaning" was "the real and true one"; John Calvin added that the historical meaning corrected extravagant allegories. Neither reformer altogether rejected allegorizing, but they did establish the historical reading as the foundation.[10]

Ministers in New England, then, read the Bible primarily as a history, not as an allegory, a repository of moral esoterica, or a catalog of references to a heavenly realm. Their first appeal was always to what Thomas Hooker in Hartford called "the letter"—the straightforward grammatical meaning. Samuel Willard, the minister at Groton and at Boston's Old South Church, summarized a consensus when he taught in the 1680s that the Scripture had but one sense, which could be discerned through close attention to grammar and context. Hooker's letter and Willard's one sense both referred to the Bible as "historia," a forthright account of historical sayings and doings.[11]

Willard observed, however, that the one sense could "include diverse things," and he expressed a consensus. To read the Scripture as a historical drama did not mean to view it as a flat report. The Boston minister John Cotton argued that the same text could easily bear two interpretations, one literal and the other metaphorical. The historical meaning had priority, but biblical texts could transcend their historical setting. So the clergy extended the scriptural history from the past into the present through a variety of interpretive moves. In addition to searching for express commandments and propositions, they appropriated the biblical past by using three other principles of interpretation.[12]

They became known for their reliance, first, on an exemplary reading of the Bible. During the 1570s in England, the Puritan theologian Thomas Cartwright and Bishop John Whitgift debated about the status of Biblical examples—narratives that entailed specific practices. Cartwright employed such narratives to criticize the Church of England. Observing that Jesus preached in public synagogues, for instance, he concluded that sermons and sacraments should never be "privately preached or ministered." Whitgift responded that it was "never lawful, neither in divine nor in human matters, to argue *a facto ad jus* (of a deed or example to make a law)." He insisted that examples could guide practice only when they illustrated a rule or commandment. But Cartwright disagreed; commandments "to the contrary" could override examples, but to "admit neither the general examples of the new testament, nor the commandments and examples of the Old" was to endanger "the chief and principal pillars and buttresses of our religion."[13]

The clergy who came to New England had no trouble choosing sides. They agreed with John Cotton that scriptural examples were "patterns for imitation." The quest for exemplary analogies therefore became a standard exegetical method. The heart of the method was the narration of a biblical episode as a precedent that permitted or required a course of action. It demanded no great degree of theological sophistication; anyone could find exemplary precedents. When John Winthrop, who would become the governor in Massachusetts Bay, wanted to assure himself that the English had a right to purchase Indian lands, he recalled that Abraham had purchased land in Canaan from Ephron the Hittite. When the Bay Colony's military commander John Underhill wanted to justify his tactic of dividing his soldiers into small bodies during the Pequot War, he said that he took "the ground from the old and ancient practice" of Israel recorded in Exodus and Deuteronomy.[14]

The clergy—and many of the laity as well—hoped to find biblical warrants for all the "sacred sciences," including "ethicks, eoconomicks, politicks, church-government, prophecy, academy." The minister Thomas Shepard had concluded when he was a student at Cambridge that only strict adherence to biblical precedent could reform the Church of England. After being silenced by the archbishop, he fled to New England in 1635 and announced his conviction that "the [biblical] word descends to the most petty occasions of our lives; it teacheth men how to look, (Ps. cxxxi.16;) how to speak, (Matt. xii.36;) it descends to the plaiting of the hair, (I Pet. iii.5,) [and the] moving of the feet, (Is. iii. 16;)." The Bible prescribed perfect rules not only for the directing of an individual soul but also for "the right ordering of a mans family, yea, of the commonwealth too." In practice New Englanders followed

English customs as much as they did biblical precedents, but the exemplary reading of biblical history nevertheless had vast persuasive power.[15]

Such a reading of the past proved indispensable to the clergy who defended New England's churches against English critics. Shepard claimed that the "great work of this age" was "the kingdome and government of Christ in his churches," and the clergy felt sure that they had recovered the original pattern of biblical governance. They published during the 1630s and 1640s at least a dozen books, treatises, and sermons defending New England's way of organizing churches. All were exercises in persuasion; all rested on a reading of the Bible as a sacred history filled with binding precedents. All defended New England's church order and worship by pointing to "the example of the Church of Israel in the old Testament, Of the Church of *Corinth*, the Churches of *Galatia*, the 7 Churches of *Asia*, and others in the New Testament."[16]

Because the church at Antioch was small enough to gather together and the church in Corinth could assemble and meet together, the true church could be "onely Congregationall." Because the apostle Paul referred to the church in Corinth as people "called to be saints" and addressed the church in Ephesus as the saints, the members of true churches had to be "saints by calling." Because John baptized his converts only after they confessed their sins and Peter required repentance before baptism, the saints had to "give an account of the worke of grace" in them before they could be admitted to membership. And because "the Lord accepted and entered Abrahams family into a Church estate, by receiving them and their children into . . . a Covenant with himself," those churches of saints could be formed only through explicit covenants.[17]

The ministers debated ecclesiastical issues with arcane logic, and their logical assumptions often governed their reading of the biblical text, but all the dialectical maneuvering returned finally to a few historical examples. In his magisterial *Survey of the Summe of Church-Discipline*, Thomas Hooker at Hartford defended congregationalism with arguments "logicall, or Scholasticall." Hooker had learned his logic at Cambridge and tested it in English parishes before Archbishop Laud drove him out of England. Arriving in New England in 1633, he remained confident that he could reduce biblical forms of thought to the categories of scholastic and Ramist logic. He distinguished the efficient, material, and formal causes of the visible church; arrayed his exegetical points in Aristotelian categories and Ramist dichotomies; appealed to the rule of reason; and depended heavily on the philosophical argument that a genus existed and acted only in its species. But in Hooker's view the function of the logic was simply to aid in interpreting the biblical pattern: "As Moses saw his pattern in the Mount, according to which he was to mold, all things in the Tabernacle: So we have ours left upon record in the holy Scriptures, unto which we must not adde, and from which we must not take any thing."[18]

The historical examples proved to be ambiguous. Even when New Englanders could agree that the church should be congregational, they disagreed about what that meant. Some believed that the biblical examples required candidates for church membership to narrate their conversion; others thought they required only orthodox belief and pious behavior. Some thought that the Bible located governing authority solely within the members; others believed that it accorded a distinctive power to the ministers. Some even argued for a "presbyteriall" organization of the church, though that term too proved flexible; it could refer merely to someone who upheld the minister's special authority in doctrine and discipline, or it could designate proponents of a national church organized hierarchically in the Scottish fashion. So the appeal to biblical examples produced no consensus. If anything, it generated persistent conflict, even after the colonists, assembled at Cambridge, produced a document that specified the proper church order. The Cambridge Platform of 1648—overflowing with biblical examples—supposedly recorded their meeting of minds on such issues.[19]

Despite the disharmony, the exemplary reading of the biblical narrative provided some enduring images of communal self-understanding in New England. By following the example of Israel, New England became a new Israel. By facing the dangers of the American wilderness, the colonists reenacted the journey of the Israelites through their wilderness. By remaining faithful, or falling away, they repeated the history of the Jews and thus became God's chosen people, with the dual sense of privilege and burden implied in the scriptural account of Israel's chosenness. By the time Samuel Danforth formulated in 1671 his account of "New Englands Errand into the Wilderness," the colonists who paid attention to sermons were accustomed to thinking of themselves as children of Israel who had left "their cities and houses in Egypt" to "go forth into the wilderness."[20]

A second means of linking New England to a biblical past was the ancient method of typological interpretation. A type, everyone agreed, was "some outward or sensible thing ordained of God under the Old Testament, to represent and hold forth something of Christ in the New." Thus Noah, who saved his household in the ark, typified Christ, who saved his people through the church; and the Jewish exodus from Egypt prefigured the Christian deliverance from bondage to sin and Satan. The New Testament itself had referred to types and shadows of Christ, so subsequent theologians used typology to argue both that the ancient Jews dimly worshipped Christ and that Christians inherited the divine promises of the Jewish covenants. Typology conflated the Jewish and Christian histories, giving the New England churches a history that extended to the beginning of the world.[21]

The ministers did not always agree about the definition and scope of types. Cotton said that some of the biblical examples that provided "models for imitation" were also types, suggesting that exemplary and typological readings might be equivalent. But most other preachers agreed that types were outward signs of future spiritual realities, while examples were not. Types were divinely instituted to represent Christ; examples were not. Types pointed beyond themselves; examples bore their meanings on the surface. The visible types were abolished when they found fulfillment in their Christian antitypes; examples endured as perpetual models for Christian behavior.[22]

Most ministers considered that the distinction, though difficult, was crucial. If the types were examples, they thought, then the churches would have been bound to imitate Jewish ceremonies. Bostonians would have had to make burnt offerings, circumcise their male offspring, worship on the seventh day of the week instead of the first, and sacrifice bulls and goats. But if the types contained nothing of an exemplary character, then the Puritans could not have appealed to Jewish circumcision as a warrant for infant baptism or to the Jewish magistracy as an example for Christian kings.

The solution was usually to argue that some types could be partially exemplary and that some examples could be partially typical. A synod meeting at Cambridge in 1646 to determine the power of the magistrates to enforce true worship took note of the argument that Jewish rulers were types and so no longer "of force for our imitation." The synod knew that if Israel's rulers were types "strictly taken," then "they in that exercise of their power, did but shaddow out Christs kingly power," providing no exemplary model for future magistrates. But the delegates also affirmed a looser definition of a type, arguing that the word could sometimes designate an exemplar, and they insisted that King Solomon, whom everyone saw as a type of Christ, had even said in Proverbs 20:8 that he was to be imitated when he weeded out public evil.[23]

John Cotton, who wrote the synod's report, later clarified the decision by explaining that Solomon had been a type of Christ in his kingly office over the church but not in "all the Kingly offices" he performed. If he had been typical when he executed the murderer Joab and the traitor Adonijah, for example, then it would be "unlawfull for Christian Princes to put Murderers or Traitors to death," for Christ had fulfilled and abolished the types. Solomon had been, in different ways, both a type and an example. Cotton made a similar distinction when he defended the singing of psalms in New England churches. If the psalms of Israel had been merely ceremonial types, he said, then Christians could no longer sing them, for with the coming of Christ the types would have been abolished. But the Jewish psalms had been, in different ways, both types and examples, and their exemplary features warranted their continuation.[24]

The distinction was exceedingly fine, and Cotton did not always observe it. He sometimes argued that the Jewish types did function as exemplary precedents warranting later Christian practices. In his *Of the Holinesse of Church-Members*, he insisted that Old Testament types justified the restriction of church membership to "saints by calling" who could offer a convincing profession of repentance and faith. The porters who protected the Jewish temple from the unclean, he said, typified the officers of the church who protected the fellowship from the spiritually impure. His argument, though, subverted the distinctions with which he usually spoke of types and examples.[25]

Other theologians employed scholastic argumentation to preserve those distinctions. A type, they said, could be *typus fictus* or *typus destinatus*. The latter was a true type, ordained to "shadow out Christ," and it bore no exemplary force. But the "arbitrary" or "affixed" type could intermingle with an example that carried a continuing moral imperative. Thomas Shepard used the distinction in his *Theses Sabbaticae* when he described the Jewish Sabbath as both a type and a binding example. The Sabbath, he said, could not have been wholly typical, for "then it should be abolished wholly." It must have been "for substance moral"; it was instituted in the moral law and confirmed in the fourth commandment. And yet it had a type "affixed to it." Shepard found it difficult to discern what the type might be, but he finally decided to follow the continental theologian Francis Junius, who argued that Deuteronomy 15:15 linked the Sabbath to the Exodus, which typified deliverance by Christ; therefore the Sabbath contained an annexed or affixed type of deliverance. Such an argument supported Shepard's contention that certain ceremonial aspects of the Sabbath had been abolished but that Christians still had a moral obligation to observe a day of worship once every seven days.[26]

None of the first-generation ministers tried to argue, in any case, that New England constituted in any strict sense an antitype of ancient Israel. The early New England clergy agreed that Israel typified the true church, not any civil society. Roger Williams once accused John Cotton of describing New England as Israel's antitype and England as an antitype of Babel, but Cotton denied the accusation and explained that he affirmed a familiar Protestant position: Babel typified Rome, the Roman Catholic church, and the sinful ceremonies and practices the papacy had introduced. Israel typified the true church. Cotton thus contended that Babylon had a local antitype, from which one should physically separate, but when Williams accused him of implying that New England was "a locall Judea, a Land of Canaan also, into which the Saints are called," he denied the accusation. The saints are called, he said, into "visible Churches of Christ, as was Judea and Canaan, of old." He never tried to say that New England fulfilled the type of Israel.[27]

He thought, in fact, that it would be "sacriledge" to contend that a courtroom of Boston magistrates, or any other civil officers in New England, should fulfill, or imitate, types that Christ had fulfilled. Cotton could argue that New England magistrates should imitate kings like Jehoshaphat, who forbade idolatry in Israel, because he considered most of the Jewish kings to have been examples, not types: "For though *David* and *Solomon* were Types of Christ, (and so the Scripture holdeth them forth:) yet the Scripture giveth no hint, that the other Kings either of *Israel*, or *Judah* were Types." If all the Jewish kings had been types, then the incarnation would have abolished all kings, and it would be a "sacrilegious and Antichristian usurpation for any Kings to be set over Christians, or the people of God. For the Body being come, Types and shadowes vanish."[28]

A number of historians have argued that the early New Englanders saw themselves as the antitype of Israel and therefore introduced into American intellectual life an incipient notion of manifest destiny. It is true that by the end of the seventeenth century some New England exegetes were playing with expanded notions of typology; it is also true that the New England clergy continually referred to Israel as an exemplum for the colony. It became common to refer to New England as a New Israel. But to say that the founders viewed the colony as an antitype of Israel is to misunderstand the function of typology in early colonial religious rhetoric. Far from suggesting that New England was a harbinger of a manifest American destiny, typology located the colonists within a larger Protestant world—a world of churches, not of nations. Typology pushed against New English triumphalism by reminding the colonists that no civil commonwealth could be the true antitype of Israel. The typological reading allied New England congregationalists with true churches everywhere. It promoted a Protestant triumphalism but not a national one.

Neither the examples nor the types could cover every circumstance. Biblical examples abounded to guide individuals, families, churches, and commonwealths, but they did not suffice for every contingency, so New England's biblical interpreters also sought a third way to recover the sacred history. Cotton knew, for example, that the careful exegete could also discern the revelation of God's will in Scripture "by Proportion, or deduction, by Consequence, as well as by expresse Commandment, or Example." He knew as well that these proportional readings were essential to the achieving of his ideal for New England churches and government. Had the clergy depended solely on the examples, they would have stood dumbly before a host of "varieties and mutabilities" that corresponded to no specific narrative. But deductions from general rules, said Thomas Hooker, could ensure conformity to the sacred past even in the absence of commandments and clear examples.[29]

Proportional exegesis could assume various forms. The expositor could open the letter of Scripture, for example, by both "synecdoches" and "metonymies." The synecdoche—a figure in which a part represents a whole—enlarged the scope of a biblical rule or example; the commandment against graven images forbade the worship of God through any ceremonies that could be attributed to "the imaginations and inventions of men." The metonymy—a figure in which an attribute of a thing stands for the thing itself—could be used to discern the implications of a text. Thomas Hooker observed that when the apostle spoke of order in Colossians 2:5, the term extended, "by a Metonymy," to "the managing of all Church-Ordinances." Or the proportional reading could proceed through simple syllogisms. Cotton noted that when one part of a syllogism came from the Bible, the conclusion embodied a "divine proposition" though the other premise came from "our human knowledge."[30]

The reading of sacred history by proportion figured heavily in arguments about civil law. Shepard noted that lawmakers should apply "the general rules, recorded in Scripture, to such special and peculiar circumstances which may promote the public weal and good of persons, places, proceedings." But it was not easy to know exactly how those general rules retained their force in new settings. Theologians had long debated, for example, about the extent to which the judicial laws of Moses should govern Christian commonwealths. A few contended that the laws of a rightly framed commonwealth would correspond exactly to the Mosaic legislation; a greater number argued that the "judicials" had been entirely abrogated. But some English Puritans sought a mediating position, insisting that the state could not enact every Mosaic statute but should embody in its laws the equity, or substance, of Israel's judicial legislation. And any quest for equity would require an adept use of proportional interpretation.[31]

New England law embodied a complicated balance of biblical and civil precedents. In formulating their legal codes, the New Englanders drew on the English common law, Roman civil law, manorial and borough law, and the Bible. But they intended all their laws to be consistent with the Mosaic legislation, and they understood that such consistency required a keen eye for proportion. "In concluding punishments from the judicial law of Moses that is perpetual," wrote Charles Chauncy, "we must often proceed by analogical proportion and interpretation, . . . for there will still fall out some cases, in every commonwealth, which are not in so many words extant in Holy Writ, yet the substance of the matter in every kind (I conceive under correction) may be drawn and concluded out of the Scripture by good consequence of an equivalent nature." The colonists debated the question "how far Moses judicials bind Mass[achusetts]," and when Cotton and other ministers compiled for the General Court in 1636 a "model of Moses his Judicials," they made some people uneasy. But the clergy themselves recognized that while some Mosaic formulations could be transferred directly to the seventeenth century, others could not except by proportion.[32]

Whether they appealed to propositions, examples, deductions, or types, the ministers called for the colonies to remember and reenact a specific past. Dwight Bozeman has shown how that biblical primitivism shaped both religious and social practices in New England. The yearning to escape "human inventions," the scorn for "innovation," the sense of the medieval past as a decline from primitive purity, the repeated efforts of the churches to bind themselves to biblical beginnings, the persistent appeals to biblical warrants in political and social debates—all of these manifested a virtual obsession with the ancient past.[33]

To be persuasive in New England, therefore, one had to know how to appeal to the past, and the Bible offered a model of history as persuasion. The biblical history required of the reader more than a mere "historical faith." It also conveyed a "Spirit of Grace" and demanded obedience. It combined truth and exhortation and therefore confirmed that such a combination always reappeared when historians did their proper task.[34]

The historians of New England wrote from within that biblical drama. Their histories bore resonances of the biblical history; their language suggested the nuances of biblical language; their aims embodied the biblical unity of truth and exhortation. Because the Bible constituted the chief example of a persuasive history, they could not have imagined a conflict between persuasion and truth. And partly because the biblical archetype accomplished its aims through an interweaving of disparate themes, they found themselves, in honoring those themes, compelled to write histories that moved beyond the limits of simple promotion.

William Bradford, for example, wrote his history, *Of Plymouth Plantation*, with a "singular regard," he said, to "the simple truth in all things." To some critics his truth has seemed too simple. Recognizing his book as an authentic masterpiece, they have nonetheless concluded that Bradford was a sectarian historian whose providential explanations displayed partisanship, nostalgia, and obscurantism. It is true that Bradford was partisan. In 1606 he devoted himself to a small band of separatists in Scrooby who believed that their congregation restored the "ancient purity" and "primitive order" of the Church. When the congregation migrated to Holland, Bradford went with them, and when they arrived finally in America, he became governor of their colony. He wrote his history to persuade the next generation to devote themselves to that purity and order. He wanted the "children" to see "with what difficulties their fathers wrestled . . . and how God brought them along, notwithstanding all their weaknesses and infirmities." The children would then, Bradford hoped, "confess before the Lord His lovingkindness and His wonderful works before the sons of men."[35]

It is also true that he described throughout his history an unceasing record of providential interventions. Through God's mercies Bradford's saints endured the storms and sickness of the voyage while their tormentors died; they found seed for corn in vacant Indian houses; they survived Indian attacks;

they overcame cheating business partners; they uncovered subverters; ships suddenly arrived bearing food; hostile arrows missed their mark. His doctrine of providence could blind Bradford to both ambiguity and tragedy. In 1637, during warfare against the Pequot Indians, the colonists massacred and burned an Indian fort, killing 400 persons. "It was a fearful sight," said Bradford, "to see them thus frying in the fire and the streams of blood quenching the same, and horrible was the stink and scent thereof; but the victory seemed a sweet sacrifice, and they gave the praise thereof to God, who had wrought so wonderfully for them, thus to enclose their enemies in their hands."[36]

Yet though Bradford could speak with simplistic complacence, he could also recognize ambiguity. Two contrasting biblical themes pervaded Bradford's history. The first, drawn from Deuteronomy, expressed the vision of providential destiny. The God of Deuteronomy assigned to all people "the bounds of their habitations"; entered into covenant with his chosen people; gave them a special destiny, to be achieved, if necessary, through holy war; rewarded their faithfulness with mercy; punished their apostasy; and recompensed their adversity with tokens of merciful care.[37]

The second theme, drawn from the Pauline epistles, pointed to a world filled with paradoxes. For the apostle Paul, the revelation of God's will assumed paradoxical forms: God chose the foolish to shame the wise and the weak to shame the strong; thus foolishness became wisdom and strength became weakness. Christ, though rich with divinity, emptied himself of his riches to be a divine-human redeemer on a cross, and the faithful, weak in Christ, lived in strength by the cruciform power of God. Bradford fastened his attention on those reversals. His book was a chronicle of troubles and trials in which God made the weak to stand. It was a story of poor and simple people who prevailed while those who "boasted of their strength" fell away.[38]

The combination of biblical themes meant that Bradford could tell no simple tale of providential progress. In his rendition of Plymouth's history, apparent weaknesses became hidden strengths and seeming achievements became temptations. His pilgrims underwent troubles in their efforts to leave England, but "by these public troubles . . . their cause became famous." They suffered poverty in Holland, but the poverty issued in victory. They encountered deceivers who tried to subvert the settlement, but those "troubles produced a quite contrary effect . . . Which was looked on as a great work of God, to draw on men by unlikely means." By the same token, seeming successes could prove deceptive; the prosperity from the trade of wampunpeag in 1628 made the Indians rich, armed, and dangerous. Later prosperity resulted in similar problems, for as their stocks increased they sought more land, scattering over the countryside until the town that had held them together lay almost desolate. Bradford could never be certain that either successes or failures were what they appeared to be.[39]

"God's judgments," he wrote, echoing the apostle Paul, "are unsearchable."

The disasters of colonization revealed "the uncertainty of all human things and what little cause there is of joying in them or trusting to them." God's will made itself known through concrete "necessities" of history, pushing and pulling men and women like a "taskmaster," using "unlikely means" to point a direction. Bradford therefore had to look closely into the natural and human means through which providence worked, and he had to be truthful even when the truth seemed hurtful. When the colony fell into "wickedness" in 1642, Bradford felt obliged to record the scandal. When the young Thomas Granger was executed for sexual relations with "a mare, a cow, two goats, five sheep, two calves and a turkey," Bradford preferred not to recount the event, but "the truth of the history" required it. Even the wickedness could be a clue for understanding God's purposes for Plymouth. Because God's ways were mysterious but trustworthy, the historian had to look closely at both the successes and the failures.[40]

Bradford wrote the book for a colony that had, in his view, faced some reverses, and he could make a case for persistence only if he could show that failures did not spell the end of the vision. The practical interests that motivated the writing required that he acknowledge, even emphasize, the ambiguity of providence. But Bradford also wrote this way because the biblical history that stood behind his narrative pressed upon him a host of clashing themes and images that he had to take into account. To combine Deuteronomy and Paul is to merge two conflicting visions, and yet Bradford could not have imagined a history of Plymouth that rejected either one.

Millennial History

The Bible as some New Englanders read it not only revealed the history of Israel and the early church but also contained prophecies that showed the outcome of history. The difficult task, but one that some colonists ardently pursued, was to relate those prophecies to the events of the past and the future. In the sixteenth century, John Foxe had tried that in his *Acts and Monuments*, and a few Puritan preachers in New England followed his example, convinced that an eschatological historiography—a study of clues in history that pointed to the end of this fallen world—would unveil the meaning of history. With more than casual interest they pondered the fortunes of fourth-century emperors, thirteenth-century popes, and sixteenth-century reformers, confident that by relating world history to biblical prophecy they could draw a map, however indistinct, of the journey toward the apocalypse.

A few preachers in England and in New England moved beyond Foxe's assertion that God would soon bring history to a destructive conclusion as a prelude to the final judgment. They affirmed an explicit millennialism—a belief that God would establish a new, transformed, historical order on this earth. The English theologian Thomas Brightman argued in the early seventeenth century, in exegetical commentaries on *Revelation* and the Pauline letters, that Christ, through his brightness and power, would bring about a supernatural transfiguration of earthly society, a golden age, an earthly New Jerusalem, long before the Second Coming and the end time. Brightman's ideas seemed dangerously innovative, but by the 1620s other millenarian schemes also competed for attention, and in the tense years before the outbreak of civil war, millennial visions attracted support from English Independents and New English congregationalists.[41]

From the beginning most of the New England clergy entertained conventional Protestant expectations about a cataclysmic end time, but during the late 1630s a few prominent preachers begin to outline more elaborate eschatological prospects, explicitly millennial in their depictions of a new earthly order that would precede the final judgment. Even before he came to America, John Cotton had begun, in the manner of Brightman, to interpret the Song of Solomon as a "historical prophecy" that revealed the movement of history toward a glorious transformation "of Church and State, according to the Rule and Pattern of the Word of God." Between 1639 and 1641 Cotton expounded those millennial views in a series of Thursday lectures to the First Church in Boston, which undoubtedly interpreted them, as did Cotton, with an attentive eye cast toward the political and religious turbulence in Scotland and England.[42]

Cotton used his lectures to argue that the two beasts mentioned in Revelation 13 were the "Roman Catholick visible Church" and the papacy; that God had already poured out five of the seven vials of wrath mentioned in Revelation 16, with the two remaining vials to be emptied at the final destruction of God's enemies and the conversion of the Jews; and that true churches could look forward, after the demise of Rome, to a spiritual resurrection through which they would share in the coming millennial glory. Cotton even predicted that around 1655 the beast might receive such a blow as to inaugurate a "further gradual accomplishment and fulfilling" of the prophecies. He was cautious about New England's role: "If I should say there is a Resurrection in *New England* from resting in Forms, from resting in the World, and carnall selfe-love. . . . I should say more than I could justifie." But such speculation whipped up enthusiasm in England during the civil wars, and Cotton's lectures stimulated, or reflected, a similar outbreak of millennial fervor in New England.[43]

In 1640 Thomas Lechford observed that the people talked "of nothing but Antichrist and the Man of Sin." Anne Bradstreet during the 1640s wrote poetry about the impending destruction of Turkey; Thomas Parker in Newbury expounded the prophecies of Daniel; Thomas Hooker announced that such prophecies were soon to attain their performances. The millennialism produced some intricate historical speculation as preachers instructed their congregations about the hidden meanings of such events as the invasion of Rome by Goths and Vandals, the imperial policies of Justinian and Charlemagne, and the troubles of monarchs from Theodosius to Elizabeth. In 1647 Shepard cited Brightman when he announced that the conversion of the Indians might possibly be the preparative for the "brighter day" when Turkish power would fall and the Jews would return to Zion. The missionary John Eliot went so far as to prepare blueprints for government in the millennial age.[44]

Some enthusiasts proved less cautious than Cotton in defining New England's contribution to the millennium. In 1647 Samuel Symonds asked John Winthrop an intriguing question: "Is not government in church and Common weale (according to gods owne rules) that new heaven and earth promised, in the fullnes accomplished when the Jewes come in; and the first fruites begun in this poore New England?" A few years later Edward Johnson announced to the world that the fruits had indeed begun to appear in poor New England. A joiner and military captain who came to New England in 1630, Johnson rose to become one of the leading citizens of Woburn—a selectman, militia captain, town clerk, and representative in the General Court. In spirit he remained a promoter, seeking support for a colony that in his eyes signified the imminent appearance of a millennial "new Heaven, and . . . new Earth."[45]

Johnson's *The Wonder-Working Providence of Sion's Saviour in New England* displayed little of Bradford's sense of complexity and ambiguity. In Johnson's history the ambition to persuade overwhelmed more modest historical aims. He set forth a brief for New England that was, in its ulterior meaning, an appeal for allegiance to a coming Kingdom of Christ. It was a book mainly for English readers—he probably began writing it in 1650 during the urgent parliamentary debates over church governance in England—and he addressed himself especially to English Presbyterians who scorned the New England way of governing churches and to English Independents who questioned the New England way of punishing dissenters. Johnson pleaded with them to change their policies, on the grounds that New England governance and discipline restored primitive purity and foreshadowed Christ's millennial kingdom.[46]

Announcing that "the downfall of the Antichrist is at hand," Johnson proved less the historian than the herald proclaiming Christ's commission, seeking soldiers who would enlist in that apocalyptic campaign. His history had all the subtlety of a recruiting poster. He tried to convince his readers that by building pure churches and defending them with civil power, they could "all see the dawning of the day." They had to fight: "all men that expect the day, must attend the means." But the example of New England—which had formed one true church after another—proved that the saints now had the momentum. The need was for more volunteers to "attend the service of the King of Kings."[47]

Like other promoters Johnson found that acceptance did not come easily. The book failed to sell, and the printer tried to recoup his losses by appending the unsold pages to another book by another author, a strategy that succeeded only in bringing howls of outrage from the other author. By the time Johnson got his book into print, partisans of an apocalyptic fifth monarchy in England were showing that millennial theology could make for turbulent politics, and millennial faiths were beginning to fade. After the Restoration of the Stuart monarchy in 1660, rhetoric about a fifth monarchy made almost everyone uncomfortable. "They, who of late were called fifth Monarchymen," wrote John Davenport in 1667, "did err . . . especially two ways. First by anticipating the time, which will not be till the pouring out of the sixth and seventh Vials [and] Secondly, by putting themselves upon a work which shall not be done by men, but by Christ himself."[48]

Throughout the century preachers speculated about the millennium and New England's contribution to it. In such books as Increase Mather's *Mystery of Israel's Salvation*, pious colonists studied the history of the Jews and puzzled about its meaning. But by the middle of the century they also became increasingly interested in the meaning of their own history. Without abandoning their fascination with Israel, they began to look anew at their own beginnings, and they discovered still another use for persuasive history.

History as Jeremiad

During the 1650s and early 1660s, a heated dispute among the New England churches over admission to baptism resulted in a new look at New England's history. Both sides claimed to represent the founding ideals, and both appealed to the authority of the aged patriarchs. The conflict led to a compromise known as the halfway covenant, and it also began the idealizing of New England's past. When a synod in 1662 announced the compromise, Jonathan Mitchell, the minister in Cambridge, wrote a preface to the synodical document in which he denied that the synod had departed from "former first Principles." In admitting to baptism but excluding from the Lord's Supper the children of church members who could offer no testimony of their effectual calling, the synod, Mitchell said, honored the intentions of "the first and best generation in New England." But the synod's opponents claimed that it betrayed the purity of the founders. The debate brought into the colonial vocabulary a new kind of appeal to New England's past.[49]

The squabbling also helped to account for the recovery of a traditional sermonic form that has come to be known as the jeremiad, which combined lament over declension, idealizing of the past, and expectant optimism about a better future. The jeremiad sermons appealed to the virtues of the founders as a way of both reprimanding and encouraging the later generation. They recalled "New Englands first ways" and urged fidelity to them.[50]

The next step was to call for a new history of those purer days—one in which the historian would combine historical truth and pious exhortation. It is conceivable that such a quest for pious history might have resulted in a seventeenth-century printing of John Winthrop's "history of New England." Winthrop had started writing a journal of his voyage to New England in 1630. He continued it after he became the governor of the Bay Colony, and nineteen years after he arrived he was still making entries. He combined everyday details, records of wondrous providences, depictions of colonial leaders, and labored efforts to explain conflicts, misfortunes, and political controversies. But the journal, which circulated among other New England writers, remained unpublished until the nineteenth century. More than any other seventeenth-century history, it remained a private book, not an effort at public persuasion.[51]

A journal devoid of exhortation was not what New England intellectuals considered history, though some eventually used it as a source. The colony published instead an account by Bradford's nephew, Nathaniel Morton, who made no secret of his hortatory intentions. His *New Englands Memoriall* (1669), concluded with an explicit "word of Advice to the Rising-generation" in which Morton made it clear that his aim was to shape behavior. While he might have hoped also to produce a book of apologetics for English readers, his chief end was to impress upon colonial readers the duty of remembering the founders in order to "follow their Examples."[52]

To encourage the younger generation to think of themselves as instruments in God's hands, Morton returned to some of Bradford's themes; *New Englands Memoriall* consisted largely of abridged excerpts from Bradford's earlier manuscript. Like his uncle Morton hoped to record "the memorable passages of Gods Providence to us." Like Bradford he assured his readers that God "effected great things by small means." Like Bradford he insisted that God's glory, and no lesser end, justified any human endeavor, including the writing of history. But Morton never shared Bradford's sense for the complexity of God's workings; he omitted, for instance, Bradford's musings on Pauline paradoxes.[53]

Morton simplified Bradford's vision, omitting not only his reflections on ambiguity but also his accounts of murders, executions, and sexual scandal. Morton could lament New England's current shortcomings—"God did once plant a Noble vine in *New-England*, but it is degenerated into the plant of a strange vine"—but by sanitizing the past, he turned his history into a nostalgic sermon designed to shame and inspire "the Rising-generation." The impulse to persuade coincided again with the tendency to oversimplify.[54]

Morton's book, though well received, did not satisfy the demand for such histories. By the 1670s a variety of voices called for a renewed look at New England's past. The General Court in Massachusetts Bay voted in 1672 to encourage the collection of historical providences, events "beyond what could in reason have been expected," as a means of bringing citizens to serve the Lord. The next year, Thomas Shepard, Jr., the minister at Charlestown, tried to get the magistrates to show more enthusiasm for protecting orthodoxy and piety. He also hoped that they would encourage some faithful historian to draw up a "Book of Records" chronicling "the mercies, judgements, and great acts of the Lord." Such a history would reveal, he thought, that "the Fathers of the Common Wealth" had shown no hesitation in making "wholesome laws" to "punish the disturbers of Christs order."[55]

Urian Oakes, the minister at Cambridge and the acting president of Harvard, seconded the motion. He also urged in a sermon to the General Court that New England consider the consequences of its "defection and declension" from its original purity. As a way to encourage awakening he suggested that "all the loving kindnesses of God, and his singular favours" to the colony "might be Chronicled and communicated (in the History of them)." It is, he said, "our great duty to be the Lords *Remembrancers; or Recorders.*" And in 1676 Increase Mather, the teacher at Boston's Second Church, added his voice to the call for more history: "I earnestly wish that some effectual course may be taken (before it be too late) that a just *History of New England* be written and published to the world." No one could be better suited for the historian's task, he added, than the ministers.[56]

Mather was writing to people who had suffered through "the most troublesome year that ever poor New England saw." In 1675 the colonists declared war against an assortment of Indian clans led by the Wampanoag sachem Metacom, or King Philip. Plans for a history of New England had to be laid aside, but King Philip's War called forth its own historians, some of them with notions that countered Mather's ideal of hortatory history.[57]

The earliest accounts of the war bore little relation to that ideal. A Rhode Island Quaker, Edward Wharton, published in London in 1675 an account that Mather found "fraught with worse Things than meer Mistakes." In his *New England's Present Sufferings, Under Their Cruel Neighboring Indians*, Wharton interpreted the war as divine retribution upon Plymouth and Massachusetts Bay for their persecution of Quakers. Another Quaker from Rhode Island, John Easton, in his "Relacion of the Indyan Warre" gave a sympathetic account of Indian grievances, claimed that the English had made no proper declaration of war, and suggested that English forces took out frustrations on "the women and children and impotent" when the warriors proved difficult to find. He had some jaundiced views of the Indians as well, but that hardly sufficed, in Mather's view, to compensate for the charge that Puritan "priests" were somehow the cause that "the law of nations and the laws of arms have bine violated in this war."[58]

Mather felt further dismay after he read an account by a Boston merchant, probably Nathaniel Saltonstall, describing for English readers in 1675 *The Present State of New-England with Respect to the Indian War.* Saltonstall had no doubts about New England's righteousness, but Mather found his treatise abounding in mistakes. It is not entirely clear what he found so offensive, but in addition to making a few factual errors Saltonstall also expressed reservations about the loyalty of Christian Indians. When the English captured eight of them and sentenced them to die, both John Eliot, the missionary to the Indians, and Daniel Gookin, who decided legal matters for them, protested on their behalf. Saltonstall made it clear that the colony's common men and women had no sympathy for softhearted Indian lovers. While he praised Eliot for his work as a missionary, he also revealed that "Mr. Eliot and Captain Guggins" had "pleaded so very hard for the Indians, that the whole Council knew not what to do about them." He made it clear that he shared the feeling of a "very worthy Person" who told Gookin that "he ought rather to be confined among his Indians, than to sit on the Bench." Saltonstall concluded by observing that the colony now took care "to satisfie the (reasonable) desires of the Commonalty": those "Praying Indians," better described as "Preying Indians," properly languished in secure confinement, much to the "general Satisfaction."[59]

Mather read Saltonstall's account, disliked it intensely, and decided that "a true History of this affair should be published." The result was his *Brief History of the War with the Indians in New-England* (1676), in which he emphasized that the "one thing" about which he felt most deeply was "the *Conversion* of the *Heathen* unto *Christ*." He even suggested that "the Lords Holy design in the *War* which he hath brought upon us, may (in part) be to punish us for our too great neglect in this matter." Mather's history had to tread a narrow line; he had to show, against Quaker critics in Rhode Island, that New England was fighting a just war against a barbarous enemy; yet he also had to show that New England flouted the will of a sovereign God if it decided that praying Indians were no longer worth the effort.[60]

He filled his history with accounts of providential interventions and divine signs, of omens appearing in the skies and phantom ordnance exploding in the countryside. He saw the finger of God in English victories and Indian disunity, and he treated the "monstrous birth" of a deformed infant in Woburn as an event fully as meaningful to the historian as a battle won or lost. Yet he acknowledged that divine providences could remain ambiguous even to a Mather. Convinced that the war signified God's wrath against the sins of New England, Mather used his history to call for collective repentance.[61]

His selection of social sins lingered on the trivial; periwigs, swearing, and excessive tippling ranked high on the list. Mather's piety often skewed his perspective, causing him, for example, to gauge the progress of war by counting the churches that had been spared the torch. In his exhortation, however, Mather also scored some of the social impulses that lay at the heart of the conflict: "*Land! Land!* hath been the Idol of many in *New-England*."

58

He told his readers, in reporting Indian grievances, that he found it "greatly to be lamented that the heathen should have any ground for such allegations, or that they should be scandalized by men that call themselves Christian." Instead of venting their wrath on Christian Indians, the colonists should recognize that "some *Praying English*" were fully as perfidious as "some *Praying Indians*" and that English Christians who scorned Christian Indians would one day "see a number of them sitting down with Abraham, Isaac, and Jacob in the Kingdome of God."[62]

Mather, when angered, could be a petty man, but it was not simply pettiness that aroused his ire when his rival William Hubbard, the minister of Ipswich, published a competing version of the war, *Narrative of the Troubles with the Indians* (1677). Hubbard had already provoked Mather by informing the General Court that magistrates need not feel constrained to persecute Baptists and Quakers. Now he published a history of the current "Warrs of the Lord" with passages that seemed utterly indifferent, if not hostile, to the work of converting Indians. "Whatever hopes may be of their conversion to christianity in after time," he wrote, "there is but little appearance of any truth in their hearts at present." The Indians were not "uncapable subjects for divine grace to work upon," he admitted, but he hastened to add that there were "some natural vices proper to every nation in the world," implying that even conversion might not overcome the "subtilty, malice, and revenge" that seemed "a part of their essence." Hubbard offered little support for Mather's defense of praying Indians.[63]

Hubbard has attracted praise because he supposedly elevated natural causes over divine providences. His ideas are said to have been relatively advanced in comparison to the views of people like Increase Mather. But Hubbard's *Narrative* contained ample reference to providences. Some places seemed to him "by special providence" marked out for preservation and others for destruction. He described "the Lord of Hosts" fighting from heaven for the English by sending thunder and rain, letting prisoners escape, alerting towns to danger, determining strategies, and deciding battles. No more than any other seventeenth-century historian did he hesitate to point out "remarkable passages of divine providence."[64]

He also showed little reluctance to exhort his readers. Hubbard claimed that he had written his narrative as a "private essay." His intention, he said, was simply to present the truth. But he also hoped that his book would move future generations by securing "the memory of such eminent deliverances and special preservations granted by divine favour to the people here" and that some of his reports would awaken the complacent from their security and confidence in earthly goods. In other words, he wrote a conventional Puritan account.[65]

Increase Mather, a conventional Puritan, did not like it. He accorded the book grudging praise; Hubbard's "pains and industry" deserved an acknowledgment. But he implied that Hubbard had failed as a historian. Despite the availability of Hubbard's narrative, Mather told his readers, "it hath been thought needful to publish" another one, "considering that most of the Things here insisted on, are not so much as once taken Notice of in that *Narrative*." Therefore Mather felt justified in publishing his own *Relation of the Troubles Which Have Hapned in New England*, a rambling account of conflicts stretching back to the first decade of the century. The book contained the usual complaints about treacherous Indians, but in his conclusion Mather insisted that the problem all along could be traced to a division between two groups of settlers: those who "came hither on Account of Trade and worldly Interests, by whom the Indians have been scandalized," and those who "came hither on a religious and conscientious Account, having in their Eye the Conversion of the Heathen unto Christ." The first group had drawn down "blasting ruining Providences" on the colonies; the second had drawn the natives into six Indian churches. The moral of the history was clear, and Hubbard had failed to see it.[66]

Few shared Mather's interest in continuing to think of Indians as persons worthy of persuasion. The poet Benjamin Tompson published in 1676 a verse history, *New Englands Crisis*, complaining that "Indian spirits need / No grounds but lust to make a Christian bleed." Thomas Wheeler, who fought in the war, described the Indians in his *Thankful Remembrance of Gods Mercy* as "cruel bloodthirsty Heathen," who blasphemed and mocked while killing and torturing. And Mary Rowlandson, whose narrative of her capture by the Narraganset endured as the most popular piece of writing to emerge from the war, depicted Mather's beloved praying Indians as barbarians. A praying Indian, she said, wrote the letter demanding ransom money for her; another betrayed his father to the English to save his own life; another fought the English at Sudbury; still another, "wicked and cruel" wore a necklace "strung with Christians' fingers." In the face of such dramatic testimony, Mather's exhortations stood little chance.[67]

In one sense Mary Rowlandson's narrative suggested a complex vision. Her captivity altered her sense of the world: "I remember the time when I used to sleep quietly without workings in my thoughts, whole nights together, but now it is other ways with me." She became aware, she said, that God's works were truly "wonderful" and "awful." Not for a moment, if we are to believe her, did she lose her Puritan faith, but she came to a disturbing awareness of how providence could defy her understanding. By providence she was delivered, but by providence, she wrote, the English army had to return home for provisions just when they could have had an easy victory; by providence the army delayed pursuit after the disaster at Lancaster; by a "wonderful providence" her captors crossed a river that the English pursuers could not cross; by providence the destruction of Indian crops failed to accomplish its ends. And the complex vision appeared also in her depiction of her captors, for she recounted not only the cruelty but also moments of kindness that belied wartime stereotypes of the enemy.[68]

Increase Mather had hoped that his history of the war might contribute "light or Help in writing an *History of New England*." Probably to his chagrin, the author who forged ahead with that history was William Hubbard, whose *General History of New England* earned him in 1682 fifty pounds and a resolution of gratitude from the General Court. But the manuscript was not published, and although it proved useful to subsequent historians, its reception must have disappointed Hubbard. Most of the book consisted of paraphrases and borrowings from Winthrop's journal and Bradford's history, and when he no longer could use those two sources, Hubbard often fell into the habits of a chronicler, listing unusual events or relating anecdotes.[69]

The work showed that Hubbard did, after all, approve of the mission to the Indians. He devoted a chapter to tracing its history, making no mention of the malice and revenge that had once seemed to him to mark the Indians' essence. The "christian Indians," he now wrote, maintained and defended their faith even at "the peril of their lives."[70]

One must assume, though, that Increase Mather remained critical, and not simply for small-minded reasons. Hubbard's history lacked the larger vision, the sense of awe, that had marked Bradford's earlier account. The difference between the two works appeared in their attitudes toward the dispersion of settlement: Bradford had worried about it as a threat to community, but Hubbard concluded his account by describing New York—a "country being capable of entertaining many thousands"—partly "for the encouragement of any that may have a mind to remove themselves thither." Bradford had written his history in order to persuade a generation that it should keep faith with the founders. In Hubbard's history, while pious exhortations recurred throughout his pages, the larger sense of purpose seemed dim. Not until Cotton Mather published his *Magnalia Christi Americana* in 1702 would a New England historian resume the older pattern of hortatory history.[71]

four

Persuasion Across Cultures

In 1626 Fray Alonso de Benavides, the guardian of the Franciscan order in New Mexico, traveled through his mission territory to visit the Indians who had been "converted and pacified" to God and Philip IV and to convince others to "give up their idolatries and sorceries." Arriving once at a mission accompanied by soldiers, he engaged a Navaho leader in a religious discussion. He began by telling him that the Christian God was "Creator and Lord of all that is created, and that to deliver us from eternal pains He had died upon a Cross," illustrating the argument by gesturing toward a painting above the altar that presented the Christian doctrines of creation, redemption, and damnation. Benavides told the Indian "that he who should not adore [God], and be baptized, must be damned and go to burn in those eternal pains."[1]

The Navaho gave his assent: "From this moment I say that I adore this God whom this Father tells of." Benavides sought to reinforce that assent by drawing his convert immediately into the sphere of gestures and sounds that distinguished a Spanish Catholic culture from that of a Navaho. He had other Christian Indians "peal the bells and sound the trumpets and clarions" at the mission church—"a thing which pleased [the new convert] much to hear, since it was the first time." The friar robed himself in his "best vestments" to celebrate Mass but forbade the unbaptized convert to see the holy proceedings at the sacred altar on the grounds that "he could not see God in the Mass." When the man objected, Benavides ordered the choir to divert him by singing "the Salve [Regina] in an organ-chant with all simplicity and solemnity, and with trumpets and clarions." He then resumed his original argument, with more "words concerning the mystery of the Creation and Redemption, wherewith he remained each time more confirmed in the faith." When Benavides called for further displays of Catholic ceremonial practice, the convert responded as the friar wished; he exclaimed "that well he perceived the truth of our Holy Catholic Faith, since it was celebrated with so much solemnity."[2]

The interchange between the two men embodied far more than any simple discussion of concepts. To understand it, one must remain aware of the soldiers in the background, the paintings on the wall, the vestments and trumpets, and the singing and chants that gave emotional force to the belief. For both men ceremonial gestures, musical rhythms, and esoteric chants symbolized profound convictions about the ultimate nature of things. For both the ritual ordering of experience represented a way of interpreting and altering the world. In that respect the conversation between Benavides and the Navaho chieftain revealed a pervasive feature of the European attempt at persuasion across cultures.

When men and women in early America encountered the ceremonial forms of other cultures, they usually reacted with disdain or apprehension. This was as true of the native Americans, who often remarked on the absurdity or malicious consequences of Christian ritual, as it was of the Europeans, who frequently described native ceremonies as demonic in origin. Unlike the native groups, however, pious Europeans felt obliged by their faith to convert others to their religion. Although they remained ambivalent about the conversion of African slaves, they announced from the beginning their intention to convert the native Indians to Christian truth and European civility.

Although they coexisted in the same geographical regions, the Europeans, the native Americans, and the Africans inhabited different symbolic worlds. Each group had its own ideas about truth and appropriate behavior, and they embedded those ideas within a complex web of rituals and symbols. They had distinctive ways of denoting the passage of time, orienting themselves within space, and expressing their ideas through symbolic sounds and gestures. This created problems, especially when the Europeans sought to persuade the Indians to leave one symbolic world and enter another.

In the seventeenth century as many as 250 native American groups may have lived in the area stretching from coast to coast north of the Rio Grande. No two tribal groups were exactly alike. They spoke different languages and dialects; bands that lived in close proximity often could not understand each other. To look at only three groups—the Pueblos of the southwestern deserts, the Hurons in the Great Lakes region, and the Algonkian-speaking people of the northeastern woodlands—is to glimpse something of the complexity and diversity of native American cultures. The African cultures represented in America were also drawn from numerous tribal and linguistic groups in West

Africa. The Spanish brought them to the New World as early as 1502; the first report of their presence in the English colonies on the mainland came in 1619. For most of the century, they constituted only a small percentage of the population in the mainland colonies. But they too, like the native Americans, confronted the Europeans with strikingly unfamiliar conceptions of space, time, gesture, and sound.

Each of the groups had a profound encounter with Europeans. In 1540 Spanish Franciscans started their mission into New Mexico. French Jesuits and Recollects began in 1611 to penetrate the territories of New France. In 1620 English Puritan separatists in Plymouth Colony first came face to face with the Algonkian sagamore Samoset. More than twenty years would pass before Puritans from Massachusetts Bay would begin a mission to the Indians, and it took many of the English even longer to decide whether Africans should be induced to accept Christianity. But regardless of the chronology of the missions, the clash of religious traditions in the New World slowly revealed the complexity of exhortation across cultures.

Pueblos and Franciscans

In 1597 the natives of Guale Island, off the coast of what is now Georgia, rebelled against the Spanish. They explained their revolt with the lament that the Franciscans had presumed to "obstruct our dances, banquets, feasts, celebrations, fires, and wars, so that by failing to use them we lose the ancient valor and dexterity inherited from our ancestors: They persecute our old people calling them witches; even our labor disturbs them, since they want to command us to avoid it on some days." To the Guale Indians revolt became necessary when the Spanish suppressed their sacred sounds and gestures, extinguished their sacred fires, and imposed on them an alien conception of sacred time. The Guale revolt thus returns us to a world in which dances and feasts expressed deeply rooted ideas and ideological conflicts often had ceremonial dimensions.[3]

By 1597 New Spain stretched from the vicinity of the Colorado River in North America to the southern tip of Peru. What began as a tiny colony of forty adventurers whom Columbus deposited on the island of Hispaniola in 1492 had become a colonial empire. It took only half a century for the conquistadores to overrun the Aztecs of Mexico, the Incas of Peru, and the Mayas of Guatemala and the Yucatán Peninsula and to establish a society of cities and plantations with Mexico City as its metropolis. The part of new Spain that extended into what is now the United States consisted by the 1630s of little more than scattered settlements of farmers and soldiers and a few dozen Franciscan missions—twenty-five in the vicinity of Santa Fe and forty-four in Florida—but they viewed themselves as the outposts of a vast dominion.

In 1552 the Dominican priest Bartolomé de Las Casas published his chilling revelations of the coercion that held that dominion together. His *Very Brief Account of the Destruction of the Indies* depicted a world in which the conquerors enslaved, tortured, and murdered untold numbers of Indians. Las Casas had fought in the conquest of Cuba in 1512 and received land and Indians as a reward. But in 1514 he chanced to read in Ecclesiastes that "the gifts of unjust men are not accepted." Troubled, he released his slaves and began to preach against slavery. When his plan for a humane colony failed, he entered the Dominican order and began his crusade for justice. Because it coincided with the interests of the monarch, Las Casas received a sympathetic hearing in the court. Charles I in 1542 promulgated his New Laws designed to limit colonial exploitation of the Indians. For the moment Las Casas rejoiced, but when colonial pressure forced the crown in 1545 to retreat, his writings became more bleak and desperate.[4]

In a flurry of polemical treatises, he claimed that the American natives were rational creatures, not barbarians designed for slavery; that the church should persuade, not coerce, them; that Spanish warfare against them was murderous, not heroic and just; and that Spain held title to the New World only to convert the Indians, not to exploit them. His opponents said that the Americans were slaves by nature, that their paganism justified warfare against them, and that their barbarism required their subjection to rulers "wiser and superior in virtue and learning." Las Casas replied that the Indians, created in the image of God, were the "brothers" of the Spaniards and that their virtue surpassed that of Spanish "thieves and plunderers."[5]

Las Casas never journeyed to either Florida or New Mexico, but he had admirers in both places. In 1549 the Dominican Luis Cancer tried in Florida to put into practice Las Casas's dictum that conversion would best occur when missionaries unaided by soldiers lived alongside the Indians they wanted to convert. The Carmelite Antonio de la Ascensión in New Mexico later warned Philip III against policies that would "cause the total ruin and destruction of all the Indians, . . . as the Bishop of Chiapa, Don Fray Bartolomé de las Casas, relates." Las Casas's bleak truths lingered especially among the missionaries who struggled with Spanish governors and soldiers about power and authority in New Mexico.[6]

Some missionaries favored coercion, but most preferred voluntary assent. When the Franciscans moved into New Mexico and the Jesuits resumed in 1566 Cancer's missionary endeavors in Florida, they continued a mission that had already begun to experiment with diverse means of persuasion. The missionaries to the South American Indians had used pictures, music, ceremony, elaborate architecture, processions, and plays to attract converts. The Franciscans, Jesuits, and Dominicans who journeyed northward employed similar techniques.[7]

It would be misleading to picture the Spanish as calculating schemers who merely manipulated ceremonies and symbols; they were themselves caught up in a symbolic, ceremonial world. When Juan de Oñate led his party of four hundred north into New Mexico in 1598, they advanced like a procession of medieval monks. Whatever their hard-nosed intentions to secure economic and political dominion, they remained immersed within a cosmos populated by divine forces and supernatural spirits. Oñate required that they hear frequent sermons and receive the sacraments, and he had them build chapels along the trail, some containing representations of the tomb of Jesus. The soldiers not only donned costumes and enacted sacred dramas but also scourged themselves, beating their backs and begging forgiveness for their sins. The king's instructions specified that Oñate's main purpose should be "the service of God, the spreading of His holy Catholic faith, and the reduction and pacification of the natives," and Oñate promised to convert all the Indians he met.[8]

The Spaniards had no sense of entering a region with its own sacred spaces, and they proved eager to erect their own. On special occasions— when they crossed the Rio Grande, for example, or on religious holidays— Oñate ordered the construction of chapels, and when the Spaniards occupied a village they immediately built churches that not only symbolized the sanctifying of the territory but also housed the altars where "the body and blood of the Son of God" could be offered as a sacrifice. They consecrated their buildings and altars with ceremonies and adorned them with decoration, confident that Indians who lived in the shadow of the altars would be inclined toward conversion. The traditional oral histories of the Pueblos, however, recalled only their resentment at the labor required to build the churches.[9]

The Pueblos had their own sacred spaces. By 1598 they had inhabited the Upper Rio Grande Valley for over 350 years, building a complex civilization ordered by an intricate system of rituals. Dwelling in some seventy permanent, autonomous towns, they organized their society in accord with a sense of themselves as inhabitants of sanctified space. Every pueblo had its sacred spaces, radiating in concentric circles from the center of the pueblo or from other designated locations, which could be marked by holy caves, altars, shrines, or ceremonial kivas (holy rooms connecting the surface of the earth to the mysterious underworld from which all life had emerged). Believing that they occupied the middle or center of the cosmos, the Pueblos used the sacred centers as intersections of the six ritual directions, which extended north, south, east, and west, as well as up and down. Those points on the compass of the numinous guided the ceremonial circuits of Pueblo worship and oriented the culture spatially.[10]

Both cultures, then, honored special places of ritual activity, but the sacred spaces in the two cultures symbolized conflicting religious and political conceptions. For the Catholics the high altar within the consecrated building honored an exalted deity whose heavenly abode awaited faithful individuals who conformed their lives to the commandments of a savior. For the Pueblos the *sipapu*, the pit within the kiva, recalled the host of divine beings from the underworld—"the god of the water," "the god of the mountains," and "gods of the hunt, crops, and other things"—who, from their earthly abodes, maintained the natural harmony in which the group, not distinct individuals, could flourish before returning, as members of the group, to their underworld place of origin. In a broader sense the Pueblos thought of their land as an environment ordered by spirits who had specified the duties—and the ceremonial and political leadership—that would ensure reciprocal harmony; the Spaniards asked them to conceive of the land as the creation of a remote deity and the possession of a remote human sovereign to whom they owed tribute.[11]

The missionaries came also with distinctive notions of time. European Catholics organized their year around an array of religious festivals, including dozens of saints' days, climaxed each year by the holy week of Easter. That calendar marked the rhythm of life in the Spanish missions. Oñate's friars named the Sacramento River "for the reason that [they] arrived at its banks on Holy Thursday, the feast of the Blessed Sacrament." At such sacred times as "Holy Thursday and Friday" before Easter, Indian converts in New Spain sometimes stood in shifts throughout the twenty-four hours, "praying the rosary in complete silence."[12]

In observing the Catholic calendar, those converts behaved in accordance with a conception of time quite unlike that of traditional Pueblos, who perpetuated a cycle of ritual activities determined by the natural rhythms of an agrarian calendar. No Pueblo language contained terms for abstract units like weeks, hours, and minutes. Pueblo adults, guided by ceremonial specialists, observed the passage of time through the rites that followed the changing phases of the sun and moon and ensured the success of the pueblo in the cycles of planting, irrigating, harvesting, and hunting. Their ceremonies reflected the rhythms of nature and the patterns established in the primordial time when the "ancient ones" had taught the new arrivals from the underworld how to cure, to dance, and to sing the songs ensuring that they could tap the power of the sky and earth.[13]

The shared belief in sacred days and seasons constituted a formal link between the two cultures, but the similarity was only superficial. While the sacred seasons of the Pueblos marked occasions of communal participation designed to promote the physical and social well-being of the group, the liturgical seasons of the Catholics marked a communal remembrance of historical events designed to ensure the eternal well-being of faithful individuals. Each conception had its corresponding social arrangements. The Pueblo calendar required a ceremonial specialist—the Spanish called him a *cacique*—who preserved the esoteric knowledge that guided the yearly round of ritual activities. Assisting him were the curing, hunting, and warrior associations—and, during periods of war, a war priest—who managed specialized ceremonial tasks at their proper times. The ritual calendar thus established not only the religious but also the political structure of the pueblo. But the Catholic calendar suggested no such overlapping; the priests served as moral and ritual leaders but not as governors. The Spanish therefore proposed to separate functions that the Pueblos considered inseparable.[14]

Spanish Catholics enacted their doctrine through vivid patterns of gesture and sound. For centuries Catholic theologians had argued that the faithful had access to gifts of grace through the seven sacraments, which they had interpreted as means of salvation. They had also denoted the domain of the sacred by means of vestments and devotional objects. When Oñate came to New Mexico, he made special arrangements for an ample supply of "vestments, ornaments, and whatever may be essential for the administration of the sacraments," and his friars advertised traditional gestures and objects as means of both temporal and eternal prosperity. They told the Indians that baptism healed both the soul and the body and that the cross could save both. Benavides explained that "if they worshipped this holy symbol with all their hearts they would find therein the aid for all their needs"—a message that promptly attracted a woman with a toothache who "put her teeth close to the holy cross" to obtain relief. Pueblo converts sometimes found their own ways to exalt Catholic ceremonial. One chief told his people, after baptism, that "he felt such great rejoicing and courage in his heart that he considered himself to be much braver than before," whereupon his followers immediately sought the sacrament for themselves.[15]

The Franciscans valued oral ritual formulas removed from everyday usage and enunciated in a language distinguished from the vernacular. They appreciated as well the devotional uses of chants and communal formulaic song. Fray Francisco Escobar, for instance, "taught the Indians to make musical instruments and how to play them, with which they now celebrate the divine service with great solemnity." The friars took pride in the boys' choirs that they created in the larger pueblos. The churches resonated with the sounds of plain chants, wind instruments, and trumpets, and, as the example of Benavides illustrated, the missionaries devoutly employed music as an instrument of persuasion.[16]

The Pueblos understood something of the Spanish ritual sounds and gestures because they too had created a culture in which bodily movement and ritual sound carried profound meaning. They cherished ceremony and dance in which beads and prayer sticks, bathing and head washing, and kachina dolls and kachina masks gave embodiment to corporate hopes and memories. The kachinas honored the multiplicity of spirits and the ancient ones who had directed the emergence from the underworld and who continued to ensure ample harvests and successful hunts. The dances both recalled the past and promised to control future events, and the respect for gesture in the dance found further expression in other kinetic performance. Running, for example, could serve as a mimetic ritual to speed up the clouds or hasten the growth of crops. Such ceremonies consisted in part of traditional oral prayers and shouting songs, sometimes esoteric even to the Indians, who nevertheless felt it imperative to learn them flawlessly because a misspoken syllable could shatter the unbroken acoustic linkage to the past and prevent a petition from accomplishing its purpose.[17]

When the Catholic missionaries came to New Mexico, it was natural for the Pueblos to note the similarities between crucifixes and prayer sticks, holy water and yucca suds; incense and smoking rituals; liturgical chants and sacred Indian formulas; saints and ancestral heroes. But rather than accenting similarities, the Franciscans tried to destroy Pueblo "idolatry." They told the Indians that Christian rites could accomplish everything the traditional ceremonies had accomplished—and more. The Catholic ceremonies, explained Father Roque de Figueredo, allied their devotees with a deity "so powerful and strong that, having Him on their side, they would be protected and defended from their spiritual as well as earthly enemies." So the missionaries advertised the mundane advantages of their rituals; they could bring healing, call forth rain, and create good harvests.[18]

Ritual actions assumed unusual importance in Franciscan efforts at persuasion partly because most of the missionaries never mastered the four or five Pueblo languages and their several dialects. They either used Christian Indians as translators or encouraged the natives to learn Spanish. Although they maintained a regimen of simple catechetical instruction and exhortation, this could rarely proceed beyond elementary teachings. They did rejoice when the Pueblos showed signs of doctrinal understanding, such as when one convert displayed a chamois decorated with a cross superimposed above a sun and a moon, explaining that the heavenly bodies were created objects rather than divine beings. But the Pueblos never developed much interest in the story of Jesus, let alone in doctrines of hell or sinfulness, and the missionaries worried more about ethical and ritual behavior than about doctrine. The Franciscan inclination to baptize large numbers as a prelude to later indoctrination—they reported questionable figures of 34,000 baptisms in 1626 and 60,000 in 1630—exemplified that preoccupation with ritual actions.[19]

Pueblo traditionalists fought for their ancient religion, therefore, primarily by questioning the efficacy of Catholic ritual. They warned against baptism by the priests: "they should not allow them to sprinkle water on their heads because they would be certain to die from it." They argued that such ceremonies as processional flagellations revealed the Spaniards to be deranged: "How are you crazy?" asked one Pueblo religious leader. "You go through the streets in groups flagellating yourselves, and it is not well that the people of this pueblo should commit such madness as spilling their own blood by scourging themselves." Traditional Pueblo oral histories recalled a widespread belief that a five-year drought resulted from attendance at church and neglect of the kiva ceremonies.[20]

The ceremonial preoccupations that nurtured the mission also helped to destroy it. The Pueblo Revolt of 1680 occurred after Spanish authorities began seriously to enforce older injunctions against native ceremonies. The Indians had long chafed, to be sure, under clashes about land and water rights and abuses in the labor system. In the conflict between church and state in New Mexico, each side accused the other of brutality, and indeed both priests and governors could exploit and abuse the Indians. One rebel told the Spanish that the uprising occurred partly because the Indians simply "were tired of the work they had to do for the Spaniards and the religious."[21]

Even so, the Pueblos refrained from violent rebellion until a new Spanish governor, Juan Francisco de Treviño, began in 1675 to suppress the kivas and confiscate sacred masks and prayer sticks. Earlier governors had resisted Franciscan efforts to ban Pueblo ceremonies, but when an extended drought convinced many Christian Indians to question the practical value of Catholic ritual and to resume traditional rites, the friars persuaded the governor to act. The Indians rose up only after he imprisoned and executed Pueblo medicine men. It was no accident that the leaders of the rebellion—including the charismatic leader known simply as El Popé—were the caretakers of ceremonial. El Popé secured support by telling the people that their traditional gods remained stronger than the Spanish god, that they "should burn all the images and temples, rosaries and crosses, and that all the people should discard the names given them in holy baptism and call themselves whatever they liked."[22]

The Spaniards who questioned captured rebels conveyed the same explanation. As the Indian Don Pedro Nanoba said, the old symbols and ceremonies had never disappeared:

He declared that the resentment which all the Indians have in their hearts has been so strong, from the time this kingdom was discovered, because the religious and the Spaniards took away their idols and forbade their sorceries and idolatries; that they have inherited successively from their old men the things pertaining to their ancient customs; and that he has heard this resentment spoken of since he was of an age to understand.[23]

To the Spaniards, therefore, it seemed that the revolt came from people who were "carried away by their anger and hatred of the holy faith."[24]

Religious symbols became the special objects of Pueblo wrath. The Indians burned the churches, mocked the vestments, whipped crucifixes, defaced statues of the Virgin, ridiculed Catholic ritual, and destroyed the sacred vessels.[25] To rid themselves of their baptismal names and the taint of the sacramental water and oils, they plunged into rivers and washed themselves with herbs, believing "that there would thus be taken from them the character of the holy sacraments." Then they rebuilt their kivas, recovered their sacred masks, and "danced throughout the kingdom the dance of the [kachinas]." "The God of the Spaniards," they shouted, "is dead."[26]

70

Huronia and New France

Unlike the Pueblos, the Hurons of southern Ontario and upper New York constructed no sacred buildings, shrines, or altars. They had no religious specialists bearing the same political power as the Pueblo *caciques*, although they did pay special heed to certain old men who at feasts recited the stories that bound them together as a people, and they did turn for aid to spiritual guides who claimed supernatural powers to control wind and rain, find lost objects, predict future events, and cure illness. But Huronia was a matrilineal society, in which women passed on names and bloodlines, and both men and women assumed responsibilities for transmitting religious traditions to the children. Huron religion formed no institutionally delimited sphere; it was a structure of customs, ceremonies, and stories thoroughly integrated into everyday activities. The Hurons called it their *onderha*, the foundation of their country.[27]

But although the Hurons created no sacred shrines, they did share with the Pueblos a sense of the sacredness of their surroundings. Viewing the sky as an overarching spirit, they believed also that every other object in the physical world possessed a spirit—an *oki*—friendly or unfriendly. Hills and rocks, lakes and rivers, inspired devotion because of the belief that they housed spirits. The Huron creation story—about the first woman, Aataentsic, who had fallen from the sky onto the back of a Great Tortoise—explained the origin and sanctity of the lakes and rivers. Aataentsic's beneficent grandson Iouskeha, whom the Hurons sometimes identified with the sun, not only created the lakes and rivers but also filled nature with wild game and caused the crops to grow. Unlike his grandmother, who brought disease and death and reigned over the dead, Iouskeha made the earth flourish. Along with the lesser spirits, he brought into being a sacred cosmos, and the Hurons responded with rituals—whether sprinkling tobacco on a lake or talking to fish spirits—designed to maintain harmony with that natural yet supernatural world.[28]

Although the Hurons probably followed no regular ritual calendar and had no ancestral cult that rendered the past sacred, they did schedule their primary festivals in accord with the passage of the seasons. The breaking of furniture and the destruction of other property during their main winter festival, conducted on behalf of the sick, symbolized their return to a chaotic primordial time, which produced a flurry of dreams that could be narrated in the form of puzzles and riddles. Their sense of time found further expression in their consecrating the periodic moments on which their existence depended; repeated rituals sanctified the hunting expedition, the fishing trip, or the battle. The Hurons extended those moments into an afterlife in which the hunt, the fishing trip, and the battle would continue.[29]

Like the Pueblos, the Hurons expressed cultural and religious assumptions through painstaking attention to gesture and ceremonial sounds. They believed that the dances and rites of their main feasts had been revealed by spirits, and they cultivated fixed customs that governed even the facial gestures or the inclination of the head during a particular dance. As part of their ritual, the Hurons used masks, charms, and other visible means of influencing the spirits. Dancers often wore wooden masks or appeared with other ritual disguises; medicine men had recourse to charms and amulets, as well as singing and the pounding of tortoise shell drums, to ward off evil spirits and heal the sick. In the oral culture of the Hurons, such sounds and gestures, transmitted from generation to generation, created communal identity while also serving more immediate practical purposes.[30]

The French traders and missionaries who encountered the Hurons entered a world in which meanings continually found expression through ceremonial sounds and gestures. Such a world bore a remotely familiar aspect to the missionaries who arrived in New France after Champlain founded Quebec in 1608, for they too were accustomed to expressing ideas through ritual forms. But they disagreed with each other in their evaluations of Huron ritual and in their judgments about how to transform Huron culture.

The Recollect priests who came in 1615 shared the opinion of the Spanish Franciscans that effective persuasion required the total transformation of the native culture. A branch of the Franciscan order, the Recollects maintained a suspicion of indigenous ceremonies and habits. Father Joseph Le Caron declared in 1624 that the Indians, mentally "benighted," held "nothing but what is extravagant and ridiculous" in religion, and Father Louis Hennepin, writing more than half a century later, echoed that bleak analysis. The Indians, he said, still clung to "savage, brutal, and barbarous" customs. The Recollects therefore persistently claimed that the Hurons could become Christians only if they first became civilized, and civilization required the abandonment of both ritual and traditional customs. The Hurons must become French, and then they could become Christian.[31]

The Jesuits took another position. Active in New France as early at 1611, they began to dominate the mission after 1625. Initially they too believed it necessary to refine the Indians before converting them, but after 1640 they changed their minds. In accordance with a long-standing assumption of Jesuit missionary activity, moreover, they sought, unlike the Franciscans, to discover points of commonality between Catholicism and native religions that would serve as starting places for conversion. Father Jean de Brébeuf expressed pleasure in discovering that the Hurons worshipped the sky, for he believed that he could move from that symbol to the Catholic doctrine of God. It was common among the Jesuits to affirm that all people bore at least a remnant of a primal revelation. Father Julien Perrault, reporting in 1635 that he had discovered among the Indians no signs of any natural knowledge of God, assumed that if he persisted he could find the remnant, "for it is not credible," he said, "that the light of nature should be altogether extinct in them." The Recollect Louis Hennepin disagreed with such beliefs, arguing that the Indians were "incapable of reasoning the most common things of Religion and Faith," but the Jesuit confidence in the remnant endured.[32]

Hennepin complained that the Indians liked "the outward ceremonies of our Church, but no more." The Jesuits again disagreed. Because they made it a point to learn the native languages, they could engage the Hurons in extended theological disputations. Brébeuf tried to convince them that the obvious order and design in nature proved the Creator to be "some beneficent *oki*, and some supereminent intelligence." He also prepared a Huron catechism with teachings about the Apostles' Creed, the Trinity, the remission of sins, the necessity for faith and good works, purgatory, the four kinds of sins, the seven sacraments, and the Ten Commandments.[33]

Jesuit reports contained ample evidence of theological discussion. The Jesuit missionary Paul LeJeune disputed with a Montagnais priest named Carigonan over the origin of the universe, the nature of evil, and the composition of the soul, leading the Indian to conclude that the Jesuit was an "ignoramus" with "no sense" and the Jesuit to reply that the priest wallowed in superstition. They also debated for several days in 1633 about the afterlife. LeJeune contended for a celestial heaven; Carigonan argued for a "village of souls" that resembled the villages of Huron society. Other similar debates covered such topics as hell, which many Hurons found incredible, and sin, which the Hurons understood as specific misdeeds rather than a universal condition. "As for me," insisted one Huron disputant, "I do not recognize any sins."[34]

Such debates often tested the Jesuits' rhetorical skills to the limit. The Hurons admired rhetorical power, and Indian orators displayed an elaborate, emphatic, highly metaphorical style of delivery. The Jesuits often complained that the Indian languages, lacking abstract and universalizing terms, hindered them in debate. The Hurons had another point of view; they found the missionaries "to possess little intelligence in comparison to themselves."[35]

As in New Spain, symbols and ceremonies deeply informed French efforts at persuasion. Clashing perceptions of space and time, gesture and sound attracted the curiosity of the Indians and governed the strategy of the missionaries. By encouraging a blending of Huron and Catholic ritual, the missionaries hoped to give a Christian character to Huron usages. But eventually the rituals generated resistance and conflict.

Like Spanish Catholics the French thought of the church not only as a universal society but also as an array of geographical parishes, sacred spaces encompassing a territorial region. Partly for this reason the Recollects began their mission with the hope of forming mission towns and sedentary farming communities for the Indians, and the Jesuits at first pursued the same goal. Both groups also believed, moreover, that mobile clans of hunters would prove impossible to convert and that towns—in which most Hurons lived, in any case—could become nurseries of civility. The Jesuits' decision to travel with wandering Huron bands therefore meant that they no longer considered it necessary to make the Indians over into Europeans before they converted them. It represented an abandoning of parochial assumptions and an assertion of confidence in the innate qualities of the Indians.[36]

The Jesuits did not abandon their Catholic notions about holy places; they always thought that conversion would proceed more easily in the shadow of sanctified sites. Thus they normally restricted sacramental worship to consecrated space "to cause the Sacrament to be more highly respected." For similar reasons they also decorated their chapels and churches as splendidly as possible. When they built their central residence at Saint-Marie in 1639, they placed large crosses at the four corners of the enclosure, and after they consecrated the chapel and cemetery, the site became a reliquary containing the remains of the martyrs. When they left the town ten years later, they burned it to the ground, "for fear," said one missionary, "that our enemies . . . should profane the sacred place."[37]

Disagreements about such notions of consecrated space could have profound implications. During the early 1640s baptized Hurons announced that they did not wish to be buried in the traditional ossuaries; they preferred the Catholic cemeteries. The announcement disturbed Huron traditionalists because the custom of holding festivals for reburial of the dead in large bone pits had reflected both social solidarity and a common worldview. The mixing of the bones symbolized the sense of social commonality, and the festivals also gave expression to the conventional Huron view of the soul. Believing that every person has two souls—one that animates the body and one that transcends it—the Hurons viewed the pit burial as the occasion when one soul traveled westward to join those who had died earlier, while the other soul remained in the ossuary as part of a larger community of souls awaiting rebirth. To question the need for the ossuary was implicitly to question this view of the soul. Without the notion of the dual soul, much of the Huron ritual would lose its inner coherence.[38]

The notion of the dual soul underlay, for example, one of the central themes of Huron ritual: the importance of the dream. In a dream, the Hurons believed, one soul left the body and underwent separate adventures. When it returned, it could not reunite with the other soul unless the person could enact the dream. Hurons therefore turned to religious guides to help them interpret and fulfill their dreams, even if only in symbolism. At least one yearly festival, the Ononharoia, existed solely for the purpose of dream fulfillment, and the high status of the medicine men depended largely on their capacities to interpret the dreams. When Christian Indians chose consecrated cemeteries over pit burials, therefore, they called into question not only the festivals and the shamans but also a central assumption in the culture.[39]

The title page of Thomas Hariot's *A briefe and true report of the new found land of Virginia. (British Museum)*

"The Conjurer," by John White from Thomas Hariot's *A briefe and true report of the new found land of Virginia. (British Museum)*

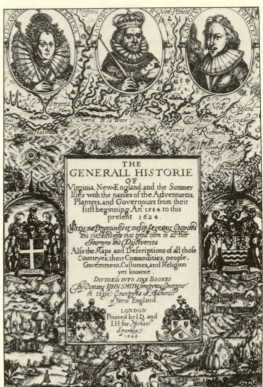

The title page of John Smith's *Generall Historie of Virginia, New-England, and the Summer Isles* (1624), with depictions of Queen Elizabeth, King James, and Prince Charles. The map at the top is of Virginia and New England.

Captain John Smith's map of Virginia, with drawings of Powhatan before his council and of a "giant-like Sasquesananoug" warrior, from Smith's *Generall Historie*.

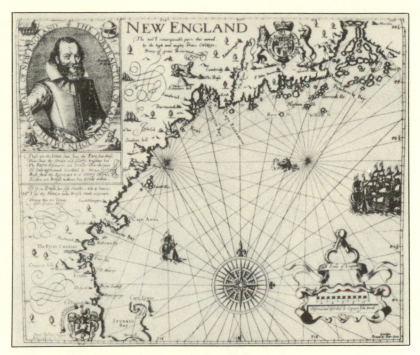

Captain John Smith's map of New England, with a drawing of Smith in the upper left hand corner, from his *Generall Historie*.

"King Powhatan commands Captain Smith to be slain," from Smith's *Generall Historie*.

Governor John Winthrop of the Massachusetts Bay Colony. *(American Antiquarian Society)*

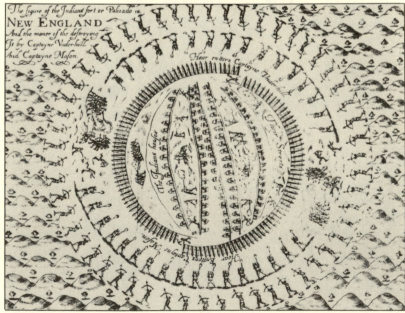

John Underhill's drawing in his *Newes from America* (1638) of the massacre of an Indian village during the Pequot War of 1637. *(New England Historical and Genealogical Society)*

The Old Brick Church (St. Luke's) in Smithfield, Virginia, an English brick Gothic parish church with wall buttresses and lancet windows, 1632. *(Sandak)*

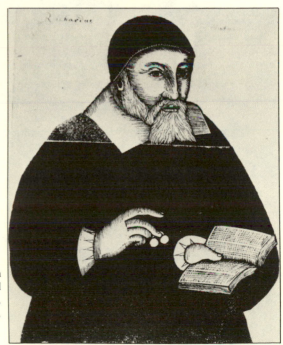

The earliest surviving American print, a woodcut of Richard Mather, minister at Dorchester, by John Foster. *(Houghton Library, Harvard University)*

Governor Peter Stuyvesant in New Amsterdam, from an anonymous painting. *(New York Historical Society)*

San Esteban, built by Franciscan missionaries on the mesa of Acoma, probably completed around 1642. *(New Mexico Economic Development and Tourism Department)*

and much more from play on [*s*] the Lords day; that we may draw nigh to God in holy duties.

s Isa. 58. 12, 13. Exo.32.6.

Q. *What is the fifth Commandement ?*

A. Honour thy Father and thy Mother, [*t*] that thy dayes may be long in the Land, which the Lord thy God giveth thee.

t Exo.20. 12. *u* Pro. 23. 22

Quest. *Who are here meant by father and mother ?*

x Kings 5. 13. and 2. 12.

Answ. All our Superiours, whether in [*u*] Family, School, Church, and Common-wealth.

1 Cor. 4. 15. 2 Chron. 29. 18. 1 Tim. 5. 1.

Quest. *What is the honour due to them ?*

1 Sam. 25. 8. Gen. 4. 2c, 21.

Anf. Reverence [*w*] Obedience, and (when I am able) Recompence.

w Mal.1.6. Heb. 12. 9. Eph. 6. 1.

Quest. *What is the sixth Commandement ?*

1 Tim. 5. 4. *x* Exo. 20. 13.

Answ. Thou shalt do no (*x*) murther.

y Mat. 5. 22.

Q. *What is the meaning of this Commandement ?*

2 Cor. 7. 10. 1 Sam. 26. 24. Mark 3. 4.

Answ. That we should not shorten the (*y*) life, or health of our selves or others, but preserve both.

Q. *What*

A page of John Cotton's *Spiritual Milk for Babes*, a catechism first published in London in 1646. *(Houghton Library, Harvard University)*

An anonymous painting of the Reverend John Davenport, Puritan minister in New Haven. *(Yale University)*

A drawing of the *Stadthuys*, a brick house with tiled roof, in New Amsterdam in 1679. *(Museum of the City of New York)*

Mrs. Freake and Baby Mary, an anonymous painting from New England in 1674. *(Worcester Art Museum)*

The Jesuits also proposed an alternative observance of sacred time. The Hurons initially ridiculed the Jesuit emphasis on the ordering of time, especially the notion of calendar-oriented fasting. But the missionaries went to great lengths to ensure that converts would order their devotion in accordance with a Catholic sense of time. They sought discipline and punctuality, with bells calling the faithful to divine service sometimes three times a day, and they honored Sundays and feast days. The converted Indians, wrote one priest, "take with them to the woods a memorandum or short catalogue of the Festival days, which they observe with much respect," and the missionaries carefully provided pictorial reminders on which the converts "distinguished the days and the months and Feasts by different marks." Like burial in a Catholic cemetery, the observance of the Catholic calendar in Huronia constituted a journey from one religious and social world to another.[40]

It was, however, the French Catholic patterns of gesture and sound that both fascinated the Hurons and deepened hostilities. Jesuit dress furnished the Indians with descriptive categories for naming the intruders. The Jesuits became known as "black gowns" and "black robes"; Ursuline nurses as "women in white." French ceremony and ritual often consisted of elaborate processionals, the priests wearing surplices and sashes, chanting psalms and singing prayers, carrying candles and crucifixes, tapers and censers. Catholic worship proceeded to the sound of songs, violins, flutes, bells, and organs, with solemn priests intoning the ancient rubrics of worship. At the celebration of the Mass, the priests genuflected reverently before the Blessed Sacrament while other worshippers stood silently. The Missionaries recognized fully the persuasive power of such ceremony. When Father Jean Enjalran wrote for "things which may help us win these poor Indians," he asked for medals, crucifixes, small crosses, rings, and rosaries. Both the Recollects and the Jesuits made use of ornate dress and furnishings to impress the Indians. The Recollects liked to show unconverted Hurons a splendid chasuble given them by the queen. "The mere sight of it," wrote one missionary, "would comfort them, and seem to alleviate their sufferings."[41]

The Jesuits did not hesitate to claim that Catholic sounds and gestures conveyed unusual powers. They taught that the crucifix and the sign of the cross could ward off and exorcise devils and that "the application of the Crucifix and holy water" could heal physical maladies. Huron converts therefore sought to master or possess such instruments of power. "Crosses, medals, and other similar Articles," wrote one observer, "are their most precious jewels."[42]

When tensions between the French and the Hurons periodically intensified, those gestures and sounds became the symbols of the cultural differences. The Jesuits condemned the songs and dances that marked the annual gatherings of the Hurons. They rejoiced at any sign that "the chants and

Drums of the sorcerers or jugglers are losing their influence." The Huron revitalization prophets who led the resistance against the French in the 1640s, on the other hand, insisted that the Hurons maintain their traditional rites, and they concentrated their attacks on the Catholic ceremonies. By the late 1640s they charged that Catholic spells and charms destroyed their crops and caused disease. Some associated baptism with premature death and images with harmful magic. Others suspected that the French concealed dangerous spells and charms in their books and inkstands; reading and writing assumed a sinister aspect to people who could neither read nor write. Still others demanded that images be removed from French chapels.[43]

Many of the Hurons rejected what the Jesuits had to offer. "Your world is different from ours," one of them said; "the God who created yours did not create ours." As early as 1616 a Jesuit missionary had reported the sad news back to France: "For all your arguments, and you can bring a thousand of them if you wish, are annihilated by this single shaft which they always have at hand, *Aoti Chabaya* (they say), 'That is the Savage way of doing it. You can have your way and we will have ours; every one values his own wares.'" Hurons sometimes spoke of heaven as a French place. "I have no acquaintances there," said one Huron woman, "and the French who are there would not care to give me anything to eat." One of the new cults that arose during the 1640s to oppose the Christian missions announced that the French heaven was a place of torture for Huron converts.[44]

As Huron culture collapsed under the force of Iroquois pressure after 1646, the number of baptisms rapidly increased. The Jesuit strategies of affixing Christian meanings to Huron rituals, of seeking points of commonality with Huron belief, and of spending their lives in Huron villages built bridges that made it easier for the Indians, their society in disarray, to accept a new faith. By the time the conversions came, however, the Hurons had dwindled in number and in the capacity to sustain their society. Only as they abandoned their own sacred spaces under the threat of violent destruction did they enter in large numbers into the consecrated churches of New France.[45]

Preachers and Powwows

Compared to the Pueblos, the native Americans of southern New England were almost like Puritans. They had no permanent sacred kivas, apparently preserved no formulaic chants that required letter-perfect rendition, maintained no ritual societies devoted to the proper celebration of sacred seasons, displayed no sacred art equivalent to that of the Kachina dolls and masks, and distinguished political and religious leadership. Any analogy between Puritans and the Algonkian-speaking people of the northeast woodlands is far more misleading than revealing, however. The southern New England Indians—especially the Wampanoag, the Massachuset, and the Narraganset, who lived near the English—developed a mental world rooted in the soil, tradition, and the authority of ceremonial specialists.

No one knows when the native peoples of southern New England became primarily farmers rather than hunters and gatherers, but the transition was manifest by the seventeenth century, and it enhanced not only the economy but also the conceptual richness of the Algonkian-speaking societies. While maintaining ritual and belief from earlier periods, they expanded their symbolic world in the quest for harmony with the land. The agricultural changes promoted new perceptions of space and time. Their pantheon maintained the respect for animal spirits characteristic of a hunting society but also exalted both spirits of the earth and a creator.[46]

The creator deity was Cautantowwit—some called him Kytan—who resided in the Southwest. The Narraganset acknowledged that the English deity created the English, but they knew that Cautantowwit "made them and the Heaven, and Earth where they dwell." Dissatisfied with the first man and woman, created from a stone, Cautantowwit had broken them into pieces and created from a tree a second couple, the ancestors of all Indians. Equally important Cautantowwit had sent the corn and beans from his field in the Southwest, which helped to explain why the winds from that direction brought "the pleasingest, warmest wind in the climate . . . making faire weather ordinarily." To that warm and fruitful region "the soules of all their Great and Good men and women" would one day return.[47]

In Cautantowwit's creation lived other gods, dwelling within the sun and the moon, the fire and the water, the deer and the bear, and elsewhere. Roger Williams said that the Narraganset had given him the names of thirty-seven gods, though he also observed that they used the term *manitou*—a god or spirit—to designate any variety of both strange and familiar aspects of their environment. They had *manitous* of the sky, the wind, the directions, corn, colors, men, women, and children. "A stranger that can relate newes in their owne language," said Williams, "they will stile him Manitoo, a God." And when they talked of English ships and buildings, or books and letters, they would "end thus: Manittowock *They are Gods.*"[48]

Such beliefs helped shape the Indians' conception of the land as a place overflowing with countless spiritual forces who demanded respect and gratitude. In their festivals they acknowledged—and tried to control—the gifts of the land. A dry year could call forth "solemne meetings" that lasted for weeks. To them the land was no simple commodity to be exploited or even to be possessed. They cultivated individual fields, and Winslow noted that every sachem knew "how far the bounds and limits of his own country extendeth," but they shared ownership with the spirits and with each other.

77

Notions of individual ownership of land for exclusive use apparently never occurred to them until the English arrived. The land was a sacred space, granting its bounty in mysterious ways.[49]

The agricultural cycle informed their ideas about the passing of time. The Narraganset appear to have directed rites to Cautantowwit in harvest and winter festivals, sometimes held in "great, spacious" houses where thousands might meet to distribute gifts ritually to the poor and sacrifice material possessions to the spirits. Some of their rites recalled older, preagricultural hunting cycles; their hunting rituals tried to soothe the spirits of the animals they killed. But most of their festivals occurred at the time of planting, the appearance of green corn, or the harvest.[50]

Such rituals displayed a profound respect for tradition. No theme appeared more often in Massachuset and Wampanoag discussions with the English than their respect for the "old men" whose memories contained sacred lore, and they resented the English "censoriousness" of their "old ways." "Are we wiser than our forefathers?" they asked. The answer was usually the same: "Why should not we do as they have done?" The forefathers had handed down the songs, dances, and plays that constituted their festivals; they also had transmitted wisdom about Cautantowwit: "Never man saw this Kiehtan," wrote Edward Winslow; "only old men tell them of him, and bid them tell their children, yea to charge them to teach their posterities the same."[51]

The rites reflected a widespread admiration for the gifted powwows, part-time religious specialists who could cause and cure illnesses, interpret dreams, commune with spirits, and interpret the future. The powwows derived their authority in part from their access, through visions or dreams, to the *manitou* Hobbamock, or Chepi, who appeared, Winslow said, only to "the chiefest and most judicious." One might become a powwow by dreaming of Chepi in the shape of a serpent and informing others of the dream in such a manner as to elicit ritual responses of dancing and joy. A powwow on Martha's Vineyard told Thomas Mayhew that he had seen Chepi as a man in the air, a crow, a pigeon, and a serpent. The powwows communicated not only with Chepi—who possibly represented the collective souls of the dead—but also with other spirits who conveyed knowledge and power. Their status depended on their effective use of that power through a repertoire of gestures and sounds. In curing the sick, Williams reported, "they howle and roare, and hollow over them, and . . . all joyne (like a Quire) in Prayer to their gods for them."[52]

Sacred gesture and sound permeated the Algonkian-speaking cultures. In mourning they painted their faces black, in joy red. In curing, the powwows spent themselves, said Williams, "in strange Antick Gestures, and Actions even unto fainting." In festivals the people sang and danced and sometimes cast possessions into a fire. These were not sounds and gestures that the English were prepared to understand.[53]

Thomas Morton concluded that the Indians had "no worship nor religion at all"; William Wood believed that they worshipped "something," but he found it hard to understand what it was; Edward Winslow first concluded that they had no religion but later decided that they had a "knowledge of . . . God," however "barbarous." The English inevitably interpreted Indian beliefs in terms of their own religion and culture, and their Puritan, Calvinist form of Christianity made them exceedingly uneasy with Algonkian ritual and belief. Some viewed it as a confused vestige of the original revelation; others saw it as a desiccated remnant of Jewish belief; most concluded that it came from the devil.[54]

The Puritan clergy and their congregations had repudiated the sacred times, spaces, gestures, and sounds of medieval Catholicism and contemporary Anglicanism. English Puritans had urged that the Church cease "the observation of dayes and tymes"; they had demanded the abolition of "monuments of Idolatry," whether "Temples, Altars, Chappels" or "other place[s]." They had decried special garments for the clergy, discarded most traditional ritual gestures—like the sign of the cross in baptism or kneeling at the sacrament—as human inventions, and abolished chants and hymns. American Puritans sought to form a community free of consecrated altars, saints' days, surplices, censers, and plainsong.[55]

Thomas Shepard proclaimed that "under the New Testament, all places . . . are equally holy." He meant that no place—no building, no altar, no shrine—bore any special aura of holiness. The Puritans conceived of the church as a congregation of the faithful, not a geographical parish. They built general meetinghouses, not special church buildings; they built them in a square or rectangular, never a cruciform, shape; and they tolerated no hint of a central sacred space, an altar, where divine mysteries occurred. They despised the adornment of churches and ridiculed Catholic efforts to "satisfie the eyes" with "gorgeous Temples." They discarded the rites with which Anglicans consecrated church yards and village boundaries.[56]

Even colonists without Puritan inclinations had no way of understanding native American ideas about the land. To the English it was no sacred space shared with supernatural beings but a source of commodities. Indian methods of farming, which used neither enclosure nor tillage by deep-cutting plows, suggested to the English that the American land lay empty, "spacious and void." According to the doctrine of the *vacuum domicilium*, the Indians had never "subdued" the earth and therefore possessed only a "natural," not a "civil," right to it. The civil right was what counted. Englishmen and Indians therefore had irreconcilable differences about the concept of land rights. The Indians believed that their land belonged to the band or tribe.

The English thought that civil title belonged to the king as sovereign lord, whose patents then permitted individual ownership by the colonists. Land disputes between the two groups seldom addressed this fundamental issue, for the English usually kept the Indians ignorant of the king's grandiose pretensions. The conflicts focused on more limited questions about the authority of individual Indians to cede the land of the group or about the means the English used to gain their consent. Although Indian resentment toward English land hunger mounted steadily, Roger Williams was the only prominent settler to worry much about colonial usurpation.[57]

The English expressed bafflement at the migratory habits of the Indians, who felt free suddenly to abandon one region and move to another, only to return later. The colonists, who bounded space within fences and organized it in geometric patterns, thought of the land either as a "wilderness" or as "improved," "dressed," and cultivated. Improvement, in their view, required stability. By 1646, therefore, the General Court even proposed to purchase land on which the Indians could be encouraged to live in an "orderly" way. Most Indians preferred another form of order.[58]

English notions of time also provided little occasion for mutual understanding between the natives and the settlers. The Puritans had repudiated calendrical rites, including the Catholic array of sacred times. They found no biblical warrants for saints' days and holy days. New Englanders could not openly celebrate Christmas until 1681, when a royal governor forced them to repeal their laws against it. The ban included all Christian holidays, even Easter, which until 1687 made no appearance in any New England almanac. New England's sacred time was the primordial time of the biblical beginnings, and that ruled out most other sacred times.[59]

They did, however, believe in the sanctifying of the Sabbath, for the Fourth Commandment enjoined them to remember the Sabbath day and keep it holy. Some New Englanders questioned the holiness of the day, arguing that the Sabbath laws of the Old Testament had been merely ceremonial, but the people in control accepted the position that "a stated time of worship"—one day in seven—was a moral duty. Thomas Shepard contended in 1649 in his *Theses Sabbaticae* that both Scripture and experience proved "that religion is just as the Sabbath is, and decays and grows as the Sabbath is esteemed," and the New England churches remained tenacious in their support for painstaking observation of the day. But the one sacred day observed widely in New England had no parallel in the sacred calendar of the Indians.[60]

The Puritans lacked also the array of gestures and sounds that Catholic missionaries had employed to attract the interest of native Americans. They had rejected medieval vestments as unbiblical; they abandoned most traditional rites as forms of unlawful worship. John Cotton described the Catholic ceremonies as sinful concessions to "naturall sence." Catholics tried to "satisfie the eyes" with "goodly Images, and Pictures . . . and Vestures"; they appealed to the smell through "incense and sweet perfumes"; they lured the taste through "Feasts full of luxury and ryot." The Puritans would have none of it. They rejected five of the Catholic sacraments, and they reinterpreted baptism and the Lord's Supper so as to preclude altogether the missionary methods of the Franciscans in New Mexico. The Puritans thought of the two sacraments as "seals of the covenant," and they would baptize only the faithful and their children; they offered the Lord's Supper only to church members.[61]

Cotton also ridiculed Catholic attempts to satisfy "the eares": "You know in their Cathedralls what curious musique they have, both vocall and instrumentall." New England wanted no curious music in the churches. Since King David was a type of Christ, some argued, and since Christ fulfilled the types, it seemed problematic whether New England Christians should even sing David's psalms. Richard Mather, in his preface to the *Bay Psalm Book* in 1640, conceded that David was a type, but he denied that this fact precluded singing. Paul had commanded psalm singing, he said, and the primitive church had practiced it, so New Englanders could sing if they avoided songs of human invention. But the psalm book failed to resolve the matter. Seven years later John Cotton published his *Singing of Psalmes A Gospel-Ordinance* to prove that singing could be considered a holy duty, that the psalms were not merely ceremonial types, and that the biblical history contained ample precedents for singing in church. But music in New England could never become the instrument of persuasion that it was in New Spain and New France.[62]

The Puritans despised almost everything—the sounds, the gestures, the ceremonies—that had evoked the initial interest of the Pueblos and the Hurons in the Catholic missions. They also lacked any consuming passion to persuade the Indians to become Christians. The promoters insisted that "the most eminent and desirable end of planting colonies" was the "propagation of religion," and the royal patent for Massachusetts Bay described the conversion of the Indians as the "principall Ende of this Plantacion," but the Bay Colony waited sixteen years to send forth a missionary, and he had to contend with skepticism from his neighbors. Even the Indians wondered aloud why the English waited so long.[63]

The English had an array of explanations: the Algonkian languages were too difficult, the Indians were insufficiently civilized, the preachers lacked miraculous gifts, and no mission could succeed until the Jews were converted. They also expected that their own good example would change the Indians without the need for any special efforts. But John Eliot, the minister at Roxbury, recognized that the English simply thought of the Indians as "dry and rocky ground." Their viewpoint contained an ample measure of sheer cultural disdain; Eliot's critics in New England said openly that "Indians be all nought."[64]

The mission began almost accidentally on Martha's Vineyard in 1643 when an Indian named Hiacoomes requested Christian instruction from Thomas Mayhew, Jr. Three years later Eliot tried out his new skills in the Massachuset language by preaching to some natives near Dorchester. When he invited questions, they showed no interest in salvation but curiosity about the cause of thunder, the ebbing of tides, and the nature of wind. But Eliot persisted, convinced that the Indians were remnants of the ancient Jews and that their conversion signaled the last days. He and his allies believed that "the time of the fulfilling that Promise is neere," and their excitement about end times permeated their promotion of the mission.[65]

Eliot believed that "the Lord hath made [the] Word the only outward instrumental means to bring home these wandering sinners." This meant that the Puritan mission consisted mainly of preaching, exhortation, catechetical instruction, and the exposition of Scripture. By 1654 Eliot had translated the Westminster *Shorter Catechism* into Massachuset, and by 1663 Indian translators, working closely with him, published the complete Bible in an Indian tongue. He eventually translated fourteen works into the Natick dialect. In his writing, as in his preaching, he tried, he said, "to communicate as much Scripture as I can." But he returned constantly to a few themes. He offered proofs for the existence of the Christian deity, instruction about sin and redemption, and warnings about heaven and hell. But as he trained native preachers, the instruction expanded to include the intricacies of trinitarian doctrine, sometimes prompting the criticism that the preachers made "long and learned discourses to us which we do not well understand."[66]

Assent did not come easily. Eliot invited inquiries and found that the Indians had "a faculty to frame hard and difficult questions." Why, they asked, did God not kill the devil that made all men so bad? If God made hell in one of the six days of creation, why did he make it before Adam had sinned? Why did not God give everyone good hearts? Why does God make the good sick? Why did Christ die for us, and who killed him? How do we know that you have not invented these stories? The Indians also had some practical questions about the new religion. Would prayer to the English God bring "food, gladness, and garments"? Did not Christian Indians remain as poor as the others? And what about sickness? "If they leave off Powwowing, and pray to God, what shall they do when they are sick?" Roger Williams once discovered, in any case, that Indian assent could be discriminating: "When I had discoursed about many points of God, of the creation, of the soule, of the danger of it, and the saving of it, he assented; but when I spake of rising againe of the body, he cryed out, I shall never believe this."[67]

The English complicated things by pushing the Indians to abandon their culture. Eliot never surrendered the conviction that it was "absolutely necessary to carry on civility with religion." Sometimes when he used the term *civility* he referred to the technical Protestant doctrine that God's law had both a civil and a theological use. To civilize meant to bridle and restrain sinners as a prelude to their later humbling through God's redemptive use of the law. But he often used the term to refer merely to "common civility," by which he meant English habits.[68]

"What more hopefull way of doing them good," asked Thomas Shepard, "than by cohabitation in such Townes, neare unto good examples. . . . What greater meanes at least to civilize them?" Beginning in 1651 at Natick Eliot slowly organized fourteen towns of praying Indians. He tried to order them in strict accord with the precedents revealed in the Bible, having them follow Exodus 18 and choose rulers of a hundred, rulers of fifty, and rulers of ten. But inevitably Eliot also had his towns follow English precedent, both for laws and for physical arrangements. The streets, lots, and fenced gardens reproduced English notions of the proper ordering of space.[69]

The mission countered traditional Indian understandings of time by insisting on the strict observance of the Sabbath. The native preacher Anthony reportedly explained that "the doctrine of the sabbath is a great point in religion." By profaning the Sabbath, he said, we turn all religion and good order out of doors and open a door unto all sin and wickedness. Indian converts worried as much as any other Puritans about the proper observance of the day. Some expressed deep dismay about the felling of a tree or the kindling of a fire on the Sabbath; the sachem Cutchamaquin solemnly rebuked his wife for her worldly discourse during the Sabbath hours. The sabbatarianism acquired a tone of worldly prudence when native preachers suggested that observing the days of rest and labor would produce riches. But the day had a deeper meaning to some of the converts.[70]

The Puritans could not introduce the Indians to elaborate ceremonial worship, but they did teach them one ritual gesture that became the mark of a convert: prayer. Eliot taught, moreover, that prayer normally required specific postures and gestures. Those symbolic actions appealed to the native preachers: "Let none lie along or sit, which are postures of unreverence," exhorted the preacher Piumbukhou, "but either stand like servants, or kneel like sons and daughters before the Lord." Eliot told Shepard in 1647 that the Christian Indians "call all religion by that name, praying to God," and that they observed morning and evening prayers, prayers at meals, and prayers at church gatherings, lifting both their eyes and their hands heavenward as they prayed.[71]

Eliot's notions of holy gestures included far more than the ritual enactment of prayer. He wanted the Indians to change entirely the way that they presented themselves to others. He wanted them to halt their healing ceremonies, abandon their mourning rites, and dress like the English. Having agonized over the symbolic meaning of hair length during the civil wars in England, the Puritans fretted about Indian hair styles, which suggested unseemly pride. The missionary's ideal was an Indian who would abandon all the "old Indian customs, laws, fashions, lusts, pauwauings, and whatever else is contrary to the right knowledge of the true God, and of Jesus Christ our redeemer." Such an ideal meant the destruction of native culture.[72]

The missionaries hoped for voluntary assent, but they could also use coercion. One week after Eliot's first mission sermon the General Court declared that "no person," Christian or pagan, could reproach the holy religion of God. The court later decided that no Indian could "performe outward worship to their false gods, or to the devill." The Mayhew mission, which began at the initiative of Hiacoomes, displayed unusual respect for the Indians; the mission in Massachusetts Bay proved more willing to apply political pressure for religious ends. Non-Christian Indians complained to Roger Williams of threats from Christian Indians that "if they would not pray, they should be destroyed by war."[73]

Some converts, however, had their own reasons for turning to Christianity. The collection of Indian confessions that Mayhew and Eliot published in 1653, *Tears of Repentance*, revealed a range of motives. Nataous decided to convert when he heard that his sachem had become a Christian; Tother-swamp accepted Christianity so that "the English should love me"; Waban became interested when he observed that the English seemed "strong to labor"; Monequassun started to pray, albeit skeptically, because he liked living in the praying town of Cohannet; Ponampam became interested when someone convinced him that God made the world. John Speene offered yet another common explanation: "When I first prayed to God, I did not pray for my soul, but only I did as my friends did, because I loved them." The missionaries waited for more satisfying accounts before they formed the first Indian church, but the confessions suggest the variety of motives that got the mission underway.[74]

Accustomed to judging ritual by practical results, some of the Indians were willing to try a new religion to see if it worked. Two sachems told John Winthrop that they desired "to speak reverently of Englishman's God" because they saw that "the Englishman's God doth better for them than other Gods do for others." Another group told Edward Winslow that they admired the English God because he once answered English prayers by sending a "gentle and seasonable rain" instead of the storm that their own prayers had produced. The Pequot Indian Wequash considered the English God to be a mere "Musketto God, or a God like unto a Flye" until the English defeated the Pequots in war; he then decided that England's God "was a most dreadful God." The tendency of the Indians to judge the gods in such terms proved useful to the missionaries. Thomas Mayhew, Jr., attracted converts when his prayers seemed to heal a man whom the powwows had given up for lost; it also helped when his convert Hiacoomes survived a general sickness. Any sign that the English God could outperform Cautantowwit or Chepi attracted attention in the Indian cultures.[75]

More than once after 1616 the Indians had suffered catastrophic losses from epidemics. "They died," said Thomas Morton, "on heapes." Those epidemics probably undermined confidence in the healing power of the medicine men, and it is no surprise that the missionaries had most success among the groups weakened by disease, the loss of land, and the surrender of political autonomy. The missions offered them some real benefits. They could retain some group identity in a familiar setting and secure a measure of physical security. For some of them, moreover, the new religion provided a satisfying explanation for the disarray and a hope for a better future.[76]

The Puritan missionaries—English and Indian—succeeded by 1674 in gathering some twenty-three hundred "Souls yielding obedience to the gospel," but they remained marginal in both the English and the Indian worlds. "Because we pray to God," complained one, "other Indians abroad in the country hate us and oppose us, the English on the other side suspect us, and feare us to be still such as doe not pray at all." When King Philip's War erupted in 1675, the converts suffered from the brutality of both sides. In the end, some thought, they could trust only in the certainties of their new faith: "God who knowes all things, he knowes that wee do pray to him."[77]

Africa in America

For the Africans who came to the New World as slaves, communal identity had to be forged anew. They came from various ethnic backgrounds, spoke different languages, and shared no unified religion. They represented a wide variety of cultural groups—Fulani, Mandinke, Yoruba, Ibo, Ashanti, Bakongo, and Malagasi—and had to begin building a culture from diverse traditions even while they suffered on the slave ships.

They brought no uniform conception of sacred space. Some West Africans entertained a conception of a high god associated with the sky, while also sharing a devotion to pantheons of the lesser gods—water divinities and nature spirits—who sanctified the natural world surrounding them. A traveler to Guinea observed that the natives "worship the sun, and believe that spirits are immortal, and that after death they go to the sun" but that they also worshipped the first natural object that they saw after recovering from an illness. Another traveler to Guinea, however, reported that the people he saw, far from worshipping the sun, felt so frustrated with its heat "that in many places they curse it when it riseth." Still another traveler, after residing with a group of Mandinkes who had converted to Islam, recalled that they worshipped only "the one true God whom they call Alle," permitting no devotion to other spirits, no images of divine things, and no "places they dedicate to holy uses."[78]

The sense of time in the West African cultures could be equally diverse.

It could find expression in periodic calendrical festivals; it could entail a "fetish day" once a week, maintained "more solemnly and stricktly than the *Hollanders* do their Sunday"; it could, in Islamic groups, require a day of worship on Fridays, though with no necessary abstention from trade and other worldly activities. Most of the West African groups did share a respect for the past, manifest in a reverence for ancestors, who were honored as the founders of villages or of kinship circles. Believing that dead ancestors watched to ensure that the living preserved traditional customs, many West Africans attached great importance to burial rites and to rituals designed to reassure the ancestors. The sacralizing of time appeared also in cultic practices associating various gods with the days of the week. Even in America, Africans retained the traditional day names used in ancient tribal customs of naming children. A male born on a Friday could bear the name Cuffee, a female born on a Monday the name Juba, and the other days provided other names. As many as 15 to 20 percent of African children in America bore African names during the colonial period, and many were day names. But time still had diverse meanings in the different West African cultures.[79]

Some practices did provide a formal basis for a common culture in America. Most West African rites, for example, made generous use of gesture and sound as symbols of tribal identity and religious sensibility. An observer on Barbados remarked in 1680 on the Sunday dances with which the Africans sought to procure rain or other benefits. Not only did African societies develop complex dances, but they also made ample use of tangible objects as means of access to sacred precincts and powers. Charms and amulets could protect; divination with entrails or through water gazing could ensure knowledge of the future. Even the Muslims among the Mandinkes, who permitted no pictures or resemblances of divine things, wore special religious objects containing sacred writings to protect them. Throughout the seventeenth century Africans enslaved in Barbados placed their trust in "Figures" and "Representations," which they enshrined in stately earthen vessels. Their rituals proceeded to the repeated sound of song and rhythm, especially the rhythm of the drums. Singing and drumming, along with dreams, could serve as means for ecstatic possession by the gods. They could also establish common cultural patterns in an Afro-American society.[80]

The slave traders went out of their way to destroy those African cultures. They preferred cargoes of people with different customs and different languages. Initially the enslaved Africans did not share even a community of speech. They shared certain broad assumptions and orientations, but they became a community and shared a culture only insofar as they created something new out of their past. They had to build their own culture, partly because the Europeans had few inclinations to invite the Africans into theirs.[81]

Africans could be highly visible or hardly visible at all. In the sixteenth century in Mexico City they outnumbered white immigrants; by 1660 they outnumbered whites in Barbados and lived in great numbers on other Caribbean islands. John Rolfe recorded the arrival of "20. and odd Negroes" in Virginia in 1619, but thirty years later only about 200 Africans, 2 percent of the population, labored there. New England in 1680 had only a few hundred; New York's African population also remained low during the seventeenth century.[82]

Not all the Africans were bound to hereditary lifetime service. New Netherland had some free blacks in 1650; in Virginia some labored the same term as white servants and then gained their freedom, while others purchased freedom from their masters. A few like Anthony Johnson in Northampton County became prosperous planters who flourished within English institutions, even winning court cases against white competitors, while retaining pride in their African past. Johnson's grandson named his own small plantation "Angola."[83]

Even in the sixteenth century, however, some in England thought of blacks simply as slaves, and by 1640 some Africans in America clearly served for life, their children inheriting the same obligation. The attitudes of colonial whites varied in different times and places. In New England they were more flexible than in Virginia, and in Virginia they were far more unpredictable in the 1640s than they were thirty years later. But toward the end of the seventeenth century, as the black population increased in the Chesapeake colonies, the restrictions intensified. The Anglican preacher Morgan Godwin, who lived in both Virginia and Barbados, complained in 1680 that in the sugar and tobacco colonies "the two words, *Negro* and *Slave*," had "grown Homogeneous and Convertible."[84]

Europeans remained undecided about persuading Africans to adopt either European civility or Christianity. The Spanish and Portuguese baptized Africans, and Puritans in Massachusetts Bay allowed them to join the church. Somebody in Virginia managed to preach to them; free blacks there left wills bequeathing their souls to Christ. But all the rhetoric about conversion that preceded the mission to the Indians rarely surfaced when Europeans wrote about Africans. Because medieval tradition forbade the enslavement of baptized Christians, they worried that conversion might raise questions about enslavement. In 1664 Domine Henricus Selyns in New York refused to honor African requests for baptism because he feared that "they wanted nothing else than to deliver their children from bodily slavery." Beginning that year in Maryland, colonists enacted laws stating that baptism did not free a slave. The laws suggested that somebody was converting Africans to Christianity, but they also revealed continuing unease with that fact.[85]

Baptism was not the only problem. Godwin charged that by 1680 slaveholders in America had invented numerous reasons to forbid evangelical appeals to their slaves. They complained that conversion would render the slaves ungovernable and lead to the loss of Sunday labor. They claimed that Noah had cursed Canaan, that the Africans were his posterity, and that the curse both required slavery and forbade conversion. They derided the Africans as barbarous and mentally incapable of rational Christian belief. They said that blackness itself was sufficient cause not to convert them.[86]

The argument that Godwin found most distressing was the assertion that "Negro's were Beasts, and had no more Souls than Beasts," so that "Religion did not concern them." One English gentlewoman told him that he "might as well Baptize a Puppy, as a certain young *Negro.*" The argument might not have been fashionable even in 1680; Godwin noted that its proponents said that they were joking. But he thought their actions revealed that they were deadly serious. And he felt obliged to demonstrate that African mental capacities—as well as the biblical history—revealed the slaves to be fully as human as anyone else. The slaveholders, he charged, were merely repeating Spanish fallacies. He published his *Negro's and Indians Advocate* to counter those fallacies.[87]

He did not, however, call slavery itself into question. In fact he assured the slaveholders that Christianity "establisheth the Authority of Masters, over their Servants and Slaves, in as high a measure, as even themselves could have prescribed." With that assertion few European settlers would have disagreed. To them the Bible seemed to authorize and tradition to confirm the practice of enslavement, especially of prisoners taken in just wars. New Englanders enslaved Indian captives and exploited Irish prisoners. But the gradual debasement of blacks in the colonies meant that they would bear the heaviest burden.[88]

A handful of theologians and lawyers in New Spain criticized slavery in the sixteenth century; an occasional English preacher criticized it in the seventeenth; a few more fretted about the proper treatment of slaves. The Quaker George Fox urged in 1657 that the gospel be preached to everyone, and by 1676 he was suggesting that it would be "very acceptable to the Lord" if masters freed their African slaves after a term of faithful service. His Quaker ally William Edmundson made a similar appeal in the same year. Some idealistic Rhode Islanders even passed a law in 1652 that "no blacke mankind or white" could serve longer than ten years, but the law remained a dead letter. The colonists were disinclined to pay much attention to critics of slavery.[89]

Even John Locke helped to write into the Fundamental Constitutions of Carolina the provisions that "every freeman of Carolina shall have absolute power and authority over his negro slaves" and that church membership would have no effect on enslavement. Few of the European colonists had much interest, in any case, in persuading Africans to become church members. A great many would undoubtedly have nodded agreement with a Barbadian slaveholder who told Morgan Godwin that he "went not to those parts to save Souls, or propagate Religion, but to get Money." In their encounters with the Indians and the Africans, the American colonists discovered, far more quickly than some of them might have wished to admit, the limits of their interest in persuasion.[90]

five

Theologies of Persuasion

During his days as a student at Cambridge, Thomas Shepard puzzled about the mysteries of persuasion. Beset with doubts and fears of death and divine wrath, he discovered "that strength of reason would commonly convince my understanding that there was a God; but I felt it utterly insufficient to persuade my will of it, unless it was by fits, when, as I thought, God's Spirit moved upon the chaos of those unbelieving thoughts." Twenty years later Shepard would warn his congregation in the New English Cambridge against thinking that a sinner "is not to be persuaded to beleeve, under a shew of letting the Spirit of Grace do all." By that time Shepard had joined the one group of colonial Americans who gave sustained and explicit attention to the topic of persuasion. The Puritan preachers of colonial New England viewed themselves as experts in the persuasive arts, and since they viewed divinity as "the art and rule of the will," they felt compelled not only to instruct and exhort their congregations but also to discern the function of persuasion within the workings of divine providence.[1]

Their ideas remained within the boundaries of Calvinist convictions about sin, redemption, and God's covenant with a chosen people. But they did not always agree about the implications of their Calvinism. In 1636 they fell into a dispute so severe that it threatened the stability of the Massachusetts Bay Colony; in the 1650s they quarreled about baptism and the church, and although a synod in 1662 reached a seeming resolution to the quarrel, the colony remained divided about the requirements for church membership. Yet as late as 1675, when the churches initiated the practice of mass covenant renewals, a rough consensus about the theological understanding of persua-

90

sion prevailed, at least in Massachusetts and Connecticut. It remained largely unchanged throughout the seventeenth century.

The New England clergy were a unique group in America. In no other region did the clergy have access to a local printing press or sufficient celebrity in Europe or England to draw the interest of printers there. No other region, therefore, produced a body of theological literature even remotely comparable to the books and sermons of the ministers in New England. The Jesuit *Relations* in New France mainly contained ethnographic information and reports of missionary activity; the Franciscans in New Mexico left behind only reports and narratives; one Lutheran pastor in New Sweden translated a catechism; the Dutch clergy in New Netherland left traces of their ideas only in letters and church and civil records dealing with practical issues; and the clergy of the entire Chesapeake region managed to publish only a handful of letters and sermons. But the New England ministers published enough theology to fill a small library, and the treatises of such ministers as Thomas Hooker, John Cotton, Thomas Shepard, and Peter Bulkeley attracted both support and opposition from divines throughout the English-speaking world.

To pore through the sermons of the well-known Puritan preachers is therefore to explore the ideas of an elite. But they directed their sermons to the men and women in the pews, and they displayed their learning in the midst of pastoral duties in local communities. The preachers spent most of their hours "visiting and comforting the *Afflicted;* Encouraging the *Private Meetings; Catechizing* the Children of the Flock; and managing the *Government* of the Church; and attending the *Sick,* not only in [their] own Town[s], but also in all those of the Vicinity."[2]

They introduced their congregations, however, to the celebrated names of English and continental theology, not only Augustine and Aquinas, Luther and Calvin, but also Catholic scholastics like Suarez, Vasques, and Bellarmine; continental reformers like Theodore Beza and Peter Martyr; Protestant scholastics like Wallaeus, Chamier, Pareus, Chemnitz, and Junius; English exegetes like Brightman; English and Scottish Presbyterians like Robert Baylie and Samuel Rutherford; and English congregationalists like Paul Baynes, Robert Parker, Henry Barrow, Francis Johnson, Henry Ainsworth, and John Robinson. However much the clergy responded to local matters, they also took part in an international conversation about issues that were far from parochial and local.

When they took sides on those issues, as they often did, they allied themselves with the Reformed, or Calvinist, tradition. If Calvinism is construed as slavish adherence to every position that John Calvin ever defended, their Calvinism can be adjudged as mildly revisionist. With other seventeenth-century Reformed theologians, they stressed some ideas—dual covenants of grace and works, congregationalism, and precise definitions of the stages of salvation—that Calvin had not emphasized. But on the great issues of Reformation theology—grace, justification, Christology—their revisions displayed no substantial departure from Calvin's doctrines. John Cotton strayed for a while in the 1630s, but most other ministers stuck to a Calvinist consensus.[3]

In the opinion of some of their contemporaries, their Calvinism should have precluded any serious interest in persuasion. The stereotype of Calvinist theology, even in the seventeenth century, held that Calvin's doctrines of sinfulness, election, and divine sovereignty destroyed any coherent notion of persuasive exhortation. Calvin taught that men and women were so self-preoccupied that they could not of their own power choose the good. Every choice they made would be an occasion for self-aggrandizement, however subtly disguised. He also taught that their own efforts to overcome their plight inevitably turned into anxious and self-defeating attempts at self-justification. They could transcend their selfishness only by being drawn outside themselves, and when this happened, Calvin said, echoing the apostle Paul, it was an undeserved gift of God. Through his doctrine of election Calvin taught that salvation is a gift, not an achievement, and that it depends on a divine decision, not an exercise of the unredeemed will. That is what Calvinist preachers meant when they said that the "natural will"—the will before it was renewed and redirected by God's gift—had no capacity to perform "one good word or good action."[4]

Calvin advanced a second notion that seemed to make persuasion superfluous. He taught in his doctrine of providence that God governed all events, however minute. Calvin distinguished his doctrine from fatalism by insisting that providence could not be equated with any chain of causes within the natural order; it was rather the hidden ruling activity of God. And although God normally worked through secondary causes (natural and historical events that caused other events to occur), God's "secret plan" nevertheless determined all things. The Calvinist John Norton, the minister at Ipswich, could therefore speak of God as "the cause, and disposer of all things, the Antecedent and disposer of all events," and could marvel at God's "eternal-free-constant act, absolutely determining . . . the future being of whatsoever is besides himself." Such a determinism also seemed to make persuasive exhortation a mere show.[5]

But Puritan theology permitted more flexibility, or ambiguity, than such bald assertions might suggest. Norton explained that every natural man and women was a "dead creature," unable to will the good, but he also added that every man and woman nevertheless remained a "reasonable creature." Because of their rationality, God "proceedeth with [them] by way of Arguments." Because of their deadness, God "must work in [them] that which he persuades thereunto." Both sides of the argument had to be preserved: no one could choose the good, but no one could receive the good without choosing it; divine grace determined the choice, but the choice had to be voluntary and heartfelt. On that paradox of grace the Puritans built their theories of persuasion.[6]

A Theology for Persuasion

To justify their confidence in persuasion, the Puritan preachers gave two reasons. The first was a claim about the incarnation (the embodiment of God in the human form of Jesus) and the second a claim about human nature. Crucial to the first was the medieval scholastic distinction between God's "absolute" and "ordinate" power. For the Puritan theologians this meant that God, who by his absolute power could do all things, had limited himself by revealing his will in Scripture and in the life of Christ. God had, in effect, promised to act always in accord with that revelation. He had ordained limits on his own actions by declaring that he would conform them to the pattern revealed in Christ.[7]

The ministers therefore built much of their theology around the traditional Christian doctrine of incarnation, and it provided a way for them to interpret their own function in the community. By assuming human nature, reasoned John Norton, God had declared an intention to deal with human beings through "external means" that were adapted to human capacities. Christ therefore made use of audible words, visible actions, and tangible objects like bread and wine "for the calling home, and building up of his Elect." And that, thought Norton, had vast implications for understanding persuasion.[8]

In particular, the doctrine of incarnation warranted a sure confidence in sermons. In the "common course," Hooker noted, the soul was converted by sermons. To be sure, the pulpit was not the only means of conversion. Shepard could urge his congregation to pray and read Scripture as well as listen to sermons because he thought that they could "expect and look for power from the Lord Jesus in the use of means, all known means." Every minister, moreover, warned against the temptation to rest in the means of grace, as if merely their use ensured salvation. But by assuming human nature and exercising a prophetic office, Christ had determined, they thought, that salvation in his churches would occur especially through "the sending forth the Ministry of his Word."[9]

"A powerfull Ministry," concluded Hooker, "is the ordinary meanes that the Lord hath appointed to prepare the soule of a poor sinner soundly for Christ." In the manner of later revivalists, he could even argue that the preacher's success in converting souls provided a criterion for his ministry. And he knew what kind of minister would succeed: one who disdained general platitudes and fired painful darts and arrows at the sinful soul. Hooker, Cotton, and Shepard earned a reputation even in England as preachers who hammered home the sins of their congregations. Criticized in England as "hot spirited" exhorters, prone to "rayling" from the pulpit, they replied that a faithful ministry had to make sin sound terrible and awe inspiring.[10]

To the laity who joined the New England churches, such claims seemed plausible. In the relations they delivered to the church when they sought membership, they testified incessantly to the persuasive powers of the preachers. References to preachers, and especially to their sermons, appeared far more frequently than references to family members, friends, or other saints and sinners in the community. When John Collins joined the church in Cambridge, for instance, he reported that he began his spiritual pilgrimage by reading "Mister Hooker's book called The Soul's Preparation for Christ" and that he moved ever closer to membership by listening to Mr. Hooker preaching on Romans 18, Mr. Shepard preaching on John 15, Mr. Dunster preaching on Matthew 25, and Mr. Mitchell preaching on Psalm 130. The theology in such lay conversion narratives corresponded with remarkable fidelity to the theology preached in the pulpits.[11]

But it was the touching of the emotions, not theological precision, that was the deeper issue for the laity who delivered their narratives before the churches. Mary Wigglesworth, for instance, gave her narration after she heard John Cotton tell his congregation that unconverted worshippers who regularly heard sermons but failed to undergo rebirth stood under even greater condemnation than sinners who never attended church. His admonition cast her down, convincing her that she was a "child of wrath," and she was "much troubled." But she found herself eventually able to trust that Christ acted mercifully toward sinners and that he made use of her reading of Scripture to refresh her heart. Indeed she began to find in herself signs of a true desire to return to God. When she gave her narrative, she talked mainly about those terrors, desires, and refreshings. Puritan preachers moved their congregations not by their doctrinal precision but by their capacity to touch the deeper dispositions of the heart.[12]

Ministers, although the most visible, were not the only persuasive evangelists. To a lesser degree, the laity also listened to each other, and the conversion narratives testified regularly to the importance of exhortation from friends, neighbors, and families. Ministers encouraged such exhortation; they extolled saintly neighbors as some of the "best instruments" of gracious conversation, and they urged parents and masters to exercise their own persuasive powers for good. The clergy defended the practice of requiring narrations by pointing out their edifying influence. Shepard told his congregation that a proper narrative always contained testimonies that could be "of special use unto the people of God." The Puritan ideal was a society in which earnest laity, subject to ministerial teaching, exhorted friends and neighbors to seek divine grace and lead holy lives. They trusted such exhortation because even Christ, the incarnation of God, had exhorted sinners to repent.[13]

The incarnation made means of grace possible; human nature made them

necessary. "Because we are reasonable creatures," Norton said, "God proceeds with us in the use of means." The ministers knew quite well that human beings were not "stocks or senseless creatures." They were creatures of
will, understanding, and affection, and God's decision to respect human nature required God's preachers to master the intricacies of human psychology,
for even the infusion of grace into the soul did not alter the structure of
human nature. The elders agreed with at least one dictum of Thomas Aquinas: "For grace when it commeth to nature doth not destroy it," Hooker
observed, "but perfect it." Grace did not destroy human wisdom but enlightened it, did not override the will but enhanced and empowered it. It drew
the soul to Christ by means of persuasion.[14]

Puritan preachers felt nervous when they said that. They cautioned their
hearers that they were not talking about mere "moral persuasion." That term
they associated with Arminians, Pelagians, and others who were supposed
to have thought that persuasion to faithfulness could be effective even without the infusion of special divine grace. A Dutch theologian, Jacobus Arminius, had taught that sinful men and women were free to accept or reject
God's offer of salvation, and a number of English divines found the idea
appealing. But Calvinists thought that it undercut the doctrine that salvation
was a gift rather than an achievement. It suggested to them that God merely
enlightened the mind and heart but then had to await the sinner's decision.
So the Calvinist clergy of New England disparaged such a "naked Arminian
illumination and persuasion." John Norton pointed out that the New Englanders had positioned themselves against both Arminians and "Enthusiasts," theologians who were alleged to believe that God transformed the
sinner without even appealing to the will through the means of grace. The
"orthodox evangelist," Norton thought, would find a way to affirm both dependence and volition.[15]

The orthodox evangelist had to understand, therefore, the dynamics of
willing, a topic about which most educated persons in seventeenth-century
New England had some awareness. Questions about the will elicited interest
at Harvard, where student notebooks and commencement theses reflected
occasional debates over the relationship of the will to the understanding.
Some of the students took the position of "intellectualists," who argued that
the will always obeyed the dictates of the understanding. Norman Fiering
has found notebooks and theses in which students pondered the claim that
"the understanding shows to the will, [what] is to be embraced and [what] to
be rejected: then the will desireth and governeth [those] inferior faculties, to
wit, the sensitive and locomotive appetite . . . for as the understanding judg-
eth, so the will desireth." For intellectualists, the understanding functioned,
in Stoic fashion, as the ruler of the soul. Men and women always chose what
they judged to be good; they willed in accordance with their understanding
of their situation.[16]

A second group defended a voluntarist doctrine that accorded the will both autonomy and self-direction. In effect they contended that the will possessed its own cognitive capacities, its own distinctive way of understanding a situation, and it could therefore act independently. The will had not only the power to direct the attention of the understanding toward one or another object but also the ability to defy the intellect's judgment. "Some question," wrote young John Stone, "whether the will or the understanding be the superior faculty, but the will is the supreme, for it hath the casting and determining vote." For the voluntarists men and women could choose what they knew to be unwise; they could refuse what they knew to be good.[17]

When the New England clergy discussed the topic from the pulpit, they blurred the neat distinctions of the collegiate disputations. They agreed that in the order of time the understanding preceded the volition. They also agreed that in the garden of Eden, "the understanding directed what should bee done, the Will embraced that, and the affections yeelded serviceably to the command of Reason and Holiness." Even in the wilderness of New England, Thomas Hooker told his congregation, "there is nothing can come to the Wil, but by the Understanding: what the Eye sees not, the Heart affects not." But Hooker, like the other clergy who wrote down their thoughts on the matter, also concluded that the will was the superior faculty: "The will can imbrace nothing but what the understanding presents to it," said Hooker, but the understanding was still only the "underling of the will."[18]

Clerical assertions about the psychology of the soul might refer to human nature before the fall, to the fallen or sinful soul, or to the soul transformed by divine grace. Hooker seems to have believed that had Adam not fallen, the will would have trotted along behind the understanding like a sheep following a shepherd. But the fall complicated matters. It distorted both the will and the understanding and therefore disordered their relations. The preacher could not draw the fallen soul to Christ simply by filling the understanding with information. In a sinful world, Shepard observed, "the heart makes the eyes blind, and the mind makes the heart fat." But even in a sinful world, the Spirit initiated conversion by illumining the mind: "We come to see how the Lord workes upon the soule," said Hooker. "First, he lets a light into the minde." This meant the preacher too appealed first to the understanding, presenting the truth of the promise. But the preacher could not assume that the will would follow the understanding's judgments. He had to appeal also to the will: "For howsoever faith be begun in the understanding, yet the perfection of it is from the will."[19]

Everyone agreed that the perfecting of faith, from beginning to end, was the work of the Spirit, which was no mere "moral Suasion." It was, said Norton, a "real Perswasion." The sinful soul faced with a real persuasion, in Norton's sense, had no option but to consent. Norton could therefore speak of a physical, as opposed to a merely moral, change of the will. Hooker also called the work of the Spirit "a physical or natural drawing" of the will: "by this the will is determined and undoubtedly carried to its object." What was utterly beyond the power of the fallen will—to choose the good for its own sake—required the supernatural power of the Spirit, which brooked no opposition. Moved by an almighty power, the will moved.[20]

Yet no one thought that the "real Perswasion" of the Spirit subverted the freedom of the will. Hooker stated the clerical consensus: one could speak of compulsion only if the will were forced against its own inclination, but God never compelled the will to act against its inclination; God simply changed the inclination. The point was important for the ministers because it allowed them still to think of a human being as a "cause by counsel"—a creature who acted "according to the proper free-motion of his own will." As long as people acted with deliberation, without external constraint, and according to their own will, human liberty remained intact. The irresistible determinism of the Spirit, said Norton, imposed no external necessity upon the will; it rather inclined the will "according to the nature and liberty of it."[21]

God determineth the Will sutably and agreeably to its own Nature, i.e., freely. He so determineth the Will, as the Will determineth it self. . . . The Efficiency of God offereth no violence, nor changeth the nature of things, but governeth them according to their own natures.[22]

Rather than forcing us unwillingly, God makes us willing, said Norton. Or as Hooker put it, God would not save men and women "against their will." So persuasion made sense even within the sphere of divine determinism. The will remained active, and the paradox remained intact; divine grace irresistibly produced a free, voluntary, and heartfelt assent.[23]

They could abandon neither side of the paradox because both sides, as they saw it, figured prominently in the Bible. The long lists of scriptural citations that filled the margins of Puritan sermons represented far more than idle gestures toward biblical authority. The Puritan preachers tried to teach in accordance with a book that taught that men and women were "dead" through sin (Ephesians 2:1). Their desires were so arrayed against each other—taught the apostle Paul in his letter to the Galatians—that they could not do what they would. And Paul claimed that God alone could save them from that spiritual death. They were therefore as clay in the hands of a potter. And yet the Bible also overflowed with appeals to the will and exhortations to repentance and faith. The Puritan theologian believed that somehow it all had to fit together.

The Covenant

The language that put it all together, that maintained all the tensions and accounted for both sides of the paradox, was the biblical language of covenant. The famous William Ames, an English Puritan theologian who never realized his desire to join the colonists but who deeply influenced them through his textbook on *The Marrow of Sacred Divinity,* expressed a common conviction. From God's "special and proper way of governing reasonable *Creatures,*" he wrote, "there ariseth that covenant, which is between God and them." The notion of covenant could balance both sides of the paradox of grace and thereby provide a subtle and effective warrant for persuasion.[24]

They employed covenantal metaphors mainly because they found them in Scripture. In Genesis God established covenants with Noah, Abraham, and the Israelites at Sinai. There were covenants with Israel in Moab and on Mount Horeb. The Psalmist sang of covenants, the prophets proclaimed new covenants, and Jesus told his disciples at the Last Supper that the blood of the covenant was poured out for many. Thomas Shepard searched the Scripture and concluded that "nor any people took the Lord to be their God, but by some Covenant, they bound themselves to the Lord."[25]

The ministers organized their thoughts about those covenants by using a logic that bore a striking resemblance to that of Petrus Ramus, a sixteenth-century French logician and Protestant martyr who had tried to reform both Aristotelianism and the church. He had proposed that logicians classify their terms, which he called arguments, according to ordered rubrics, and in a Ramist ordering the logician would usually think in dichotomies, trying to discern the two more specific and concrete terms clearly implicit within each general term. Each of the two concrete terms would then be subdivided into others even more concrete, until every notion was clear. Having analyzed the terms in that way, the logical thinker could then combine the words into either self-evident propositions or more complicated chains of reasoning.[26]

Puritans took from Scripture the dichotomy between law and grace, but they also learned from Ramist teachers how to discern the dichotomous qualities of all covenants. They spoke not only of covenants of works and covenants of grace but also of covenants absolute and conditional or of internal and external covenants. They enhanced the biblical distinctions with Ramist refinements.[27]

The New Englanders thus imposed a systematic order on all the covenant making. Defining a covenant as "an agreement between severall parties covenanting together upon mutual conditions required in both parties," Peter Bulkeley of Concord explained in his *Gospel Covenant* how God established covenants with the creatures. In the covenant of works with Adam, God promised eternal happiness on the condition of perfect obedience. Adam's fall broke that covenant, though without annulling all of its terms. Its commands, evident both in the natural law engraved on the conscience and in the moral laws of Scripture, still required obedience, but the obedience could no longer earn salvation. In the covenant of grace, however, the promise of eternal happiness rested on the condition of faith alone.[28]

Since the biblical covenants almost always had conditions affixed to them, preachers found covenantal language congenial when they made moral demands or urged reforms. But Calvinists had no desire to substitute moralism, the view that sinners could save themselves through their ethical striving, for the grace of the gospel. By the middle of the sixteenth century, they found a linguistic distinction ideally suited for their purposes.[29]

In 1562 a German Reformed theologian at Heidelberg, Zacharias Ursinus, began to distinguish between a covenant of grace and a legal covenant (a covenant based on obedience to moral laws). When the English reformer Dudley Fenner published in Geneva in 1585 his *Sacra Theologia*, he named and described, for the first time, a covenant of grace and a covenant of works. By the end of the sixteenth century the great Puritan preacher at Great St. Andrews in Cambridge, William Perkins, made the dual covenant a commonplace among the learned clerical reformers in the Church of England. The implication was that everyone stood in a covenant; everyone was fair game for moral persuasion, even though no one could earn salvation by doing good works.[30]

The preachers in New England taught, without apology, a covenant of works. Or, to be more precise, they proclaimed the substance of the covenant of works. They could say, as Thomas Hooker said in England, that the "legal covenant" was "not continued with us . . . not required at our hands," or as Peter Bulkeley said in New England, that a true fulfilling of the covenant of works was now "impossible." But those disclaimers had a precise theological meaning that did not prohibit the assertion that everyone stood in some respect under the substance of the covenant of works. Bulkeley reminded his readers that God's purpose was immutable and that the "first covenant" therefore also remained unchangeable "in respect of the substance of it."[31]

This meant, first, that New Englanders whom God had not yet called effectually into the realm of salvation remained entirely under a covenant of works. It meant, second, as John Cotton taught his listeners, that it was "the usuall manner of God to give a Covenant of Grace by leading men first into a Covenant of works." Living under the covenant of works, Shepard explained, they would discover their sinfulness and be driven inward into themselves "by terrors, and fears, and hopes." And it meant, third, that even Christians safely within the covenant of grace remained subject to the substance of the first covenant. Bulkeley pointed out that Christ did not destroy the law: "The morall law belongs no lesse to us than to them, it being the eternall will of God." Abolished as a "covenant of life," Shepard said, the law still remained as a "Rule of Life." These were the traditional "three uses of the law" in Reformed theology; New Englanders were fully in accord with Calvin's *Institutes of the Christian Religion*.[32]

When the clergy preached to their congregations, however, they wanted to ensure above all else that the saints did not trust in their works to earn their salvation. Such an error would "disanull the nature of the Covenant of grace, and turn it into a covenant of works." The preachers repeatedly out-lined the differences. The covenant of works required perfect obedience for salvation, while the covenant of grace required only faith; the first covenant required ethical duties as a means of salvation, while the second required them only "that thereby we should glorifie God, and manifest it that we are made righteous by faith"; the first cast men and women on their own abili-ties, while the second provided the grace of the Spirit; the first could ensure an orderly society, but only the second could ensure an eternal place in the kingdom of God.[33]

Thomas Hooker described to his congregation the "civil man," the paragon of public moral virtue who fulfilled the requirements of the covenant of works: "outwardly just, temperate, chaste, carefull to follow his worldly businesse, will not hurt so much as his neighbours dog, payes every man his owne, and lives of his owne; no drunkard, adulterer, or quarreler; loves to live peaceably and quietly among his neighbors." This decent human being could look forward, Hooker said, to nothing but eternal damnation.[34]

But that warning introduced a problem. The covenant of grace was a gift to the elect, and one aim of Puritan theology was to preserve the Pauline doctrine of salvation as a gift. To affix conditions to the covenant of grace, to exhort the unregenerate to enter into that covenant, even to establish faith as a necessary condition, seemed perilously close in Puritan eyes to under-cutting both the gratuity of salvation and the sovereignty of grace. Yet in the incarnation, the ministers thought, God had revealed that he would "proceed with man in such a way as is most sutable and agreeable unto a reasonable creature, namely, by perswasion and Proposal of Arguments." How, then, could they make a place for genuine persuasion and responsiveness while rejecting every temptation to compromise the gratuity of grace and refusing to abandon their conviction that the unregenerate, left to their own devices, lacked the power even to "desire grace"?[35]

The virtue of covenantal doctrine was that it proved amenable to a host of refinements and qualifications that provided an answer that, by its very am-biguity, preserved conflicting religious values. Precision was not the point. Covenantal ideas flourished because they undergirded a rhetorical strategy that enriched Puritan piety and devotion. Nowhere was this more evident than in the distinctions with which the preachers refined their doctrine.[36]

They argued, for instance, that the covenant of grace was both conditional and absolute. By its nature, a covenant had conditions, and the condition of the covenant of grace, as Paul taught in Romans 4:16, was faith. This lan-guage of conditionality permitted the preachers to urge their hearers to seek faith by using the means of grace. "Labor to get faith," Hooker said. "Labor to yield to the . . . condition of the promises." And they could instruct the troubled to "test their estate" by looking to the "conditional promises." Since God promised salvation on the condition of belief, worried saints could discern signs of belief in their hearts and gain some assurance that they had met the condition.[37]

John Cotton felt wary of all the talk about covenantal conditions. He granted the other ministers their right to "speak of conditions," but he admonished them to remember that "the Lord doth undertake both for his own part and for our parts also." God would freely call and preserve his elect, whose effectual calling was not "built upon any Conditionall Promise" but rested on the "absolute free Promise unto the Soule" of the elect saint. But Cotton need not have fretted. The other ministers also believed that in the end everything depended on God's free grace. Shepard wrote that the covenant of grace was "absolute": God had "undertaken to fulfill the Covenant absolutely" for his elect. Hooker spoke often of covenant conditions, but he too thought that "the Lord, as he requires the condition of thee, so he worketh the condition in thee." Bulkeley insisted as well that the God who required the conditions also fulfilled them "for us."[38]

Citing William Ames, Bulkeley pointed out the advantage of this equivocal language. By saying that the covenant was conditional the preachers reminded the faithful and the faithless that salvation would "not be brought to passe but by means, in which mans care is required." By saying that the covenant was absolute they reaffirmed the Reformed doctrine that the promise of salvation would "certainely be fulfilled" through the sovereign grace of God. Such ideas, derived from Calvin, provided an attractive way to maintain two conflicting ideas that were deeply valued in the religious culture.[39]

All the talk about absolute promises, however, evoked some criticism from an upstart Baptist movement that disliked the sacramental implications of covenantal terminology. The Puritan preachers defended infant baptism by arguing that it sealed the covenant, as circumcision had sealed God's covenant with Abraham. But did it seal an absolute promise? If so, the preachers were unwittingly espousing, so some Baptists charged, a doctrine of baptismal regeneration—the view that the sacrament itself conveyed a grace sufficient for salvation—which everyone in New England associated with Catholicism. Or did it merely seal a conditional covenant, thus making the efficacy of the sacrament contingent on future faith and repentance? Some ministers took that position, but they also responded to the Baptists by making still another distinction.

The covenant of grace, said Hooker, could be "considered in a double notion": "I finde a double covenant, an inward and an outward." In the inward covenant stood the faithful elect, who by baptism were sealed for salvation. For most people, however, the sacrament sealed only an external covenant membership, granting rights to the means and ordinances of the visible church. Most New England ministers shared Hooker's opinions. Shepard announced that baptism was annexed to an outward covenant and that baptized infants were therefore by no means "always in inward covenant." Cotton also distinguished "a double state of grace": saving grace, from which there was no fall, and federal grace, by which the children of believing parents were holy. Because of their federal grace, such children had a right to the "outward dispensation of the Covenant and to the seale of it," but neither the covenant nor its seal would benefit the nonelect "seed of the flesh."[40]

The distinction served again to hold in tension the two conflicting ideas in the paradox of grace. The language about the inward covenant reasserted the doctrine of divine sovereignty; the notion of an external covenant preserved the sense that the human activity of administering means of grace remained important, especially since the ministers asserted in their Cambridge Platform of 1648 that covenanted, baptized children were "in a more hopefull way of attayning regenerating grace." Cotton explained that baptism entitled infants to the means by which the elect would eventually experience "the grace of the new birth." The sacrament brought them within the reach of a "visible Ministery, visible sacraments, and censures." It brought them into the sphere of evangelical persuasion.[41]

Conflict

Some of the New England clergy had firm—their critics said harsh and severe—ideas about evangelical persuasion. They thought it necessary for the persuasive evangelist to pound home the demands and threats of the law in order to shatter sinful self-confidence and make people feel miserable about themselves, for only then would they despair of saving themselves. Shepard tried, one of his hearers recalled, "to pound our hearts all to pieces." Giles Firmin, who lived about fifteen years in New England, thought it was a dreadful mistake "to preach and print of such strong convictions, such dreadful legal terrors, deep sorrows and humblings, as being the common road through which men go that come to Christ," and he charged that Shepard's sermons cast people into despair and distraction, but Shepard replied that it was necessary for the heart to be "prepared" for conversion.[42]

"Preparation" meant driving the soul to contrition and humiliation, and the leading New England ministers were considered experts at it. Even before he came to the colonies, Thomas Hooker had devoted to the topic the major part of at least eight books. John Cotton, preaching in England, declared that "the Spirit of grace will not come but into an heart in some measure prepared," and he continued after moving to New England to insist that God prepared sinners by dashing their worldly confidence. Bulkeley thought it possible that faith might be created "without any preparation," but he too pointed out that God's "usuall course" was to break the heart before scattering the seeds of faith.[43]

One matter at stake in the discussion was rhetorical strategy. Hooker thought that the need for preparation required a ministry that would uncover the secrets of the soul and drive it to see its own nakedness. That meant preaching the law. "There are a generation of preachers," Cotton complained in an English sermon, "that would now have no Law preached, but onely to draw men on to Christ, by the love of Christ." He thought that such smooth and comforting sermons would be worthless; the heart had to be wounded unto death before it would abandon its pretension. Shepard, writing to his English critic Firmin, ridiculed rhetorical "dainties" that might "tickle and ravish some," advising instead the use of "Axes and Wedges" to "hew and break this rough, unhewn, bold, yet professing Age."[44]

The intent of the preaching was to push the unregenerate soul toward self-denial; the soul sunk in humiliation lost all "self-confidence in any good it hath or doth." What especially offended Firmin was the conclusion that even the regenerated soul should be, as Hooker phrased it, "content to bear the estate of damnation." Firmin thought that only a saint could be that unselfish, though he also thought the idea odd even for saints. Hooker's position, however, did not imply that Puritans repudiated all self-concern. He recognized that everyone naturally desired self-preservation and that saintly souls could rightly prefer their own temporal good to that of their neighbors. But when they talked about preparation for conversion, both Hooker and Shepard argued that a soul "truly prepared and empty" would willingly abandon itself to damnation.[45]

Hooker thought that such "legal humiliations" were the harbingers of faith. But he went a step further, arguing that self-denial of that magnitude suggested "a saving worke of Christ" in the soul even before the onset of faith. It followed that troubled and despairing souls might find in their very self-doubt a promise of salvation. But when Hooker tried in 1636 to convince his colleagues in New England that preparatory works were saving, most of them seem to have demurred. One observer reported that this was only "Hooker's position, the rest of the Ministers do not concurr with him." John Cotton suggested that others—though not he—shared Hooker's view, but neither Shepard nor Bulkeley accepted the doctrine of "saving preparatives."[46]

At stake once again was an issue of pastoral persuasion. Before coming to New England, Hooker had tested the practical implications of his doctrine when he counseled a despondent noblewoman named Joan Drake, who believed herself to be damned. Hooker persuaded her to look upon her distress as an indication that she was chosen; her despairing thoughts could be interpreted as signs of a broken heart. Joan Drake underwent a remarkable spiritual recovery, and it seemed that her despair indeed contained seeds of saving grace. But "the rest of the Ministers"—so we are told by our anonymous reporter—feared that Hooker's doctrine obscured the doctrine of grace by implying that God was obligated to save the self-critical soul.[47]

But Hooker's notions of preparation, like those of his colleagues, preserved the paradox of grace. "Nothing but grace doth all, workes all, prepares all," he wrote. "He that doth prepare is the Lord; he that doth receive the work, and is prepared, is the soules of those whom God hath elected to salvation." No preacher suggested that preparation was a matter of human striving. "These saving preparations," wrote Hooker, "are no acts of mine, therefore not my fruit. . . . They are wrought in me, not by me." Yet God wrought them through the means of grace, which he blessed so that they would "worke upon the soules of men." Preparation occurred through God's "effectual perswading"—effectual because it could not fail of its aim, persuasive because it involved both the understanding and the will.[48]

Hooker and Norton were talking about preparation for conversion, but other ideas of preparation also suffused New England piety. Shepard wrote his *Parable of the Ten Virgins Opened and Applied* to examine the church's preparation for the coming of Christ. Ministers and laity "prepared" for the Sabbath; they engaged in "preparatory meditations" before receiving the sacrament; they urged one another to "prepare" for death and the day of judgment. In all these "acts of the new creature," said Shepherd, "the Lord is pleased to use morall and rational perswasions." But the Lord, he thought, always did more than appeal to the mere "strength of reason." All depended finally on irresistible grace, on "effectual perswading."[49]

Or did it really require persuasion at all? That was one question implicit in the turbulent theological and civil quarrel that has come to be known as the Antinomian controversy. Early in 1636 Thomas Shepard heard John Cotton lecture in Boston, and he thought he heard him imply that it was necessary for troubled saints, doubtful of their conversion, to wait for an immediate "revelation of the spirit" rather than taking comfort in biblical promises. Cotton's reply was not reassuring. He told Shepard that Christians must "close" with Christ before they could rely on the covenant. The reply disturbed Shepard because it sounded like the slogan of a zealous party of Boston laity who had "secretly begun" a "quarrell."[50]

In fact the quarrel was no longer secret by 1636. One of Cotton's admirers, Anne Hutchinson, had begun holding open meetings in her home to discuss the previous week's sermons, and she let it be known that, apart from her continuing admiration for Cotton, she did not like what she heard in New England pulpits. She accused the ministers, Cotton excepted, of preaching "legal" sermons that encouraged saints and sinners alike to trust in their own works rather than in Christ. She and other members of the Boston congregation were caught up in a style of piety about which Cotton too seemed enthusiastic; when he wrote to Shepard about "closeing with Christ," Cotton sounded the keynote of the awakening.[51]

Union with Christ and the witness of the Spirit: those were the themes that shaped the new form of piety in Boston. Cotton remarked in later years that "it was the judgment of some of place, in the Countrey, that such a Doctrin of Union, and evidencing of Union, as was held forth by mee, was the Trojan Horse, out of which all the erroneous Opinions and differences of the Country did issue forth." The judgment was understandable. Cotton's rhetoric in 1636, even in his replies to his critics, resounded with metaphors of "closing" with Christ.[52] He wanted to redirect the attention to Christ. He told his followers that they could find assurance of salvation not by looking to their holy works and dispositions but only "upon the sight of Christs righteousness imputed to us." He told them that all the biblical promises had been fulfilled in Christ and that they had right to them "only by right of union with Christ." They lived by faith, he said, only when Christ lived within them; they were spiritually active only when Christ acted within them. And the only testimony to the union with Christ that could be trusted had to come immediately from the Spirit.[53]

The other New England preachers also believed that "the best man without Christ can do nothing and through Christ can do all things," but Cotton was drawing implications that seemed to conflict with the standards of Reformed orthodoxy. Although the idea of union with Christ was familiar, Cotton was doing unfamiliar things with it. He diminished the prevailing notion of faith as an activity of the understanding and the will. In the standard Reformed position, justifying faith, a human activity made possible by divine grace, preceded the union with Christ. Justifying faith was the divinely conferred trust that allowed one to embrace that union. Empowered by an infused principle of grace, the soul could move in an act of trust toward union with Christ. But Cotton, swept up in the new Christ piety, insisted that union with Christ preceded the activity of faith, the act of trust. Justifying faith for Cotton was merely the recognition of a union with Christ that had already occurred through Christ's agency. The tendency of Cotton's doctrine was to accentuate the agency of Christ to the detriment of any notion of activity on the part of reasonable creatures.[54]

The same tendency reappeared when Cotton and his admirers denied that sanctification—the progress in holiness made possible by grace—could serve as evidence of justification, or God's accepting of the sinner as righteous. Most New England ministers, like most other Reformed theologians, thought of sanctification as spiritual growth resulting from new principles of action—new "graces"—in the soul. They thought that by observing the actions and dispositions arising from the new principles, the doubtful might find evidence of their effectual calling and union with Christ. Cotton disagreed. He acknowledged that the saints displayed new created graces, but he denied their evidential status: "Neither word nor Spirit do teach us to take comfort so much from the work of Christ in us, as from the object of it," Christ himself. Hypocrites could appear to be as loving and pious as saints. An act of sanctification could not be adjudged gracious except insofar as it was done in faith, and this meant that the evidence of justification had to precede the evidence of sanctification.[55]

The New England elders were accustomed, furthermore, to saying that one test of regeneration was adherence to the conditional promises. Viewing faith as a condition of justification, they could appeal to people to be faithful and point to the presence of faith as a sign that the condition had, by grace, probably been met. Or recalling the requirement that true Christians love each other (1 John 3:14), they could point to the presence of love as a sign of faith. Cotton disagreed. He used the conditional promises as grounds for exhortation, but he thought that they had no place in discerning justification. Only by recognizing oneself as an heir of the absolute promises—the free promises of salvation—could one recognize one's love as a faithful love. "No man can see his gifts and duties of sanctification in himself, but hee must first have seen Christ by faith."[56]

Cotton could therefore trust only the immediate witness of the Spirit. Ruling out any evidence from the observation of the created graces in the soul, he grounded assurance in immediate divine testimony. The elders also believed in the witness of the Spirit, but they claimed that the Spirit spoke mediately through scriptural words and the works of the saints. Cotton came close to severing those connections. The Spirit, he said, bore witness "immediately . . . though not without the word of God nor without (sometimes in some cases) the work of God, yet with his own immediate power above the power which either the word hath of it self, or the work of any creature."[57]

He did not entirely abandon the paradox of grace; he accorded a limited value to acts of the will and understanding. But he came close to saying that the regenerate acted only as they were acted—*acti agimus*—by Christ. If the elders meant to imply, he said, that regenerated saints were able "by the power of the gift of grace received" to be "active without his renewed help," then the elders erred. Even elect saints, effectually called and sanctified, remained unable to activate their gift of grace unless Christ acted within them.[58]

Cotton had no intention of calling into question the need for "holy duties"—means of grace like prayer and preaching—but wanted only to prevent their abuse. Yet his piety in 1636 raised questions about the theological grounding for all the means of persuasion in the colony's churches. While the elders appealed to both the incarnation and to human psychology, Cotton formulated a doctrine of incarnation that overrode the psychology and threatened to undo the doctrine of means of grace. The elders thought that he was close to discarding "ordinances and duties." So did some of his admirers, who were eager to go even further.[59]

Cotton eventually repudiated those admirers, thereby beginning his own rehabilitation in the eyes of his fellow clerics. It came slowly. Thomas Shepard in 1639 commented that "Mr. Cotton repents not, but is hid only." The English Presbyterian Robert Baylie believed that the New Englanders let matters drop "to save Mr. Cotton's credit." But by the 1640s Edward Johnson could say that some of Cotton's seeming disciples simply misrepresented him, and Cotton's polemics against the Baptists in 1647 enhanced his reputation. Second-generation ministers admired Cotton, but they also took care not to repeat his mistakes.[60]

Reason and the Psychological Order

New England ministers thought of a person as a microcosm of a hierarchical universe. The human body, they believed, participated in and represented the lower levels of the cosmos, the world of material objects. The vegetative soul, or ability to grow, marked each person's kinship with the world of plants. The locomotive soul, or capacity to move, exhibited a point of commonality with the stars. The sensitive soul, or capacity to perceive, think, remember, and feel, represented the proximity between human and animal life. The rational soul, or power of knowing, judging, and choosing, demonstrated the likeness between human beings and angels. A person was a hierarchy of powers, and each ascending stage integrated the lower stages into a higher unity, the highest being reason.[61]

The clergy did not insist that each capacity was a separate soul. "Whether they have so many distinct Souls in them, as they have Kinds of Life, or whether they perform all these Functions by one and the same Soul, let Philosophers dispute," wrote Samuel Willard of Boston. Ministers also did not intend to denigrate the lower levels of the psychological hierarchy. But because each higher stage both transcended and integrated the lower, the "Life of Reason"—the will and the understanding—perched atop the biological ladder, rightfully assumed command and government over the other powers. By nature men and women were supposed to be rational and therefore susceptible to persuasion. Yet the psychological order, like the cosmic and social orders, was forced to withstand rebellions from the lower depths, and it was the task of the clergy to support the proper ordering.[62]

One potential rebel was the body, the lowest level of personal life. The clergy did not disdain it; it was, they thought, "Essential and Integral" as the seat not only of motion and sense but of reason itself. It became a problem only when physical desires overwhelmed rational restraint or when physical maladies engendered spiritual stress. The body could rebel against the fragile imperium of reason, and a successful rebellion was often signaled by the onset of melancholy. Impressed by the medical writings of the second-century Greek physician Claudium Galenus, a few English authors in the sixteenth century began to popularize a distinction between the true afflictions of conscience and a melancholy that occurred when gross elements in the blood settled in the spleen and created vapors that pressed upward to the brain, causing it "without external occasion to forge monstrous fictions."

Even as Robert Burton in England was writing his rambling *Anatomy of Melancholy* (1621), clerical casuists were beginning to caution spiritual advisers that such problems as scrupulosity might be rooted in "Melancholy, or some such like constitution of body." And the clergy recognized that melancholia could not be cured by persuasive arguments. The cure, when there was one, was not introspection but action. An active life might be the only way to preserve spiritual equilibrium when the body rebelled against the soul.[63]

A second possible source of rebellion lurked in the affections. In theory, thought Thomas Shepard, "the eye or mind of a man sits like a coachman, and guides the headstrong affections." He also believed that when God illumined the understanding of the godly, their affections flowed forth unerringly in hope and love toward Christ. But Samuel Willard noted that the exorbitant power conferred on the affections by the fall into sinfulness gave them a "crooked bias," causing them to move "in a wrong way, and on wrong objects." With the connivance of a fallen mind, perverse affections could continually disrupt the soul's internal equilibrium. Disordered passions could resist the appeal of persuasion; one large field of ministerial labor was to assist the forces of rationality to maintain internal order in people who had fallen prey to the unchecked power of the unruly affections.[64]

Throughout the century the clergy always claimed that reason remained subordinate to biblical revelation. The first-generation clergy believed that reason could, as Hooker observed, show "what God is, in his Power, Glory, Majesty, and Bounty, and that he is to be worshipped." Reason, thought Shepard, could prove the existence of "the Being of beings, or the first Being" by examining the evidences of order and design in the creation. It could also "prove the Scripture to be the word of God." But reason could not know God as the reconciler and Christ as the redeemer. Reason could know *that* God was but could not know *what* God was.[65]

The second-generation clergy held the same view. Samuel Willard argued that reason approximated revelation, carrying the mind step by step to the boundaries of the higher revealed truth. Reason found in the human spirit a yearning for an infinite good that would satisfy the soul; it could prove that a transcendent and infinite God was real; it could then uncover the moral order—the law of human nature—to which one must conform in order to live in accord with the infinite God. But reason also showed that human beings, as sinful creatures, did not naturally possess the good for which they yearned. Hence reason pointed beyond itself and beyond the natural order to a higher order revealed in Scripture. Reason could validate that revelation; there were rational proofs for the truth and authority of biblical teachings. And reason could interpret revelation, showing again and again exactly how it fulfilled our natural knowledge. But reason could never reveal knowledge sufficient for salvation, which came only through a revelation in Scripture to a will and understanding renewed by the Spirit.[66]

Just as the second-generation clergy retained the traditional Reformed conception of the relation between reason and revelation, so also they held on to the paradox of grace. "The Spirit," wrote John Davenport of New Haven, "causeth the soul to yield," but since the soul was "reasonable," God drew it through "perswasives." The assurance that God lured saints persuasively stood in the background of the techniques devised by the second generation to preserve piety in New England, including their expanded emphasis on such means of grace as baptism and the Lord's Supper.[67]

In the struggle over admission to baptism that resulted in the halfway covenant of 1662, some ministers argued that the Spirit could elicit assent without having to rely on the external means of grace that baptism made available to the children of the saints. The majority conceded that point but replied that baptism and the privileges it conveyed nevertheless made those children more receptive to the Spirit. The Synod of 1662 therefore reaffirmed a traditional belief in the suasive power of the means of grace.[68]

In 1675 James Fitch, citing earlier precedents, demanded from the children of his Norwich congregation a pledge to fulfill their baptismal obligations by "owning the covenant," or pledging themselves to strive after faithfulness. The practice of covenant renewal, which received official sanction in a 1679 Reforming Synod in Boston, embodied the clerical confidence in persuasion. "Let us," Increase Mather urged his congregation in Boston, "be exhorted, perswaded, and prevailed with to return unto the Lord our God." Samuel Willard explained to his congregation the theory that underlay Mather's appeal. To renew the covenant, he said, is "a judicious and voluntary act, it is an act of a Cause by Counsel, acting according to the dictates of right reason, and freely resting in this conclusion." But the ministers remained sure that the covenant renewals could engender true conversion only in the soul renewed and empowered by divine grace.[69]

The ministers who called for covenant renewal experimented with differing rhetorical styles, some preferring "prophetic" sermons that bristled with threats while others urged "gentleness." The second generation of ministers paid more attention to rhetoric than had their predecessors, but the underlying theories of persuasion remained unchanged. The New England clergy never abandoned their conviction that lively sermons and divine promptings of grace could coincide in such a way that their listeners would be "perswaded and prevailed with to return unto the Lord our God."[70]

six

Dissenters

In 1647 former New England minister Nathaniel Ward offered his readers a simple lesson in geometry. "If two centers (as we may suppose) be in one Circle," he wrote, "and lines drawn from both to all the points of the Compass, they will certainly cross one another, and probably cut through the Centers themselves." Society, he pointed out, needed one center, one ruler, one religion, one truth. Writing during the chaos of the English civil wars, Ward exhorted Parliament to create a "state united," which could be achieved, he thought, only if England submitted itself to the one Truth.[1]

The ideal, he assumed, was a culture in which men and women would give unbroken allegiance to a unified body of thought, with only minor individual differences. But whatever cultural consensus New England achieved, it did not overwhelm dissent and diversity. New Englanders offered their allegiance to a variety of competing ideas and ideals, generating conflict and disagreement, and the moment one stepped beyond the borders of New England, the diversity intensified.

Religious dissent in England had flowed from two different, though overlapping, sources. Ever since the fourteenth century, when the "Poor Preachers" who followed the reformer John Wycliffe began to excoriate the church for its supposedly unbiblical practices, a tradition of radical dissent persisted on the margins of English Christianity. During the sixteenth century it expanded by appropriating ideas from the continental Anabaptists, who wanted to abandon comprehensive national religious establishments and reconstruct the church as a voluntary community of the faithful. The second pattern of dissent originated with the Calvinists. Their ideas of reform molded English Puritanism, which during the reign of Elizabeth I (1558–1603) split into competing factions: moderates who disliked the church's vestments and ceremonies but accepted its bishops; more zealous reformers who wanted to replace the bishops with synods and presbyteries; and even more revolutionary groups that proposed to relocate English Christianity in a host of pure and independent congregations subject neither to synods nor to bishops.[2]

In 1581 two ministers, Robert Browne and Robert Harrison, announced that there could be no reformation without separation from the Church of England, and an illegal Separatist movement began to flourish, first in London and then among religious refugees in Holland. By 1612 some of the Separatists who had fled to Amsterdam took a further step, repudiating their baptism in the Church of England and deciding that Scripture permitted only the baptizing of faithful adults. Their leaders soon rejected the Calvinist doctrines of predestination and limited atonement (the belief that Christ died only for the elect), so when some of them returned to England they became known as General Baptists. Their critics viewed them as more radical than the Calvinist Particular Baptists who emerged in England after 1633.

To the enemies of dissent it seemed that the conflicts that produced the English Civil War in 1642 released a swarm of such "sectaries and schismatiques"—men and women prepared to "preach (or prate) in woods, in fields, in stables, in hollow trees, in tubs, on tops of tables." During the 1640s Presbyterians strove to abolish bishops; Independents to abolish presbyteries; Baptists to abolish infant baptism; and Quakers to abolish all forms of public worship and ministry that impeded the motions of the Spirit. Other dissenters found religious reasons to expand the range of abolitions: Seekers renounced allegiance to every existing form of the church, which in their view no longer represented the original gospel; Levellers sought radical political reform; Fifth Monarchists envisioned an imminent Kingdom of Christ to replace the kingdoms of this world; and Ranters discarded the notion of sin and therefore any need for the moral restraint that the respectable took for granted. By 1649, when the Parliament executed Charles I, the dissenters appeared to have carried the day. Their victory proved to be temporary, but the decades of turmoil in England left a mark on America.[3]

The Puritans who in England had been dissenters became in America the targets of dissent. Criticism could be heard as early as the 1620s; the tempo increased when Roger Williams came to America in 1631 and denounced the Boston church for refusing to denounce the Church of England as a false church. In 1636 Williams had to leave the colony and established the earliest Rhode Island settlement at Providence, but his departure brought no peace. In 1637 Boston struggled through the Antinomian controversy, which pitted a charismatic woman, Anne Hutchinson, against the ministers she accused of being "legalists." By the time the magistrates banished her in 1638, a radical spiritist named Samuel Gorton initiated yet another dissenting movement, which led to still another banishment, when the Gortonians joined Williams and the Hutchinsonians in Rhode Island.

Before long the dissenters were too numerous for the authorities to banish them all. During the 1640s Baptists challenged the New England churches, while Anabaptists and Lutherans challenged Dutch Reformed dominance in New Netherland. By the 1650s Quakers made turbulent appearances in every colony along the Atlantic coast. The colonies therefore had to decide just how much persuasion they were willing to tolerate. Lord Baltimore tried, with limited success, to compel his settlers in Maryland to tolerate each other, and Charles II finally intervened to ensure a measure of tolerance in New England. But there was no universal ideal of toleration in the seventeenth century, and American colonists in positions of power found it as difficult as anyone else to listen to the voices of dissent.

Dissent in New England

One way of interpreting dissent, especially in New England, is to see dissenters as people who pushed accepted ideas to logical extremes, forcing more moderate Puritans to acknowledge the implications of their own dissent from the English establishment. This accent on consistency is then often combined with a view of dissent as a series of transit points along a spectrum. According to this interpretation, the drive to purify the church, combined with the pronounced accent on the inner experience of the Holy Spirit in Puritan piety, inevitably led devotees of consistency to attack, with varying degrees of intensity, first one and then another of the external structures of medieval tradition until finally they left nothing unchallenged. This was the way conservatives were accustomed to viewing dissent in both England and New England. One English critic charged in 1650 that separation from the Anglican establishment served as "an ordinary step to *Anabaptisme*," which led to other forms of "*Seeking*, being above *Ordinances*, and *Questioning* everything revealed in the *Scriptures*, and in high *Raptures* and *Revelations*," and this led to still more radical ideas of "*Levelling*" and libertinism in the social order.[4]

There is much to be said for such an interpretation. It recognizes the extent to which Puritan reform displayed a centrifugal force that appeared to have its own inner logic. It calls attention to the overlapping interests among such diverse groups as Puritan Congregationalists and itinerant Quakers. On occasion, moreover, some dissenters explicitly included the argument from consistency among their polemical strategies. Roger Williams, defending his separation from the Church of England, observed that "the grounds and principles of the Puritans against Bishops and Ceremonies, and prophanes of people professing Christ, and the necessitie of Christs flock and discipline, must necessarily, if truely followed, lead on to, and inforce a separation from such wayes, worships, and Worshippers." Williams himself became a Baptist before proceeding further into lonely spiritual isolation, waiting for Christ to reestablish a church that no longer existed.[5]

Despite its usefulness, the interpretation of dissent as a logical progression along a spectrum of interconnected positions can obscure the diversity among the dissenters. They differed not merely in degree but also in fundamental principles. They developed their thoughts not simply by following the inner logic of existing ideas but also by appealing to distinctive forms of piety and different sources of authority. As Roger Williams discovered when he debated the Quakers, dissenters often had little to say to each other.

If dissent is defined as any principled and outspoken opposition to a prevailing consensus, then dissenters surfaced early in New England, and among them were a few beleaguered proponents of Anglican tradition. In 1628 Thomas Morton erected a maypole on his estate, Merry-mount, to express disdain for Plymouth's piety, and although his satirical *New English Canaan* (1632) could hardly be described as a plea for Anglican piety, Morton did ridicule the Separatists at Plymouth for their departures from the Book of Common Prayer and traditional Anglican ceremonies. A year later Samuel Browne and his brother "began to raise some trouble" at Salem by calling the ministers there "Separatists" and gathering a company "distinct from the publick Assembly" for reading the Book of Common Prayer according to "the Orders of the Church of England." The magistrates shipped the troublemakers back to England, but others of a different spirit quickly took their place.[6]

From the beginning the dominant group of Puritans in New England had to encounter dissenters who appealed to the criterion that had consistently guided Puritan reform: the example of the primitive church as described in the Scripture. This became a frequent theme among Separatists who refused to think of the Church of England as a true church. In the Bay Colony, which defined its churches as congregational but denied having separated from the Anglican church, the Separatists represented a dissenting voice. Most of them usually moved on to Plymouth, where Separatist ideas were more acceptable, but a few made their stand in Massachusetts Bay colony. One year after disavowing Separatism, for example, the minister Samuel Skelton in Salem appeared to adopt the "pattern of separation" by "refusing communion with the church of England." He barred Winthrop and other new immigrants from communion with the Salem church, much to the dismay of John Cotton, who wrote from England instructing him about church covenants. But Skelton's views had popular support, and Salem soon joined Plymouth as a haven for people with Separatist sympathies.[7]

In 1631 Roger Williams, questing for purity, arrived in Boston, only to be disappointed. The congregation there "would not make a public declaration of their repentance for having communion with the churches of England."

So he accepted an invitation to become the teacher in the Salem church, which "was known to profes separation." When the General Court objected, Williams moved on to Plymouth, but after a couple of years he returned as Salem's teacher, with results that greatly distressed Winthrop: "He . . . so far prevailed at Salem, as many there (especially of devout women) did embrace his opinions, and separated from [even] the churches [of Massachusetts], for this cause, that some of their members, going into England, did hear the ministers there, and when they came home the churches here held communion with them." Under Williams's guidance the Separatists at Salem assumed a stance of public dissent.[8]

During the two years he remained as the teacher in Salem, Williams made the case for separatism partly by appealing for consistency. He accused the nonseparating Congregationalists of having halted midway between the Antichrist and Christ. By leaving the English parishes, he said, they practiced separation, but they refused to acknowledge it publicly by repenting for their earlier worship in a false church. Instead they criticized Separatists who did repent, and they allowed their members to hear sermons in parish churches when they returned to the homeland. That was inconsistent and hypocritical. For the Bay churches to be consistent they must truly separate and repent. For the church in Salem to be consistent it must refuse communion with the unrepentant churches in the Bay Colony. For Williams to be consistent, he decided, he must refuse communion with the Salem church until it refused communion with almost everyone else.[9]

Williams' case for separation in New England rested on primitivist arguments. He appealed repeatedly to the primitivist contention that "the first *Churches* of *Christ Jesus*" had established "the *lights, patternes* and *presidents*" for "all succeeding Ages." His complaint was that the Bay churches did not follow those ancient patterns; they ignored plain scriptural injunctions. To Williams it seemed clear that biblical precedent required Christians to separate themselves from uncleanness, and his early debate with John Cotton over separatism consisted mainly of commentary on precedents: Paul told the Corinthians to separate from idolaters (2 Corinthians 6:17); John conveyed angelic admonitions for Christians to come out of Babylon (Revelations 18:4); Ephesian Christians confessed all their sins when they entered the church (Acts 19:18). Since the New Testament churches used the Old Testament Scriptures, Williams could add examples from the prophets: Isaiah had commanded the faithful to depart from unclean things and purify themselves (Isaiah 52:11), and Haggai (2:13–15) had warned that when the unclean touched holy things the result was uncleanness and profanity.[10]

Despite such clear and binding precedents, he said, most New Englanders not only refused to separate themselves fully from their unclean past but also allowed—even compelled—the unclean to touch holy things. They made the ungodly take oaths, even though oaths were holy acts of worship, forbidden to the unclean. They encouraged the unregenerate to pray, even though prayer was an act of worship reserved for the holy. They promoted prayer in New England families, even though the presence of unconverted family members would profane the prayers. After he left Salem, Williams would argue that the unregenerate had no more right to hear sermons than to receive the Lord's Supper, for sermons too were among the holy things that could be profaned by the unclean.[11]

Before he left Salem he had some other disturbing things to say. He claimed that magistrates had no right to punish religious offenses unless they threatened civil peace, that all religions should be tolerated, and that the colony's patent from James I gave no title to the land, which the colonists could rightly possess only after they purchased it from the Indians. We do not know how he argued for these views while he lived at Salem. He probably opposed the patent because he found no scriptural grounds for the popular idea that a Christian prince could claim the lands of heathens and heretics. In his later writings he defended his opinions about the church and the state primarily through exegetical arguments showing that "Christ Jesus never directed his Disciples to the civill Magistrate," whether to vindicate their doctrines, convert the unsaved, or protect the church from heretics.[12]

His extended literary debate with John Cotton over liberty of conscience dealt largely with how to interpret the Bible. Williams relished a confrontation over biblical texts, and he condemned religious persecution mainly because he found scriptural evidence that Christ was "King alone over conscience." The precepts of the primitive church confirmed him in that judgment: Christ said that the anti-Christian tares should be allowed to grow up with the godly wheat until the harvest at the final judgment (Matthew 13), and he reproved his disciples when they wanted fire from heaven to destroy his enemies (Luke 9:54–55). In the same spirit Paul taught the early church that the weapons of spiritual warfare were not carnal but only spiritual (2 Corinthians 10:4).[13]

When Cotton reminded Williams that the Jewish magistrates had protected Israel's worship, Williams countered with typology. The magistrates of Israel, he said, were types of Christ; their swords of steel prefigured the spiritual swords of Christian ministers. They were no examples for New England's civil rulers. Cotton used typological exegesis too, but he pressed the point that some types could also have an exemplary force. The kings of Israel were typical in some respects, exemplary in others. Williams replied that "the whole *Church* of *Israel*" was "*figurative* and *Allegorical*." Israel had been both a holy church and a holy nation, but only to foreshadow the incarnation. After the coming of Christ, who brought the types to fulfillment, holy nations and sanctified princes no longer existed.[14]

With the incarnation, the sword of the spirit replaced the fleshly sword. The purpose of princes now was to protect the bodies and property of their subjects, not to care for their souls. They could regulate moral behavior but not piety. When they presumed beyond their bounds, they pulled "God and Christ, and Spirit out of Heaven, and subject[ed] them unto naturall, sinfull, inconstant men, and so consequently to Sathan himselfe."[15]

Williams believed that Christians remained subject to the precedents established in the primitive churches, but after 1639, when he became a Baptist for a few months, he decided that the primitive pattern of church order could be restored only through a supernatural intervention by Christ at the time of the millennium. The church's apostasy under Constantine in the fourth century had cut off the succession of true churches and true ministers. Williams knew this because he could find neither in the medieval past nor in the present any signs of a ministry that conformed to "the first *Institution* of the *Lord Jesus*." According to the primitive precedent, true churches had to be founded by true apostles and evangelists and nourished by true pastors and teachers. But they no longer existed. For now, God's witnesses could not hope to restore the church; they could only testify against the "Inventions" that subverted the "true Pattern" of the primitive past.[16]

When the magistrates of Massachusetts Bay expelled Anne Hutchinson from their colony in 1638, Roger Williams, true to his convictions about religious liberty, helped the refugees establish a colony in Rhode Island. But Williams and the Hutchinsonians were no kindred spirits. He looked to the biblical past and the millennial future; they cast their hopes on the presence of the Spirit. He worried about the external orders and ordinances of the church; they exulted in the inner experience of spiritual freedom.

Anne Hutchinson could cite a text for every doctrine she taught. She reported that God's revelation came to her when she was reading the first letter of John; she discovered her own false devotion to a covenant of works when she read the prophet Isaiah's injunction to the "stubborn of heart"; she decided to follow John Cotton to New England after meditating on Isaiah's reference to the teacher who would not hide himself. When she appeared for trial before the church in Boston, she engaged the ministers in intricate exegetical arguments about the soul, mortality, and the resurrection. When the ministers challenged the right of a woman to teach, she answered by recalling the admonition to older women in Titus 2:2 to teach the younger ones what is good and the prophecy in Joel 2:28 that God would pour out his Spirit on the daughters and they would prophesy. John Winthrop noticed, with some dismay, that the "Rule she pretended to walke by, was onely the Scripture."[17]

Yet though she appealed to Scripture as often as Williams, Hutchinson sought not to recover a primitive church order but to confirm a belief in the indwelling of Christ through the Holy Spirit. He sought communal purity; she sought inner assurance. He read the New Testament as a source of precedents; she read it as a guide to the acts of the Spirit. She eventually attracted support from at least 187 men and perhaps a similar number of women. Her advocates ranged from the barber William Dinely—"so soon as any were set downe in his chaire," complained Edward Johnson, "he would commonly be cutting of their haire and the truth together"—to the new governor, Henry Vane. By 1637 the tensions had become so severe that the General Court, with Winthrop now serving as governor, felt it necessary to disarm her more zealous followers in Boston.[18]

Her true convictions lie hidden beneath documents written and preserved by her opponents, but even John Cotton finally said that she had pushed far beyond him. Before coming to New England she had begun to absorb ideas from the fringe movements of English sectarian piety, which she easily combined with ideas from Cotton. She became an active proponent of the Christ piety prevailing in Boston. "The foundation she laid," John Winthrop observed later, "was (or rather seemed to be) Christ and Free-Grace." Like Cotton she exalted union with Christ above all else, but she lacked Cotton's inclination to wrap the piety in scholastic distinctions.[19]

Cotton said that the saints were spiritually active only when Christ acted within them; Hutchinson reportedly taught that "Christ was all, did all, and the soule remained alwayes as a dead Organ." Cotton denied that obedience to the law could signify a gracious state; so did Hutchinson, but she seems also to have taught that "the law is no rule of life to a Christian." Cotton identified habitual faith and the union with Christ; she was accused of saying that the Christian lived not by faith in Christ but by the "faith of Christ." Whatever Cotton said, Hutchinson's rhetoric seemed to carry one step further—or so it appeared to her antagonists and some of her disciples.[20]

Despite her biblicism she entertained notions of Scripture that Williams and the other New England ministers could never have accepted. Cotton had said that the witness of the Spirit transcended the letter of the Scripture; Hutchinson was charged with having said that "the whole Scripture in the Letter of it held forth nothing but a Covenant of works." In her examination by the General Court she made it explicit. "They that were ministers of the letter and not the spirit," she said, "did preach a covenant of works." She seems to have meant that only the saints who received an immediate witness of the Spirit could discern the true meaning of the biblical text. Thomas Leverett, the ruling elder of the Boston church, quoted her as saying that until the New England ministers "received the witness of the spirit they could not preach a covenant of grace so clearly." And some of her followers apparently proposed that the presence of Christ through the Spirit could stand in conflict with the teachings of Christ in the Scripture: "All Doctrines, Revelations and Spirits, must be tried by Christ the word, rather than by the Word of Christ." She implicitly subordinated Scripture to the Spirit; some of her followers were more explicit.[21]

Her great mistake before the magistrates was to make her own explicit statement about spiritual revelations. Under pressure from her judges, she asserted that she could distinguish between the voice of Christ and the voice of Moses in Scripture by means of "an immediate revelation" from God, "the voice of his own spirit to my soul." Magistrates and deputies quickly recalled other instances when she seemed "inquisitive after revelations." Some of the magistrates, including Winthrop, believed that she and her followers were saying that "their owne revelations of particular events were as infallible as the Scripture." That was unacceptable in a colony whose leaders looked to Scripture for the precedents to maintain communal order and harmony. Fearing the consequences of spiritist immediacy, the magistrates banished her.[22]

The crushing of the Antinomians failed to end the dissent by radical spiritists. One woman announced that she was "a Prophetesse" who must prophesy like the Prophet Ezekiel. A "lusty big man" insisted that "the spirit of Revelation came to him as he was drinking a pipe of Tobacco." The most provocative of the spiritist dissenters was Samuel Gorton, an English clothier who maintained ties with dissenting religious movements in London and exemplified the close links between spiritism and social radicalism. Arriving in Massachusetts Bay in 1637 during the Antinomian crisis, he moved the next year to Plymouth, where he fell into disfavor after he condemned the government for mistreating his wife's servant. His private lay preaching refreshed some Separatist spirits in Plymouth, but when his banishment in 1639 led him to Aquidneck in Rhode Island, a small settlement composed mainly of Boston's former Antinomians, they too whipped him for sedition and banished him. By 1640 Roger Williams was complaining that at Providence "almost all suck in his poyson as at first they did at Aquedneck."[23]

Gorton's "poyson" consisted partly of an incorrigible tendency to launch into what Williams described as "uncleane and foule censures of all the Ministers," but the chief ingredient was an esoteric religious mysticism that resulted in a dramatic reinterpretation of traditional Christian doctrines. Gorton's writings, cryptic and confusing, appear to have taught that an incarnation of Christ in Adam made all human beings divine. As the divine image of God, Christ became flesh when God created Adam. Adam's loss of that image through sin was the death of Christ, whose resurrection came when God began to restore the image through the regeneration of human beings. Symbolized by the biblical story of Jesus and appropriated through inward experiences, these events, in Gorton's eyes, entailed a radical egalitarianism that made ministers unnecessary and restricted other earthly rulers.[24]

At the heart of Gorton's message was the notion of "the equal nearness of the divine spirit to [both] the sinner and the saint," which made possible, he thought, a spiritist principle of scriptural interpretation. Gorton could therefore reinterpret the biblical narratives to conform to his ideas about divine immanence. Like Anne Hutchinson he quoted copiously from the Bible, but he too felt no constraint to remain within the merely literal sense of scriptural meaning, and he had no interest in the recovery of a primitive past.[25]

His enemies in Providence insisted that his true interest was "licentious lust" and that the Gortonians "put no manner of difference between houses, goods, lands, wives, lives, blood, nor any thing will be precious in their eyes." He denied the accusations, but to most colonists his political doctrines were almost equally outrageous. The Gortonists believed, if Roger Williams was accurate, that "the Saints are not to submit to the powers of the world or worldly powers, and that the powers and governments of the world have nothing to doe with them for civil misdemeanours." To the chagrin of the rulers in the Bay Colony, who once sent an expeditionary force to capture him, Gorton by 1648 had convinced some powerful people in England to protect him as he put his ideas into practice in an isolated colony called Shawomet, south of Providence. In Shawomet spiritist dissent found a haven.[26]

It seemed initially that spiritism might also have found a home among the Baptists. As early as 1638 some church members at Plymouth "fell into the error of Anabaptistry." During the next five years Baptist sentiments surfaced in Salem, Charlestown, Lynn, Hingham, Watertown, and Essex County. In Rhode Island Roger Williams and other members of the Providence church rebaptized each other in 1639, and by 1644 a congregation in Newport practiced believer's baptism. Within seven years Baptists also worshipped openly in Seekonk (Rehoboth) in Plymouth Colony. The Bay Colony magistrates were alarmed, but it was only a matter of time until Baptists had their own congregation even in Massachusetts Bay.[27]

When Baptist ideas first surfaced in New England, ministers and magistrates panicked, thinking of the seizure of Münster, Germany by violent radicals in 1534. Fearing "incendiaries of Commonwealths, and the infectors of persons in maine matters of religion," the General Court in 1644 banished the colony's few outspoken Baptists. But the law failed to stifle the movement, and the issue divided the colony.[28]

The initial evidence suggested that unconventional views about baptism represented a continuation of spiritist agitation. During the Antinomian crisis one of Anne Hutchinson's followers proclaimed that baptism was anachronistic: "In the New Testament there are no signes, no not our baptisme, for the baptisme of water is of no use to us, when once wee are baptized with the Holy Ghost." The early Baptist movement also seemed to have spiritist associations. Winthrop thought that it was Katherine Scott, Anne Hutchinson's sister, who in 1639 emboldened Roger Williams to seek rebaptism. The Baptist congregation that John Clarke founded in Newport in or about 1644 consisted largely of refugees who had departed from Massachusetts Bay after Anne Hutchinson's banishment. And some Baptists, like Lady Deborah Moody in Salem, eventually moved from Baptist piety into radically spiritist forms of dissent.[29]

When John Clarke published in 1652 his *Ill Newes from New-England*, however, he argued the Baptist case almost exclusively on primitivist grounds.

He wanted to persuade the ministers and magistrates, he said, to reform their churches and restrain themselves from violence against Baptists. And he would use "but these two arguments." He could find, he said, among "those churches that first trusted" in Christ no sign of infant baptism. And he could also find in the New Testament no authority for the use of the civil sword "to correct errour." He could make the case for the Baptists, he added, merely by recovering "the precept of Christ or . . . the president [precedent] of primitive Christians."[30]

The appeal to the New Testament church reappeared whenever Baptists defended their views. After the president of Harvard, Henry Dunster, refused to have his child baptized, the Cambridge church dispatched Jonathan Mitchell, who had been Dunster's student in the college, to reclaim the erring educator. Mitchell found it an unnerving experience and failed miserably; he himself began having doubts about infant baptism. The General Court commissioned nine more ministers and two ruling elders to change Dunster's mind, but Dunster held to his argument that "John the Baptist, Christ himself, & [the] Apostles did none of them baptize children." Such an argument was no monopoly of college presidents. The farmer Thomas Goold, John Winthrop's tenant, countered his minister's admonitions with the same reply: "we have no command in the gospel, nor example, for the baptizing of children." Throughout the seventeenth century the Baptist argument remained the same. Puritans who practiced infant baptism fell away from the primitive church, but Baptists maintained the ancient precedents.[31]

In 1656 the Quakers arrived in Boston and announced that both the Baptists and the "hireling priests" of the Bay Colony churches cared too much about precedents and too little about the inner voice of the Spirit. The two Quaker missionaries Ann Austin and Mary Fisher resumed the spiritist demand for immediacy. Quakers could, to be sure, make use of the Puritan appeal to the primitive church. They delighted in reminding the New England magistrates that the church in ancient Corinth and Galatia had never fined and persecuted other Christians and that Christ had never commanded his churches and disciples to whip or fine either Jews or Gentiles. George Fox, moreover, claimed that the Friends were reestablishing the true primitive church, but the Quakers could hardly have been described as a restorationist movement.[32]

Believing that they lived in the new dispensation of the Spirit, Quakers hoped not to restore primitive forms and structures but to recover "the everlasting gospel," preached unto both Abraham and the apostles and now renewed through the pouring forth of the Spirit. The difference between primitivist dissenters and the Quakers appeared especially in their conflicting attitudes toward Scripture. The Quakers cited the Bible, but they subordinated "the written Word" to the inner word given to the soul through the light of the eternal Christ. They also elevated the eternal Christ, known through the Spirit, above the merely historical Christ who had lived in ancient Israel. This meant that the continuing revelation of the Spirit provided the criteria for interpreting the Scripture. It meant also that the restitution of primitive forms seemed far less important than the millennial harbingers implicit in the activity of the Spirit.[33]

In 1672 Roger Williams debated three Quakers in a meetinghouse in Newport before an unruly crowd of Quaker spectators. Williams complained that his opponents often fell to their knees in ecstatic prayer rather than respond to his criticisms, but he managed to show how he viewed the differences between a primitivist and a spiritist style of dissent. He complained that the Quakers elevated "their pretended new found Light within them" above the Scripture. Whereas he looked to the precedents of "the first primitive Churches," they seemed to him to speak only of an invisible church without visible forms.[34]

New England's dissenters, then, often disagreed with each other, but they also adopted some of the same strategies of persuasion. The literature of dissent, after all, consisted of far more than syllogisms. Dissenters tried to move the emotions as well as convince the understanding. Abstract arguments often gave way to graphic descriptions and narratives. Although primitivists and spiritists used different arguments, they often displayed similar styles of suasive appeal.

First, they described their sufferings, sometimes with the apparent aim of merely eliciting sympathy but often with deeper intentions. Roger Williams considered it a point of immense significance that the nonseparating Puritans had "not comparably suffred" as the Separatists had suffered. Christ had taught, Williams believed, that his true followers would face "paine and sorrow, yea poverty and persecution, until the great day of refreshing, neer approaching." When Williams described how his banishment had exposed him "to the mercy of an howling Wildernesse in Frost and Snow," he was making a theological point: "I acknowledge it a blessed gift of God to be inabled to suffer, and so to be banished for his Names sake."[35]

In a similar spirit Anne Hutchinson "boasted highly of her sufferings for Christ," and John Clarke's *Ill Newes from New-England* made a forthright appeal to the "tender hearts" of his English readers by telling "a tragicall story" about men and women who traveled to "those utmost parts of the World, to the extreme hazard of their lives, the wasting of their estates, and upon the point, to the totall loss and deprivation of their neer and deer relations." The book described interrogations and scornful treatment, including Obadiah Holmes's account of his whipping at the hands of the Bay Colony magistrates—how he prayed for "strength of body to suffer for [the Lord's] sake," how he accompanied the jailer with his Bible in his hand, how he told the assembled magistrates that he would "seal with my Blood . . . that which I hold and practise," how the jailer spat on his hands three times before delivering the thirty strokes with the three-corded whip, and how, as a result of Holmes's suffering, many came to him afterward "rejoycing to see the power of the Lord manifested in weak flesh." To Holmes the pain provided an occasion for "such a spirituall manifestation of Gods presence, as the like thereunto I never had." It also proved useful as a testimonial to potential converts and to parliamentary sympathizers.[36]

Nobody exploited the persuasive force of accounts of suffering more skillfully than the Quakers. They carefully collected the testimonies of their martyrs and published them for English readers. Their intention was partly to persuade the crown to intervene, but they also recognized that the spectacle of suffering drew converts. After receiving fifteen stripes with rods, John Rous observed that his suffering "did prove much for the advantage of Truth, and their disadvantage, for Friends did with much boldness own us openly in it." Magistrates in Rhode Island urged their Bay Colony counterparts to ignore the Quakers, who "delight to be persecuted by civil powers." But Governor John Endecott and his assistant, Richard Bellingham, proved to be the perfect antagonists, and Quaker writers made it a point to publicize their brutal and abusive behavior. After the magistrates cropped the ears of Quaker missionaries and hanged four of them on the Boston Common, the Quakers never let them forget it.[37]

They believed that their suffering confirmed their faithfulness. Roger Williams complained that no one "did so magnifie and so exactly insist upon their *Sufferings* as the *Quakers* did," and he argued that their suffering was "not valid as to the proof of their *Religion*." By the 1670s Williams claimed that heretics had suffered just as much as the faithful, so that suffering proved nothing, but his claim contradicted the views he had held three decades earlier. It also revealed his recognition of the extent to which the narratives of Quaker suffering bore the power to persuade.[38]

A second potent dissenting strategy of persuasion was to attack the ideal of an educated ministry. Thomas Shepard complained that Separatists and Baptists were "dispisers of Gods Ministers, and therefore prefer trades-men before those whom God hath gifted, and set apart for his work in the Schooles of the Prophets." English spiritists like John Saltmarsh and William Dell led a lively attack during the 1640s on university-trained ministers, charging that their bondage to the "Arts and Sciences" inhibited the freedom of the Spirit. By 1654 Edward Johnson was lamenting the "many pamphlets" that had been written in England to deride "all kinds of Scholarship." But even before the war began, New England dissenters had promoted anticlericalism and proclaimed that pious lay exhorters taught more faithfully than ministers trained at Harvard. Johnson reported that one of Anne Hutchinson's disciples lured colonists by promising to show them a woman who preached "better Gospell then any of your black-coates that have been at the Ninneversity."[39]

Such attacks became a common feature of religious dissent. Baptists claimed that the churches were wrong to allow "none but such as had human[e] learning to be in the ministry" and insisted on the right of the laity to prophesy. Nobody was more disdainful of the educated clergy than Samuel Gorton, who boasted that he was "not bred up in the Schooles of humane learning." "I blesse God," he added, "that I never was." And the Quakers denigrated the ministers as mere "hireling priests."[40]

The Quaker condemnations prompted Roger Williams again to revise his earlier evaluations of divine learning. In 1652 he had praised the "many excellent Prophets and Witnesses of Christ Jesus, who never entred (as they say) into the Ministry," arguing that the Spirit could give them "Utterance in the holy things of Jesus Christ." He preferred their exhortations to those of the "hireling ministers" who succeeded only in turning the divine calling into a trade. But when the Quakers depreciated both the ministry and the need for biblical scholarship, Williams defended "Schools of Learning," which promoted "Divine Knowledge" by teaching "the Hebrew and Greek Tongues." Since Williams believed that no true ministers any longer existed, his anti-clericalism remained firm, but by 1672 he no longer felt comfortable with the anti-intellectualism that permeated the attacks on the ministry, for it suggested that close study of biblical texts was unnecessary.[41]

The laity in New England had long asserted the right to prophesy—expound scriptural passages and exhort other members—in their churches. The practice had been popular in England, especially among the Separatists, and during the 1630s John Cotton encouraged "the exercise of prophecy" in the Boston church, with the result that "some were converted, and others much edified." Such events also occurred sometimes in private homes. When the court admonished Anne Hutchinson for her prophesying in private gatherings, she replied that such meetings were "in practice before I came therefore I was not the first." But by the 1640s the popularity of prophesying among dissenters made the ministers uneasy. Samuel Gorton had encouraged both men and women to prophesy in his meetings in Salem. The Baptists, according to Thomas Shepard, had also permitted the same kind of "promiscuous prophesie."[42]

Gradually the prophesyings, which once had ministerial approval, began to symbolize discontent with the ministry. In 1642 John Cotton encouraged prophesying and urged the curious—"save onely for Women"—to ask questions of the prophets, but when he published two years later his *Keyes of the Kingdom of Heaven*, he placed further limits on the practice. In the primitive church, he argued, only those could prophesy who had "extraordinary gifts for it." By 1653 the General Court passed laws to curb lay prophets. But prophesying remained popular, especially among dissenting groups, who found it an effective vehicle of persuasion.[43]

A third strategy of the dissenters was so obvious that it is easy to overlook its significance: they criticized and condemned. The rhetoric of condemnation touched deep chords in New England Puritan culture. The English Puritan reformers had been marginal outsiders whose shared antipathies toward the practices of the Church of England rather than any common program for reconstructing the church had bound them together. The Puritans who migrated to New England defined themselves in part by their willingness to condemn Anglican "inventions." Although they promptly divided over the proper limits of condemnation, with the Separatists complaining that the nonseparating churches were mealymouthed compromisers, the memory of prophetic condemnation remained part of the New England heritage. The dissenters made that heritage of condemnation their own.[44]

New England already felt threatened by internal conflicts, political enemies in England, and their Indian neighbors. Their sense of fragility, when combined with traditional beliefs in popular culture about the potency of words, intensified a prevailing European sensitivity to aggressive speech. Colonists worried a lot about name calling. They evidenced a passionate concern for reputation, keeping their courts busy with complaints about slander. In one sampling of various New England courts between 1645 and 1685, John Demos found that charges of slander and defamation accounted for 27 percent of the cases. Aggressive speech also figured heavily in conflicts over witchcraft.[45]

Sensitivity to condemnation was no peculiarity of New England Puritans. The courts in Virginia severely and frequently punished men and women for slander. When the Virginian Thomas Parks described Argall Yeardley's father as "a Taylor that Lept off a shopp board in Burchin Lane" and disdained his mother as "a middwife not to the honour-Citizens but to bye blowes," a court sentenced him to thirty lashes. Because religious epithets could be especially troublesome, Lord Baltimore tried in 1649 to forestall conflict in Maryland by having the legislature declare any religious name calling a punishable crime. He forbade his colonists to call each other "heretick, Scismatick, Idolator, puritan, Independant, Prespiterian popish prest, Jesuite, Jesuited papist, Luthern, Calvenist, Anabaptist, Brownist, Antinomian, Barrowist, Roundhead, Sepatist" or any other derogatory religious name. Words in the seventeenth century could be potent weapons, and people feared their power.[46]

In a society marked by a pronounced sensitivity to abusive language, dissenters aroused profound anxieties when they condemned the churches, ministers, and magistrates. Winthrop felt aggrieved when Antinomians described the ministers as "Baals Priests" and the magistrates as "Ahabs" and "enemies to Christ." These were "sore censures" in a culture nervous about censorious speech. Samuel Gorton's rhetorical style therefore attracted about as much attention as his ideas. Gorton never hesitated to describe his opponents as apostles of the devil, vipers whose "foule and inhumane" wrongs revealed their devotion to Satan. The magistrates were "falsifiers of the word of God" who served "their own lusts," and the ministers were hypocrites and "Magicians." When Edward Winslow complained to a parliamentary committee, therefore, he concentrated on Gorton's "raylings and reproachfull language." If Gorton had been "moderate in revilings," he said, then his errors "might have been winkt at." "But to fly out into such extremity on so small provocation against their betters, as to call them Idolls, blind-guides, despisers, generation of vipers, such as crucifie Christ, men that serve their own lusts, hypocrites, the seed of the Devill. . . . This language speakes loud to what Country they belong, and of what race they come."[47]

Some dissenters took care to moderate their rhetoric, but most, like their European counterparts, believed in the persuasive force of name calling, and their opponents more than answered in kind. The Quakers proved especially adept at aggressive shock tactics. They conducted their "Lamb's war" by interrupting church services to denounce the ministers as hireling priests, refusing to remove their hats or use the customary titles of deference, and addressing everyone with the informal and egalitarian "thee" and "thou." By the 1660s they began emulating the ancient prophets who enacted their condemnations with dramatic gestures. Catherine Chatham walked through the streets of Boston in sackcloth and ashes "as a sign of the Indignation of the Lord against the oppressing and tyrannical Spirit" of the ministers and magistrates; Thomas Newhouse broke two bottles in a Boston meeting house, warning the congregation that they too would be dashed to pieces; Lydia Wardel and Deborah Wilson walked naked through Boston as a protest against New England's pride and brutality. As late as 1675 Margaret Brewster entered "Priest [Thomas] Thatcher's House of Worship" with ashes on her head, sackcloth on her shoulders, and her face colored black, protesting the cruel laws with which New England suppressed Quaker dissent.[48]

The valorization of suffering, the depreciation of educated clergy, and the rhetoric of condemnation were not the only strategies of persuasion used by dissenters, and the typology of traditionalist, primitivist, and spiritist dissent fails to encompass every form of protest. When "the greater part of the Inhabitants of Hingham" complained about their not being allowed to select their own military officers, they appealed to their "common Liberties" as English subjects. When Robert Child and six other colonists issued in 1646 their "Remonstrance and humble Petition," urging an extended suffrage, relaxed standards of admission to the churches, and an end to "Arbitrary Government," they claimed the authority of the Bible, but they appealed primarily to "the Fundamentall lawes of England." And when the merchant William Pynchon of Springfield published in 1650 his *Meritorious Price of Our Redemption*, maintaining that Christ's obedience, not any satisfaction of divine wrath, brought God's atoning forgiveness, he was introducing a style of religious thought linked more to Christian rationalism in Europe and England than to any dissenting movement in New England. That dissenters in New England did not adopt a uniform strategy of persuasion made them even more puzzling to their opponents.[49]

Historians have differed in their evaluations of New English dissenters. Some have argued that they barely rippled the surface of cultural uniformity; others have claimed that New Englanders achieved their self-definition by distancing themselves from minority dissenting movements. Dissent certainly affected some colonists more than others; some towns offered refuge to dissenting ideas, while others ignored them. Sandwich in Plymouth Colony became a dissenting stronghold; in the Bay Colony Salem was known as a dissenting town; Baptists, Quakers, and Separatists set the tone in Lynn; Quakers flourished in a few smaller villages like Amesbury, Dartmouth, and Tiverton, and they formed a strong minority in a few places like Salem, the port town of Gloucester, and the northern village of Kittery. All this suggests the importance of social and geographical proximity in sustaining dissent. It was much easier to defy convention when one's neighbors defied it too.[50]

Ministers and magistrates worried that dissenting movements especially enticed women. Winthrop complained that the Antinomians "commonly laboured to worke first upon women," hoping that they would then "catch their husbands also, which indeed often proved too true amongst us here." Ministers worried aloud during Anne Hutchinson's trial that her "fluent Tounge," if not silenced, would "draw away many, Espetially simple Weomen of her owne sex." Women did prove troublesome to the authorities during the crisis. They also drew clerical disapproval when they continued to preach and prophesy in the Rhode Island settlements founded by disgruntled Antinomian refugees. Samuel Gorton allowed both men and women to prophesy in Warwick. Quaker missionaries offered a continuing affront to the accepted ideas about the proper subordination of women. Nine of the first twenty-two Quaker missionaries to New England were women; so were twenty-six of the first fifty-nine Quaker missionaries to America.[51]

Women enjoyed somewhat less prominence in the Baptist movement. Lady Deborah Moody in Salem shocked Winthrop when she adopted Baptist views, but she eventually found the Quakers more persuasive. Roger Williams once refused even to reply to a Quaker woman's question at Newport because he "would not Countenance so much the violation of Gods Order in making a Reply to a Woman in Publick." His refusal helps explain why women were highly visible in leadership roles in some dissenting movements but not in others. Primitivist dissenters continued to feel bound by Paul's rule in 1 Corinthians 14 enjoining silence on women in the church, but spiritists found a new source of authority in the inward motions of the Spirit. The Quakers argued that the Spirit of Christ could "speak in the Female as well as in the Male" and that Paul was addressing a unique problem in the Corinthian church, restricting only certain women in one congregation.

They and other spiritists could therefore encourage women to teach and prophesy; the primitivists could not.[52]

Dissenters left a firm imprint on one other group of New England colonists. As the objects of dissenting scorn and the defenders of the New England way, the colonial clergy found that their critics often set their agendas. A good portion of clerical publishing went into the refutation of dissent. Five ministers published book-length arguments against the Baptists in treatises that resulted in some detailed revision of covenantal themes. Thomas Shepard wrote both his *Theses Sabbaticae* and his *Parable of the Ten Virgins Opened* partly to confute Antinomians. Richard Mather's *Summe of Certain Sermons*, John Norton's *Orthodox Evangelist*, and Peter Bulkeley's *Gospel-Covenant* also emerged out of the Antinomian crisis. John Cotton developed his ideas about toleration through debate with Roger Williams; John Norton and Peter Folger published treatises against the Quakers. By requiring a continued defense of New England's institutions, the dissenters helped to elicit the body of thought that defined the culture.

The Toleration of Persuasion

John Cotton insisted that New England authorities never imagined themselves to be stifling liberty of conscience. They punished no one for error, he said, unless for a fundamental error seditiously or turbulently promoted. Cotton thought that the fundamental truths were clear; dissenters who persisted in denying them in the face of good arguments for them might rightly be condemned. They underwent punishment not for their conscience but for sinning against the light of their conscience. But he was also willing to grant toleration even to "Anti-Christians" who persisted in "Fundamentall Errors," as long as they stayed quiet about it. What New Englanders actually punished, he said, was persuasion. Efforts by dissenters to "seduce simple soules," to persuade men and women to act upon erroneous assumptions, inevitably created a danger to society. Any threat to religious unity endangered "the peace of the Common-wealth," and persuasive dissent threatened unity.[53]

Cotton's distinction between the silent holding of erroneous views and the attempt to persuade others into error reappeared whenever New Englanders defended intolerance. John Norton, confronted by Quaker missionaries, explained to readers in England and New England in 1659 that magistrates dealt with matters of "fact," not of "judgement." Quiet heresy, maintained without any effort to induce others to become heretics, remained outside the bounds of the magistrate's authority: "We say religion is to be perswaded with Scripture-reasons, not Civil weapons; with Arguments, not with punishments." But blasphemous efforts to persuade cloaked a demand for liberty of error, which had public consequences. An error made public became a social fact, and magistrates had responsibility for social facts. Not until the 1670s did some ministers begin to suggest that it might be "impossible that all Consciences can quietly submit to the Religion of the state."[54]

Not only in New England did colonists view dissent with a wary eye. The Holy Office of the Inquisition, established in Mexico City by 1569, became a forceful presence in New Mexico after 1625. The commissary Alonso de Benavides arrived that year representing both the Franciscan order and the Holy Office, and he took satisfaction from his status: "As I am commissary of the Inquisition, these Teoas Indians prided themselves that I lived among them, and they painted the coat of arms of the Inquisition in the church . . . since they did not want any other church to have it." He spoke for the most powerful ecclesiastical court in the New World, which found itself in almost constant battles against heretics in New Mexico, though what the friars found heretical were usually the words and actions of governors and soldiers who engaged the church in a battle for control of the Indians and the economy. In any case, the opponents of the churchmen complained bitterly of their "strong hand," as three separate ecclesiastical tribunals kept watch in a population with a few hundred Spanish settlers.[55]

Virginia had no Inquisition, but it had its own traditions of intolerance. As early as 1609 the company's instructions to the governor required the punishment of "all Popery or Schisme," and the "articles, lawes, and orders" that Sir Thomas Dale introduced in 1610 imposed the death penalty for blasphemy. The company proposed to whip people for demeaning preachers, missing too many church services, or refusing to divulge their religious principles to the ministers. It was no innovation, then, when the first assembly of 1619 ordered the colony's clergy to "exercise their ministerial function according to the Ecclesiastical Lawes and orders of the church of Englande" and later assemblies arranged to deport dissenters. In 1643 Governor William Berkeley required all nonconformists to leave the colony. Five years later he "raised a persecution" against stragglers, driving many into Maryland, and when Quakers later entered Virginia, the burgesses promptly passed an act suppressing them as well.[56]

In 1671 Berkeley revealed that such attitudes toward the toleration of dissent could have broad implications: "I thank God there are no free schools nor printing [in Virginia], and I hope we shall not have [either for a] hundred years; for learning has brought disobedience, and heresy, and sects into the world, and printing has divulged them, and libels against the best government. God keep us from both." As late as 1682 a Virginia governor suppressed a printing press in Jamestown and prohibited the printing of anything until the king made known his pleasure. The king conveniently procrastinated in making his pleasure known.[57]

Virginians had comparatively little difficulty repressing dissent. A few Independents and Presbyterians found their way to Virginia pulpits; a handful of Quakers managed to survive on the Eastern Shore despite occasional persecutions that continued into the 1670s; a few people practiced witchcraft and magic. But the turbulence that rocked New England every few years rarely surfaced in Virginia. Not that everyone was a heartfelt Anglican; it was rather that dissent needed some hot-spirited zeal to survive, and few Virginians felt exceedingly zealous about such issues in the seventeenth century.[58]

Other colonies had more trouble than Virginia. In New Sweden, founded in 1638 on the Delaware River, for instance, the colonists symbolized their cultural distinctiveness through Lutheran ritual, but the presence of a more powerful neighbor ensured a place for conflicting voices. In 1647 no more than 183 people lived in the Swedish settlements. Yet they cherished cultural uniformity as much as the larger colonies did. The Swedish court instructed Governor Johan Printz in 1643 to decorate their church and clothe their priest in a Swedish manner to show that they were different from the English and the Dutch Calvinists. But because of the threat from New Netherland, the Swedes had to grant the Dutch an indulgence to practice their "heresy," so the ideal of uniformity remained unfulfilled.[59]

The Dutch Reformed clergy of New Netherland, who labored to protect their colony against false opinions and foreign sects, enjoyed even less success than the Swedes. When the settlement began, the company's provisional orders to the commander of the expedition included an injunction to punish anyone who "should wantonly revile or blaspheme the name of God or our Savior Jesus Christ," and the company decided in the same year to permit "no other services than those of the true Reformed religion, in the manner in which they are at present conducted in this country." This ideal of uniformity lingered even after years of diversity. The first article in the oath administered to Peter Stuyvesant, who arrived as the new director in 1646 with orders to impose some order on an unruly settlement, specified that he was to permit only Reformed doctrine and worship.[60]

The Jesuit Isaac Jogues, visiting the colony in 1643, recognized that such efforts were doomed. "No religion is publicly exercised but the Calvinist," he wrote, "and orders are to admit none but Calvinists, but this is not observed; for besides the Calvinists there are in the colony Catholics, English Puritans, Lutherans, Anabaptists, here called Mnistes [Mennonites], etc." Gravesend on Long Island became the home of Dutch Mennonites, followers of the continental Anabaptist Menno Simons. The majority of the people there, complained the domine Johannes Megapolensis, "reject the baptism of infants, the observation of the Sabbath, the office of preacher, and any teachers of God's word." English Presbyterians and Independents settled on Long Island, where they quarreled with each other about baptismal practices. When the Presbyterian minister Richard Denton at Hempstead began to baptize the children of parents who were not church members, the Independents in his congregation rushed out of the church, confirming the Dutch clergy in their impression that chaos reigned in their colony.[61]

When Lutherans entered the colony the result was further turmoil. Objecting to a phrase in the Dutch baptismal liturgy, they initiated in 1653 a series of petitions to the States General of the Netherlands seeking permission to call "a capable and faithful pastor of the Augsburg Confession." The Dutch clergy responded with a familiar argument: "Strife in religious matters would produce confusion in political affairs." If the Lutherans succeeded, New Netherland would become a "Babel of confusion, instead of remaining a united and peaceful people." In 1657, when the Quakers arrived, the domines undoubtedly thought their prediction had come true. The Quaker missionaries announced their presence by falling into a frenzy, calling loudly for repentance, and creating panic throughout the town: "Our people not knowing what was the matter, ran to and fro, while one called 'Fire,' and another something else." The Dutch, like the New Englanders, responded with whips and fines, but the Quakers eventually prevailed.[62]

The preachers knew that they had failed to maintain the uniformity they desired when the company ordered the colony not to expel the twenty-three Portuguese Jews who arrived from Brazil aboard the *St. Charles* in 1654. The clergy complained that New Netherland was already filled with "other servants of Baal," and Governor Stuyvesant urged the company that "the deceitful race—such hateful enemies and blasphemers of the name of Christ,—be not allowed further to infect and trouble this New Colony." Megapolensis made a similar appeal to the Classis of Amsterdam. Persuade the company, he begged, to send the "godless rascals" away. Their only aim, he wrote, was to "get possession of Christian property." The panic deepened when members of the Dutch congregation heard that the recent arrivals hoped to build a synagogue. But the company, while expressing its sympathy to Stuyvesant, explained that the Jews of Amsterdam had invested a substantial sum in company shares, so expulsion seemed inadvisable.[63]

A synagogue was out of the question, but the Jews could stay, and they could "exercise in all quietness their religion within their houses." In 1656 they even gained their own small sacred space. The colony granted them "a little hook of land situate out of this city for a burial place." By gaining a place to bury their dead, they confirmed at least that in New Amsterdam the sacred spaces would not be all of one kind.[64]

In 1663 a Dutch Mennonite from Amsterdam, Pieter Plockhoy, tried to expand the limits of Dutch colonial culture. Calling for the abolition of churches, ministers, and creeds, he came to Zwaanendael, in territory that later became a part of Delaware, to establish a cooperative community with a common religion held together by the public reading of the Bible and the singing of psalms. The company in Amsterdam might have allowed even Plockhoy to stay, but when the English invaded New Netherland in 1664, they displayed no tolerance for Plockhoy's commune. It took only a few English soldiers to disband the community and exile its members.[65]

A few colonies abandoned the ideal of uniformity from the start. When commissioners outside Rhode Island urged the Assembly at Portsmouth to take action against Quakers, it responded in 1657 with a reminder that "freedom of different consciences to be protected from inforcements, was the principal ground of our charter." The royal charter of 1663 also permitted no punishment for religious opinions that did not disturb civil peace, and although the colony disfranchised everybody but Protestants, it continued to tolerate an unusual amount of diversity. For this it became known as "a place of errorists and enthusiasts," the "*latrina* of New England."[66]

Lord Baltimore tried also to provide a haven in Maryland. Eager for a colony both profitable and open to Catholics, George Calvert and his son Cecil tried to impose toleration as a means to maintain social harmony. Cecil Calvert instructed the first Catholic colonists to give no offense to Protestants and to practice their religion "as privately as may be." The proprietor encouraged a Jesuit mission, but he also resisted Jesuit efforts to secure special privileges.

For a decade the Catholic minority maintained a tenuous peace with the larger, poorer non-Catholic majority. But the 1640s brought political collapse, pressure from the English Civil War, and a migration of Puritans fleeing Virginia. Baltimore tried to counter rising Protestant sentiment with the "Act Concerning Religion" (1649), which reaffirmed toleration for all who "believe in Jesus Christ" while setting penalties for either blasphemous speech or sectarian slander. But Protestant dissenters, complaining of the Calvert family's "tyrannical power against the Protestants," gained control of the colony, repealed the toleration act in 1654, and banned Catholicism.[67]

By chance the coup expanded the influence of Quaker missionaries. When Elizabeth Harris entered the colony in 1655 or 1656, sharing the "Inward word of truth," she drew about twenty converts from the Puritan areas, and some of the chief leaders of the Maryland government became Quakers. Calvert regained control in 1658, and the lawmakers promptly began to whip and fine the "vagbonds" who dissuaded people from military and jury service. Baltimore soon sought an accommodation even with the Quakers, and by 1677 Charles Calvert estimated that the "greatest part of the Inhabitants of that Province (three of four at least) doe consist of Praesbiterians, Independents, Anabaptists and Quakers." The story did not end there. In the 1680s the Protestants took over again, passed laws against Catholics, and began their efforts, eventually successful, to establish the Anglican church.[68]

By 1670 when the Carolina settlers founded Charleston, a few important people were convinced that toleration was the only right way. The proprietors advertised Carolina as a haven for dissenters, and by 1680 Quakers held regular meetings there without much opposition.

The tangled history of toleration serves as a reminder of how ambivalent seventeenth-century Americans remained about the unchecked freedom of one person to persuade another to follow an unfamiliar course. It reminds us also that dissenters refused to go away. However warily most colonists viewed dissent, they had a hard time preserving uniformity. To that extent, New Netherland, filled with people who disagreed with each other, foreshadowed the later history of America far more accurately than New England. But even in New England the dissenters left a permanent cultural imprint, and throughout the colonies the voices of dissent illustrated both the variety and the complexity of persuasion in early America.

seven

Rulers

Gentility, wealth, education, or force of character marked a few men as the natural rulers of colonial society. Ordinary colonists viewed those rulers with profound ambivalence; they believed that no society could flourish without "great men" but that great men also threatened the liberty and fortunes of the people who depended on them. One group of Dutch settlers in New Netherland, for example, wrote the directors in Amsterdam that "the power of electing a Governor among ourselves" would be disastrous because "we are not supplied and provided with persons qualified and fit for such stations." But another group in the colony exhorted the States General in Holland to permit frequent elections in the colony, observing that elections in neighboring New England served as "the bridle of their great men." Great men were necessary, but they needed bridling, and throughout the colonies their ambiguous position became the source of social and political conflict.[1]

The colonists wrote no abstruse treatises in political or social thought. They formulated their ideas about their society and its rulers by taking sides in concrete political and social struggles. The period of initial settlement produced the first flurry of political writing. Settlers in Plymouth drew up their Mayflower Compact in 1620; Virginians had to reorganize their government in 1624 when James I revoked the old charter; and the directors of the Massachusetts Bay Company transformed themselves into a civil government in 1630. An even more substantial outpouring of political and social thought accompanied the crises of the 1640s. In the Bay Colony deputies representing the towns succeeded in 1644 in creating a bicameral legislature that enabled them to check the authority of the higher magistrates. In New Amsterdam, however, the governors responded to similar pressures by simply disbanding

133

even their advisory councils, and in Maryland the tensions between poorer Protestant settlers and the largely Catholic proprietary government led between 1644 and 1646 to unchecked violence and plunder.

The civil war and Restoration in England also complicated matters for the colonists. After the execution of Charles I in 1649, Virginia announced its allegiance to the Royalists, thereby drawing the wrath of Parliament, which in 1651 forced Governor William Berkeley and his council to submit. Parliamentary commissioners also ousted in 1651 the Royalist governor of Maryland. But after the English restored the Stuarts to the throne in 1660, the commissioners came from England with a different agenda. Charles II began to impose his will on the colonies as early as 1662, when Connecticut accepted a new royal charter. In 1664 the restored English monarchy had sufficient military force to oust the Dutch from New Netherland and rename New Amsterdam in honor of the duke of York.

Another series of crises hit the colonies during the 1670s. The governor in New York had little difficulty putting down popular demands for an assembly, but governors elsewhere encountered problems more difficult to resolve. Massachusetts, suffering from the havoc of King Philip's War in 1675–76, had to endure in 1676 the arrival of a royal agent whose hostility foreshadowed the eventual abrogation of the charter. In Virginia the outbreak of Bacon's Rebellion in 1676 almost toppled the government, and discontented colonists in Maryland and the Carolinas launched brief rebellions against their own proprietary governments.

Political and social thought in the colonies always bore the aura of those diplomatic struggles and military conflicts and reflected always the clash of interests. The colonists formulated their political and social views in the course of efforts to justify, persuade, and secure allegiance. But their pamphlets and treatises also embodied some complicated ideas about the relationships of power, order, liberty, and consent.

Order, Liberty, and the Common Good

In 1659 John Norton explained to right-thinking New Englanders and to skeptical English readers why all reasonable colonists should despise Quakers. Observe, he said, "the suitableness of their doctrine unto discontented, seditious, factious, and tumultuous spirits, especially if pressed with poverty or a suffering condition." Quakers were dangerous because they subverted order, the highest of all the social values. Order, Norton explained, "is requisite in the way of means for the preservation of what is fundamentall." No society could stand without order, which preserved both "wel-doing and wel-being," even in a fallen creation. And order was no mere human creation or convenience; it was God's way: "Whilst we remember that God is the *God of*

Order: it is not hard to discern the maligning thereof, as proceeding from the Serpent."[2]

If asked to define order, Norton would have had no difficulty. It was hierarchical ranking and the deference of the lower orders to the higher: "Order is a divine disposal, of superior and inferior relations, distributing to each one respectively, what is due thereunto." Such a notion appealed also to a former servant, George Alsop, in Maryland. It was the "common and ordained Fate," he said, "that there must be servants as well as Masters." The beauty and strength of society, added the New England preacher William Hubbard, required that persons be disposed into different stations: "It is not then the result of time or chance, that some are mounted on horseback, while others are left to travell on foot." This attitude prevailed in social institutions and practices from Massachusetts to Virginia. A few of the colonies—Maryland, Carolina, New Netherland—even began as feudal societies, with patroonships, manors, baronies, and levies. The feudal dream soon faded, but colonists clung for a long time to notions of hierarchical order.[3]

Colonial society was fashioned to remind people continually that somebody towered above them and somebody else languished beneath them. Persons of every rank had their appropriate titles and designations, ranging from "goodman" and "goodwife" for the yeomen farmers and other common folk to "esquire" for some of the councilors. The titles of "gentleman" and "lady" connoted a diffuse social superiority accorded civil officers, the owners of large estates, or the highly educated. The oral forms of address for the genteel were "Mistress" and "Master," and a chance encounter on the street was a reminder of social location.[4]

Titles were not the only yardstick of rank. In New England in a procedure known as dooming the seats, the churches assigned their members to pews according to rank, dignity, age, and wealth. Each Sabbath day offered a display of local hierarchy. Similar criteria governed the seating in churches in Virginia. When Richard Price in Lancaster County sat in a chapel seat reserved for a county justice, he soon found himself before a court for "tending to the dishonor of God Almighty, the contempt of his Majesty and Mynisters, offence of the congregacion, scandall to religion, and evil example to others." Some colonies passed laws to ensure that daily apparel would mirror the ordering of society. The Massachusetts General Court, like other courts, expressed its "utter detesttion that men and women of meane condition should take upon themselves the garb of gentlemen, by wearing gold or silver, lace or buttons, or points at their knees" or other adornment reserved for "persons of greater estates, or more liberal education." Virginia, like other colonies, administered legal punishment "according to the qualitie of the person offendinge." It was not surprising that portrait painters attended carefully to the emblems of hierarchy and subordination with which their subjects distinguished themselves.[5]

Near the bottom of the hierarchy stood the "multitude," and people who wrote books or preached sermons viewed the multitude with wary suspicion. John Norton thought of them as a discontented and "irregenerate" mass, possessed of a "tumultuous nature." He warned that the multitude entertained secret hopes of "changing places with their Superiours" and usurping "their power, honour, and estates." Seventeenth-century writers rarely had anything good to say about the multitude. They recognized that rulers had a duty to protect "the commonalty"—often to protect them from each other—but they rarely assumed that common people possessed the virtue of political wisdom. "They may not be denied their proper and lawful liberties," wrote Nathaniel Ward in Massachusetts, "but I question whether it is of God to interest the inferior sort in that which should be reserved" to their superiors. Governor Berkeley in Virginia reported that the members of the colonial assembly had "this Axiom firmly fixt in them, That never any Community of people had good done unto them, but against their wills." And after Nathaniel Bacon led his rebellion against Berkeley's government, political leaders in both Virginia and Maryland pointed to the uprising as evidence of "the distempered humor predominant in the Common people."[6]

Hierarchical order was not the sole political value. From New England to Virginia articulate colonists appealed to the "common good," "the general good," or the "public good," often contrasting it to "privat gaine and interest." John Robinson advised the settlers at Plymouth to "joyne common affections truly bent upon the generall good" by repressing "all private respects of mens selves, not sorting with the general convenience." The colonies abounded with acquisitive souls seeking nothing more than what served their self-interest, and the promotional literature lured men and women to America with the promise of riches, but the conventional rhetoric of governors, ministers, and reformers repeatedly countered acquisitive individualism with the reminder that private ambitions had to remain subordinate to public ends. "It is the highest law in all Policy Civill or Spiritual," wrote Thomas Hooker, "to preserve the good of the whole; at this all must aime, and unto this all must be subordinate."[7]

It was a telling point in political debate when anyone could accuse an opponent of subverting the public good. Lord Baltimore's critics in Maryland charged him with pursuing only "his privat gaine and interest"; they accused his council of scorning "the common good." Governor John Harvey in Virginia responded to his own critics by charging them with disdain for "the generall good." Colonists never assumed that such appeals precluded a moderate and rightful quest for private gain, but they believed that rulers—the great men—bore a special responsibility to preserve a larger public good, and in the political rhetoric of the era, appeals to that public good were clearly believed to carry substantial persuasive power.[8]

Such language appeared in various settings: in sermons declaring that the touchstone for rulers was "the Publick good, and the Welfare of the people"; in efforts by company directors in New Netherland to persuade people to concentrate themselves in towns and villages; in the pamphlets of reformers in Virginia who argued that the best means to promote the "publique good" was to create well-ordered towns; and in oaths of office for judges and magistrates who were urged to do "equall right, to the poore and to the rich." The most damning political epithet in seventeenth-century America was "factious." By definition a faction was a group seeking its own ends. It stood in opposition to the good of the whole, and it called for prompt action. The Plymouth settlers drew up their Mayflower Compact when they observed a faction; Massachusetts Bay magistrates punished Quakers because they seemed factious; opposing sides in Maryland accused each other of being "factious people." In John Winthrop's vocabulary, and in that of others, to be factious was to "take up the rules of Matchiavell," to adopt the "Machevilian Principle, divide and overcome." Faction had to be resisted.[9]

By no means did the colonists disdain the political value of liberty, but they viewed it as an ambiguous notion, susceptible to misuse. Liberty did not, moreover, denote an individual right counterposed against the corporate welfare. When the colonists spoke of liberty—whether "the liberty of the freeborne subjects of England" or, more broadly, "liberty in people"—they remained fully committed to hierarchical order and the priority of the general good. To exercise true liberty, as contrasted to unbridled liberty, meant to act in accordance with the privileges inherent in a socially defined role. Freemen had the liberty, for instance, to vote or to declare their grievances but not to usurp the prerogatives of magistrates. Few colonists believed that anyone ought to have the liberty to move from one level of the hierarchy to another. Edward Johnson once described a group that moved to the Somers Islands in the Caribbean in search of the false liberty to elect "all men" to the office of a magistrate and elevate anyone to the authority of the pulpit. They returned, however, in disarray, determined that they "would never seek to be governed by liberty again."[10]

To have liberty meant to be able to act in accord with one's status. Servants had liberty when they received the freedoms that normally accrued to the status of servants; subjects of the king had liberty when they could count on exercising the freedoms traditionally granted to subjects. But when servants, subjects, or anyone else presumed the right to a boundless liberty, moving outside the social boundaries that defined them, they misused liberty and endangered the general good.[11]

The preachers in New England combined the idea of liberty with the notion of vocation or calling. As expounded by the celebrated English casuist William Perkins, a calling was "a certain manner of leading our lives in this world," ordained for each person by God for the common good. God called men and women to be Christians. He also bestowed inward gifts enabling some to be magistrates and ministers, others to be servants and laborers; some to be husbands, others wives. As a divine ordination each calling was a sacred task, but some stood higher than others. "God hath appointed," Perkins admonished, "that in every society one person should bee above or under another; not making all equall." To have liberty was to be free to act within the bounds—and the privileges—of one's calling.[12]

In 1645 John Winthrop, who had often served as governor of Massachusetts Bay, was accused of interfering arbitrarily in a local election. After he was vindicated, Winthrop made a famous speech in which he distinguished between two kinds of liberty. For him the important value was not liberty to do what one pleases but liberty to do what is right. All fallen creatures had a "natural liberty," common with the animals, to do as they willed. Since this implied the liberty to do evil as well as good, it proved to be inconsistent with authority. But men and women also had a "civil or federal" liberty, defined by either the covenant between God and humanity in the moral law or by covenants and constitutions among themselves. Civil liberty was the freedom to do what was good, just, and fitting. Rather than challenging authority, civil liberty existed only "in a way of subjection of authority"; it connoted the freedom to act in a manner appropriate to one's calling. It could not exist without the boundaries that defined it.[13]

The Great Men

Some had the calling—and the liberty—to be great men. Even in colonies where words like *vocation* and *calling* were rarely heard, most people assumed that providence had elevated a few persons to a position of singular right and ability to rule over others. John Cotton told New Englanders to "make choice of men of greatest worth for wisdom, for sufficiency, for birth." Like the settlers in New Netherland who renounced elections because their town lacked persons of quality, colonists elsewhere also placed their confidence in great men. After the early economic collapse, starvation, and violence in Virginia, the company explained that all the problems had resulted from the lack of an able governor, and they proposed the remedy of sending as governor the Lord De la Warr, "a Baron and Peere of this Kingdome." With far less confidence in the future, a distraught commoner in Watertown in the Bay Colony told a friend in 1630 that he did not know "how long this plantation will stand," for some of the "magnates" had forsaken it, and God had taken away "the chiefest stud in the land, Mr. Johnson, and the lady Arabella, his wife, which was the chiefest man of estate in the land and one that would have done most good."[14]

Six years later the minister in Watertown begged the younger John Winthrop to settle there, fearing that "the weakness of a company without a head cannot well sway and guide it selfe but is subject to many errors distractions confusions and what not." The inhabitants of Ipswich, where Winthrop was living, quickly petitioned lest they lose their great man. Their other great man, Mr. Dudley, had already departed, leaving the villagers feeling "desolate and weak." Ipswich needed someone with power and prestige: a real magistrate. The loss of such a figure, claimed the petitioners, was "too great a greif." But Winthrop grieved them anyway, moving from place to place until he settled at Pequot, where his admirers assured him that God had made him "fitt to be guid of a greater people." In 1656 he moved to New Haven, prompting the settlers in Pequot to lament that "we are Naked without you, yea, indeed we are as a body without a head." Connecticut elected him governor in 1657 without his knowledge and then persuaded him to move to Hartford to assume his office. In the competition for the great man, Hartford won.[15]

It was important to have a great man to rule, wrote John Robinson, the minister to the Separatist congregation that came to Plymouth, because common people were more likely to obey "persons of special eminency above the rest." Robinson worried because Plymouth had no such eminent persons. He urged the Pilgrims to compensate by choosing only leaders with a visible devotion to the common good—and to give them both honor and obedience even though they lacked the family connections that could naturally command loyalty.[16]

Great men—the men whose presence could naturally command loyalty—were always gentlemen. Lord De la Warr in Virginia told the company in 1610 that the colony needed gentlemen—even those "whose breeding never knew what a single dayes labour meant"—because a gentleman provided "the force of knowledge, the exercise of Counsell, and the operation and power of his best breeding and quallitie." Half a century later William Berkeley defended the colony's honor by claiming that it had managed to attract such men of quality and breeding. In New England as well the colonists longed for gentlemen. When ships arrived in 1633 with several persons of quality, the government declared a day of thanksgiving. Four years later Edward Winslow in Plymouth marveled at the rumor that New England might have attracted an undeniable gentleman. "We heare there is a noble man commen over onto you," he wrote Winthrop, "but cannot beleeve till we can receive more credible informacion." When Edward Johnson published in 1654 his history of New England, he recorded, year by year, the arrival of anyone who might be considered a gentleman.[17]

John Cotton could assure wealthy nobles in the homeland that the Bay colonists always chose their governors "out of the rank of gentlemen." He acknowledged that good Puritans required piety as well as gentility in their civic leaders. Believing that carnal men, even carnal gentlemen, were "not fit to be trusted with place of standing power of settled authority," they chose only church members as magistrates. But they did not, Cotton hastened to add, disdain gentle birth; they chose only "the eminent sort" of church members as their leaders. They chose gentlemen.[18]

Cotton even proposed a law that magistrates, if otherwise qualified, always be chosen "out of the ranck of Noble men or Gentlemen." Almost half a century later New Englanders still valued gentility as well as piety in their leaders. One colonist assured another in 1680 that Wait Winthrop, one of the sons of John Winthrop, Jr., would be an ideal magistrate because he was "a very sober discreet gentleman, much advantaged by his parentage, as well as his abilitys and fulness of estate, for publique trust." He added that "the making of rulers of the lower sort of people" would lead to contempt on the part of the ruled.[19]

Such assumptions prompted ministers and magistrates to denounce the notion of democracy. "If the people be governors," asked Cotton, "who shall be governed?" Cotton's query, written in an effort to persuade Lord Say and Seal to migrate to New England, had nothing to do with voting rights or popular participation in the choice of magistrates. He was talking about "mere democracy"—like that of the Greek city-states where the people decided every issue—which usurped the authority of the great men called to leadership. He was quite willing to accept that the people could choose their own governors. But then he wanted to let the governors do the governing, as befitted the status of great men.[20]

John Winthrop defended a similar position when he told the Bay colonists that "meere Democratie" was "among most Civill nations, accounted the meanest and worst of all formes of Government." He warned Thomas Hooker that "the best part is always the least, and of that best part the wiser part is always the lesser." Winthrop thought people had a right to elect their rulers, but he expected them to choose from the best and wisest and to obey them as "men precedinge in gifts & experience," men "whom God hath set over them."[21]

In 1645 a group of disgruntled colonists in Hingham decided that the excessive authority of magistrates threatened the liberty of the people. Winthrop reminded them that Massachusetts Bay was no mere democracy: "It is yourselves who have called us to this office, and being called by you, we have our authority from God, in way of an ordinance, such as hath the image of God stamped upon it, the contempt and violation whereof hath been vindicated with examples of divine vengeance."[22]

Only in Rhode Island were colonists prone to define their governments as democratic, and even there the meaning of the term remained ambiguous. When Newport and Portsmouth united, their General Court in 1641 declared them to have formed a "Democracie or Popular Governmt" because they recognized "the Powre of the Body of freemen orderly assembled or major Part of them" to legislate, but in fact they established an oligarchy in which only about half the men could vote. After Roger Williams secured in

1644 a patent giving powers of civil government to a larger union of the Narragansett Bay colonies designated as Providence Plantations, the freemen declared that their new government would be "Democratical, that is to say, a government held by free and voluntary consent of all or the greater part of the free inhabitants," but when it proved unstable, the old ambivalence about democracy surfaced, with William Coddington rushing to England to have himself declared permanent governor and judge of the town of Aquidneck. The other colonists countered his move, but the confusion must have served to confirm outside Rhode Island the danger in loose talk about democracy. The founders of Carolina were far more typical of prevailing sentiments when they announced from the outset their intention to "avoid erecting a numerous democracy."[23]

In Massachusetts Bay the magistrates and ministers defined the proper government as part monarchy, part democracy, part aristocracy. Cotton used the term *theocracy*, meaning any form of government approved by Scripture that referred ultimate sovereignty to God. (He did not have in mind a state governed by the clergy.) Winthrop preferred to speak of a "mixt Aristocratie." He preserved a place for the people, observing that their representatives, the deputies, were "the Democraticall part of our Government." But he made a higher place for the magistrates, and he thought it presumptuous when deputies, who merely represented the people, claimed the same prerogatives as magistrates who spoke for the entire colony and bore an office ordained by God. The magistrates, he said, were "Gods upon earthe."[24]

The men who cast the votes had little objection to the proposition that great men were destined to rule and they were destined to choose them. Not everyone, not even every free adult male, could join in the choosing. In New Mexico and New Netherland—and in New York until 1683—the colonists normally cast no votes. After the English conquest of New Netherland in 1664, English colonists on Long Island, protesting the absence of any representative assembly, were told that nothing was "required of them but obedience and submission to the Lawes of the Government." But elsewhere free male voters could have a greater voice. In New England they chose not only local officers and representatives to the General Court but also the governors and their assistants; in Virginia they could elect burgesses, though not the governor or his council; in Maryland they chose the assembly of freemen, though the proprietor appointed the governor, who named his own council.[25]

Each colony placed restrictions on the franchise. But no expansion or contraction of voting rights altered the fundamental point: the voters almost always returned to the same great men. They chose the genteel or, in their absence, the wealthy. In Virginia a planter elite without social distinction scratched their way to power in the 1630s, but during the next decade a group of landed immigrants with pretensions to greater gentility took control of both the elected and appointed offices and held on to them.[26]

Officeholding in Maryland proved more volatile, but of the 330 men who served between 1637 and 1676 in the Maryland Provincial Court, 275 were recognized as gentlemen from their first entry in the records, though many had only a dubious claim to the title in England. The ideal in Maryland was to have only "men of Estate and Ability" as the rulers; both voters and governors associated officeholding with gentility. Although a shortage of wealthy and genteel settlers resulted in the opening of offices to common men of modest wealth, the association between political office and gentility was so fixed in Maryland that a stint of public service permitted officials to designate themselves as gentlemen and to be accepted as such by the colony's recordkeepers.[27]

Most colonists did not envision their propensity for returning the same men to office—or accepting their return—as an approval of either lifelong or hereditary rule. In Maryland and Carolina the proprietors advanced claims to hereditary authority, and in Maryland the Baltimore family made good on those claims despite complaints of tyranny, but suggestions of a hereditary— or even a lifetime—right to rule met elsewhere with severe opposition. One Virginia assembly passed legislation permitting councillors to hold office for life, but a subsequent assembly repealed it. In 1634 John Cotton told the Massachusetts Bay colonists that worthy magistrates had a permanent right to office; the colonists responded by removing John Winthrop from his governorship for a year. One of them, Israel Stoughton, explained that a few wanted even "to change yeare by yeare the governorship: but the assistants more rarely, yet sometimes lest it be esteemed hereditary." When the magistrates and ministers proposed a standing magisterial council—a group of eminent magistrates who would govern for life and thereby provide oversight when the General Court was not in session—the deputies initially agreed but later ensured that the council would have no authority.[28]

Yet for all the fretting over standing councils and hereditary rulers, most colonists turned repeatedly to the same faces. John Winthrop served eleven times as the governor of Massachusetts Bay. Connecticut seemed doggedly intent on avoiding such a precedent; the Fundamental Orders of the colony ruled that "noe person be chosen Governor above once in two yeares." But in a referendum in 1660 the free men deleted that clause and proceeded to elect John Winthrop, Jr., as their governor every year for sixteen years. Great men were rare, and few wanted to waste them.[29]

Ambivalence

Great men were also powerful, and power was dangerous. Each of the colonies developed a rich vocabulary of opposition to tyrannical power; they spoke of "bounds," "liberties," "consent," and the "common good." They argued for the limitation of political power by arguing for constraints on the

great men. Rarely could the struggles be described as a simple division between the great men and the people. Although the contestants could draw
upon varying degrees of popular sympathy, they usually represented competing groups of great men—notables of the towns trying to limit provincial
magnates, gentlemen from the counties trying to restrict the cosmopolitan
elite of the capital city, great men in the elected assemblies quarreling with
governors and the other great men they appointed to their councils, or merchants and patroons resisting company directors and proprietors. In the distant background stood the immense battles over centralized power in
Europe. The conflicts there between the great men of the royal courts and
the powerful local nobles—as, for example, in England under the centraliz-
ing rule of Charles I—paralleled the conflicts in America between colony-
wide magistrates, proprietors, and company directors, on the one hand, and
local leaders, on the other. Out of those conflicts on both sides of the Atlantic
the colonists developed their political vocabulary.

Rhetoric against the tyranny of great men resounded most loudly in New
Netherland, where the company directors had neither the gentility nor the
wealth expected of rulers but displayed a decided inclination to assume autocratic prerogatives anyway. A series of temporary representative bodies,
elected at the behest of directors who wanted to use them for their own ends,
protested endlessly against arbitrary rule. The Twelve Men of 1641, the
Eight Men of 1643, and the Nine Men of 1646 sent one remonstrance after
another to Holland, decrying the "princely power" claimed by the company
officers. The colony bore the burden, they complained, of men like Wouter
Van Twiller, who boasted that he had "more power here than the Company"
and could therefore do as he pleased; or Willem Kieft, who told the colonists
that "the Prince is above the law" and applied that maxim "to his own case
with so much arrogance, as to make even himself ashamed"; or Peter Stuyvesant, who was accused of responding to criticism by reviling his critics as
"Boobies, usurers, rebels, and such like." The central theme of the various
remonstrances can be summarized in a phrase: the colony should not have to
depend on "the whim of one man."[30]

The critics in New Netherland sought no democracy, and the evidence for
designating them as spokesmen for a party of the people is unimpressive.
They worried about specific grievances more than about broad political principles, and most of them were merchants seeking prosperity, not radicals
questing for a political utopia. But they did call for representative institutions
as a way of countering directors who tried to dispose of "lives and properties"
at their own "will and pleasure, in a manner so arbitrary that a King dare not
legally do the like."[31]

In their opposition to arbitrary power, the settlers in New Netherland
voiced a commonplace. The preachers in New England gave that commonplace its most articulate expression. Thomas Hooker in Connecticut insisted

in 1638 that the ruled had the power to "set the bounds and limits" of their rulers, and John Cotton agreed that it was necessary for magistrates to recognize the "utmost bounds of their own power." The New England ministers became known as consistent, though not utterly predictable, allies of the magistrates, but they always insisted on the limits of magisterial power.[32]

They specified the boundaries of that power by employing the notion of consent. "The foundation of authority," said Hooker, "is laid firstly in the free consent of the people." Cotton demanded that rulers seek the consent of "the People, in whom fundamentally all power lyes." And few rulers had, in theory, any objection to that demand. John Winthrop went as far as to define consent as the "essential form of a commonwealth." Even allies of the autocratic Lord Baltimore in Maryland defended him from charges of arbitrary rule by arguing that the provincial assembly represented "the consent of the Freemen . . . or the major part of them." It followed that magistrates were bound to listen to the people. But not everyone agreed about what that meant. Consent turned out to be a complicated idea.[33]

In New England the idea of consent often found expression through the image of covenants between rulers and the ruled. "It is the nature and essence of every society," explained Winthrop, "to be knitt together by some Covenant, either expressed or implyed." The Pilgrims aboard the *Mayflower* tried to ensure social order by having everyone covenant into a "civill body politike," and civil covenants formed the basis of several New England towns: Exeter, New Haven, Providence, Portsmouth, Newport, Dedham, and others. In the Dedham covenant the founders pledged to love one another, exclude the "contrary minded," resolve their differences, and subject themselves "unto all such orders and constitutions as shall be . . . made now or at any time hereafter from this day forward."[34]

The Dedham covenant illustrated the narrow boundaries of consent. A civil covenant did not require that rulers accept popular participation in political decisions. Consent was a formal act through which freemen expressed their willingness to be bound by the decisions of their rulers. It implied no right to question the content of those decisions. Winthrop applied the theory to the decision of magistrates. "The covenant between you and us," he told the Massachusetts Bay settlers in 1645, "is the oath you have taken of us, which is to this purpose, that we shall govern you and judge your causes by the rules of God's laws and our own, according to our best skill." Having taken that oath, the colonists had vowed not to question magisterial decisions with which they disagreed. Although free to select new magistrates, they were not free to resist the decisions of the magistrates they had selected. To do so was to break the covenant. Winthrop conceded that the "greatest power" lay originally in the people, but he added that when they gave it over to rulers, thereby exercising their consent, they surrendered any further right to exercise that power. As late as 1671 New England preachers could promote similar political sympathies by urging their listeners to "leave the guidance of the ship to those that sit at Helm."[35]

In 1632 several colonists in Watertown revealed, in Winthrop's view, that they had failed to understand the theory of consent. They resisted a taxation levy for the fortifying of Newtown. But Winthrop and the court convinced them after much debate that they had erred. They "took this government to be no other but as of a mayor and aldermen, who have not power to make laws or raise taxations without the people." They understood consent as entailing the right to accept or reject each magisterial decision. But Winthrop told them that the Bay Colony government was "rather in the nature of a parliament" and that the consent of the people consisted only in the power to vote for the magistrates, offer suggestions to the General Court, and declare their grievances.[36]

At the time the General Court in Massachusetts contained only the governor and his magisterial assistants. Two years later, in 1634, the freemen succeeded in electing representatives from the towns to sit alongside the magistrates as deputies of the people. In practice their success expanded the notion of consent by enlarging the power of popular participations in lawmaking, but it took several years for Winthrop to reconcile himself fully to the change.

The great men responded to skepticism about their power by asserting their authority with both ceremonies and arguments. They often relied on sheer display. In 1636 the rulers of Massachusetts Bay decided to "appear more solemnly in public, with attendance, apparel, and open notice of their entrance into the court." Virginians not only made ample use of symbolic gestures—maces, swords, and processions—but also surrounded their governors with soldiers, both for protection and for honor. Cecil Calvert in Maryland, wary lest the people not defer to the colony's rulers, considered a law requiring "the wearing of habbits medals or otherwise" so that "some visible distinction or Distinctions might be drawn." Peter Stuyvesant in New Netherland went to such lengths that he drew sarcastic criticism of his "great state and pomposity." "The Word Myn Herr General and such like titles," complained his critics, "were never known here before."[37]

Convinced that solemn processions alone would not establish their authority, the politicians also advanced some arguments for it. The assertions focused attention on two large themes: the negative voice and judicial discretion. In several colonies the great men claimed the right to veto decisions by the people or their representatives. In Massachusetts Bay they also asserted a right to make determinations of equity in judicial matters. The debates over those topics represented an effort to define the prerogatives—as well as the limits—of the great men.

When the Virginia Company authorized the formation of the first Virginia General Assembly of 1619, the company retained the power to abrogate any laws the assembly might pass. The Virginians acknowledged that it was the company's "right so to doe." The company also reserved "alwaies to the Governor a negative voyce" and that veto power became a mainstay of gubernatorial authority. During the administration of John Harvey (1630–39), the governor's council tried to assert its own right to override his initiatives, but he held on to sole possession of the veto, and when the king told William Berkeley in 1641 how to rule Virginia, his instructions specified that the governor should retain a "Negative Voice as formerly."[38]

In Maryland the negative voice became a point of severe contention between the proprietors and their critics. Cecil Calvert assumed from his charter that he possessed "free, full, and absolute power" over his colony. When he concluded that his first provincial assembly in 1635 exceeded its authority by enacting laws that he had not proposed, he refused to ratify them. The second assembly, meeting three years later, responded by refusing to accept the proprietor's own proposals for legislation—thus claiming, in effect, its own negative voice—and the two sides had to arrange a temporary compromise. But the issue remained. The charter granted Baltimore a kingly power in Maryland, and he never let the colonists forget it. He told his brother Leonard, who lived in the colony and served as its governor, that as proprietor he had "the power to rebuke any authority I have given you, either in whole or in part . . . for you are but meerly instrumental in those things to do what I direct." He had no intent of allowing any greater authority to his assemblies.[39]

During the civil war in England, a Maryland settler, Richard Ingle, believing that Leonard Calvert was exercising "a tyrannical power against the Protestants, and such as adhered to the Parliament," tried to resolve that dispute and others by staging an armed revolt, driving the governor from the colony and beginning a two-year "time of troubles" that came to be known as "the plundering time." But when Calvert regained his authority, the question of the negative voice soon surfaced again as a source of provincial disquiet.[40]

During a second period of violence in the early 1650s, Baltimore's enemies complained in a pamphlet, *Virginia and Maryland, or the Lord Baltimore's Printed Case Uncased and Answered*, that the governor had "an absolute Negative Voice in all things, and in the Assembly of the Burgesses." They decried such a presumption of authority as arbitrary. "Whatever is done by the people at great costs in Assemblies, for the good of the people," they complained, "is liable to be made Null by the negative Voice of his Lordship." But his defenders had another view. No one, they said, would even undertake a plantation if factious planters should "have power to make Lawes to dispose of him, and all his estate there, without his consent." The negative voice, in their view, was the essential legal safeguard of proprietary governance. And the Calvert family held tenaciously to its power of veto. In 1676 an anonymous "Complaint from Heaven with a Huy and a Crye and a petition out of Virginia and Maryland" lamented that the Baltimore family—in the person of Charles Calvert, the third Lord Baltimore, who was both proprietor and governor—still continued to exercise tyranny by insisting on the negative voice: "what he doth not relish is of no force."[41]

In Massachusetts Bay the issue created a continuing political crisis. When the General Court expanded in 1634 to include local deputies, Winthrop and the magistrates claimed that any act of the court required magisterial approval before it could become a law. The deputies argued, to the contrary, that an act required only a majority of the whole court, thus denying to the magistrates any veto power. Viewing the position of the deputies as "dangerous . . . to the commonwealth," the magistrates sought to end the stalemate by calling for a day of public humiliation, with John Cotton as the preacher. Cotton proposed a compromise formulation. In Massachusetts Bay, he said, the magistrates, the ministers, and the people had their own strengths. The strength of the magistrates was their authority; of the people, their liberty; and of the ministers, their purity. Each of these contained a negative voice. Magistrates could exercise it to defend their authority; the people could overrule unfitting usurpation of their liberty; and the ministers could override any action that subverted the purity of the churches.[42]

Cotton's sermon skirted all the difficult political issues, and not everyone felt satisfied about "the negative voice to be left to the magistrates," so the following year Israel Stoughton resumed the arguments against it. The court disciplined him, but the question refused to go away. In 1642 Goody Sherman accused the merchant Robert Keayne of stealing her sow. The magistrates believed that she lacked the evidence to sustain the charge; the deputies supported her; and the standoff turned into yet another debate about the negative voice of the magistrates.[43]

The debate illustrated how questions about the negative voice were intertwined with prevailing ideas about the prerogatives of great men. Winthrop told the deputies that the negative voice of the House of Lords in England provided a precedent for the magistrates. The deputies replied that the magistrates could not imitate the House of Lords because they were "not of the Nobility, as the upper house there is." Winthrop answered that the magistrates represented "the Aut[horit]ye of all the people" and therefore stood in authority above even English noblemen. But he also argued that the magistrates should have special powers because they possessed a status above that of "the Common rank of the people." They were men of superior gifts and experience, men of dignity, wisdom, and learning. To abandon the negative voice was to surrender that status, and the inevitable result would be a mere democracy: "We should hereby voluntaryly abase our selves of that dignity, which the providence of God hath putt upon us: which is a manifest breach of the 5th Com[mandment]," requiring obedience to parents.[44]

147

The deputies remained unimpressed when Winthrop defined them as mere representatives of the people. In the interim between sessions of the court, he said, a deputy became "but as another freeman; and so he cannot be counted in the same ranke with the magistrates." But the deputies were the great men of their own communities, and they disliked Winthrop's suggestion that they were inferior to the magistrates in wisdom and stature. Their protests were so heated that Winthrop had to backtrack. He conceded that some of the deputies were "not inferiour to some of the magistrates." But he held to his main point. A magistrate, he said, stood in a higher rank than did mere freemen and their deputies. And although he acknowledged that voters had the liberty to turn magistrates out of office, he warned them against exercising that right. Having heard of a plan to purge the magistrates, he announced that such a course would be both "dishonorable and dangerous to our State." It would take power from men recognized as "the most able for publ[ic] service" and put it into the hands of weaker men. Winthrop's arguments were only partially successful. The magistrates kept their negative voice, but they also had to grant the same right of veto to the deputies, the great men of the villages.[45]

The second critical issue—at least for the great men of Massachusetts Bay—was magisterial discretion. In one sense the debates over the negative voice and life tenure were but a dimension of a larger conflict over the discretion of magistrates. But in a narrower sense the issue of discretion turned on the authority of magistrates to make judicial decisions in the absence of positive legislation. In Massachusetts Bay the magistrates served not only as rulers but also as judges. Could they be trusted to use their own judgment to determine fairness in colonial courts?

As early as 1635 Winthrop noticed that the deputies "conceived great danger to our state" in the fact that the magistrates, lacking positive laws, often proceeded to judicial decisions "according to their discretions." The result was the naming of a committee to "frame a body of grounds of laws, in resemblance to a Magna Charta," which would become the colony's fundamental laws, and by 1636 John Cotton was ready with his "model of Moses his judicials," a rough legal code with marginal references to biblical precedents. The court never accepted Cotton's code, but the deputies continued to push for clear, positive laws, and they had some articulate allies. Thomas Hooker told Winthrop that his defense of judicial discretion was "a course which lacks both safety and warrant: I must confesse I ever look at it as a way which leads directly to tyranny, and so to confusion." William Pynchon in Springfield complained that the magisterial assertions of discretion implied a "lawlesse law."[46]

In 1641 Nathaniel Ward brought forth his Body of Liberties, one hundred broad statutes providing for freedom of speech and assembly, prohibiting cruel and barbarous punishments, and specifying the penalties for criminal actions. The court proposed to spend three years weighing the merits of Ward's document, but it did not take that long for dissatisfaction to surface. Part of the problem was that Ward had not solved the issue of the magistrate's discretion. William Hawthorne of Salem, urging fixed penalties for crimes, charged that the magistrates sought an arbitrary government.[47]

The magistrates felt aggrieved. Their interest, they said, was simply justice. To assign a fixed penalty for theft, they thought, was to preclude the possibility of distinguishing between the pilfering of bread by the starving and the theft of a horse for merely pleasurable ends. In a just system varying circumstances would be taken into account, and that required the exercise of judicial discretion. Even Scripture, they argued, prescribed only a few penalties; it expected judges to exercise wisdom. To flout that expectation was to question the providence of God. But some of the deputies remained unconvinced.[48]

After three years of intermittent squabbling, the court decided to consult the elders, who sought a compromise. The ministers said that penalties for capital crimes and certain lesser crimes should be prescribed, but they conceded that circumstances could still alter decisions about most punishments. They acknowledged that the magistrates might vary from the penalty prescribed by an existing law, but they wanted to allow the variation only if the magistrates consulted the court. The problem, as they saw it, was the risk that magisterial discretion might lead to the appearance of favoritism. Partly for that reason they suggested that magisterial discretion should never include the authority to impose stricter penalties than the law permitted.[49]

The deputies were wary of compromise. Some continued to push for "such a body of laws, with prescript penalties in all cases, as nothing might be left to the discretion of the magistrate." A few colonists began to spread the word that "the magistrates would have no laws"—that the colony faced the danger of great men run amok. So Winthrop prepared a "Discourse on Arbitrary Government," designed to show that such wild charges had no basis. "Arbitrary Government," he explained, "is, where a people have men sett over them without their choyce, or allowance: who have power, to Governe them, and Judge their Causes without a Rule." Where the people had the liberty to elect their governors and the governors followed a public rule, no arbitrary government existed. Since the magistrates bound themselves to the patent, to the positive laws that did exist, and to "the Worde of God," they clearly accepted the authority of principles that prevented arbitrary rule. But to turn those principles into precise formulas governing every decision was to prevent the judges from making the distinctions that could ensure true justice. The magistrates, moreover, were the men selected by providence to "holde forthe the wisdom and mercy of God." The deputies were attempting to set aside that authority.[50]

Winthrop failed to persuade his opposition. The deputies, pretending not to know the author and claiming that the treatise contained dangerous principles, brought it before a committee of the court in an effort to have it censured. They failed and soon committed the tactical error of supporting an impeachment of Winthrop for abuse of his authority. The deputies made him serve as a symbol for the sentiment that the magistrates' authority "was too great to consist with the people's liberty." But Winthrop's trial turned into a disaster for his enemies, and he used it as an occasion for admonition: "When you choose magistrates, you take them from among yourselves, men subject to like passions as you are." But you also choose them, he said, from men who, being chosen, have their "authority from God."[51]

Winthrop's critics also won something from the long dispute. In 1648 the colony published its *Lawes and Liberties*, along with an explanation that law created a barrier against human corruption. Yet some people also believed that it created a barrier against the great men—a means of preserving the liberties of men and women called to a lower standing in society. Between 1636 and 1680 the New England colonies produced a panoply of legal codes: Plymouth in 1636, the Bay Colony in 1648, Connecticut in 1650, New Haven in 1656. In subsequent years New Hampshire, New Jersey, and New York published legal codes. Whatever the motives behind the movement, the codification represented a departure from notions of judicial discretion. Whatever else the lawmakers were doing, they were expressing an unwillingness to place all their trust in the discretion of great men.[52]

Winthrop's speech after his trial encapsulated the colonial problem with great men. Rulers could claim their authority from God, or their gentility, or their wealth. But in a colonial society without a traditional nobility, it remained all too evident that the men who made such claims were "subject to passions" like everyone else. The eighteenth-century governor and historian Thomas Hutchinson recognized the problem: "The generality of the colony being very near upon a level, more than common provision was necessary to enforce a due obedience to the laws, and to establish and preserve the authority of the government, for, although some amongst them had handsome fortunes, yet in general their estates were small." The great men, measured by conventional seventeenth-century criteria, were not always great enough.[53]

They were usually wealthy enough. It was widely assumed throughout the colonies that rulers would be men of wealth. In Massachusetts Bay William Hawthorne once proposed "leaving out two of the ancientest magistrates, because they were grown poor, and spake reproachfully of them under that motion." John Cotton accused him of "dishonoring of parents," but Hawthorne was expressing a familiar notion. The wealthier gentry dominated political activity in both the colony and the towns. John Hull lamented in 1665 that the colony permitted Governor John Endecott to die "poor, as most of our rulers do," but poverty was not generally a mark of the colony's magistrates.[54]

Virginians too assumed that their rulers would be men of estate, and the wealthy landholders who began after 1634 to occupy seats on the county courts eventually eroded even the power of the governors. Even in Maryland, where economic mobility turned indentured servants into burgesses, the men who dominated politics were those with wealth. Money alone did not ensure political power, but few men achieved the power without the money.[55]

John Eliot in Massachusetts Bay could take it for granted that no one cared to assign political power to the poor. The poor, he said, were not believed, not trusted, not "regarded." When men and women are poor, he added, people think that God despises them: "Every one will be bold to afflict, wrong, tread upon the poor man." It was sometimes hard for seventeenth-century colonists not to blame the poor for failing to live in plenty. Lord Baltimore in England probably expressed a widespread conviction among affluent colonists when he claimed that the poor in America were lazy: "If there be any that live in a poor manner, it is not from the low price of tobacco, but from their own sloth." Churches, towns, and counties made provision for the "worthy poor," but laws from New England to Virginia against vagabonds and the idle revealed the colonial disdain for the supposedly unworthy and landless poor.[56]

It is sometimes supposed that the Puritan preachers of New England looked on poverty as a sign of divine disfavor and damnation. They did not. John Cotton assured his congregation that "no man can certainly discern the love or hatred of God to himself or others, by their outward events or estates." Other preachers warned their listeners to expect affliction, including poverty, as part of the Christian's probation. "Every follower of Christ," said Thomas Hooker, "hath affliction allotted to him as a child's part." Indeed the Puritan doctrine of affliction assumed that poverty, piously endured, could become a means of edification, deepening the spiritual life.[57]

To a Puritan preacher wealth could be positive, though it would always pose dangers. New England preachers assumed that some people should properly be wealthier than others. John Eliot observed that "wealth is an exercise of the dominion of man," and he thought that dominion would always be unequally distributed. John Cotton probably expressed a common conviction when he said that Christians, who might have to endure poverty, might also expect prosperity. It was acceptable for the saints to yearn for wealth, though only within limits. "We may desire wealth from God," said

Cotton, "partly for our necessity and expediency, partly to leave to our posterity. Thus far a man may desire wealth. But we are never to desire more than we can make good use of." He sometimes added, moreover, that true faith should help the Christian "sit loose" from prosperity, and that sentiment became a sermonic refrain. "And what though you have got money? Yet your soul may perish, and goe downe to hell," warned Thomas Hooker. "Let commodity, let profit go to the wall, rather than let prayer and the Word to fall, and to be neglected."[58]

When the merchant Robert Keayne overcharged his customers in Boston in 1639, Cotton used the occasion to shame him for seeking excess profit. He offered the tradesman some instruction in business ethics. A merchant could not, he preached, sell above the current price, redeem losses on one product by hiking prices on another, or buy cheap and sell dear. The General Court reinforced Cotton's admonition by imposing a fine on Keayne, and the church then compelled him to repent publicly for his greed. To the merchant such scoldings were "a shame and an amazement," but they sprang from a familiar Calvinist ethic calling for restraint, mutual love, and self-denial.[59]

The irony was that an ethic of restraint and self-denial could lend itself easily to the accumulation of wealth, especially in a religious culture that interpreted self-disciplined labor as a sign of a sanctified heart and a means of glorifying God. English Christians, both Puritans and their opponents, had long taught that systematic diligence in the pursuit of a calling could be an expression of devotion to God. Even as they criticized people who overvalued wealth, the clergy promoted habits of mind and work that could, if maintained diligently, issue often in material success. A true saint, wrote Cotton, would "rise early, and goe to bed late, and eate the bread of carefulnesse." Like other New England ministers, he made no allowance for idleness. "Be busie, like Antes, morning and evening," he urged.[60]

Whatever exaggerations and errors of detail reside within the classic argument of the sociologist Max Weber about the affinity between the Protestant ethic and the spirit of capitalism, Weber recognized this connection between a style of piety and the formation of dispositions congenial to economic success. The Protestant ethic, as Weber described it, was the assertion that diligent labor in a worldly calling could become a form of piety. In certain forms of Protestant piety, he added, such diligence became a sign of election to salvation, though this was not the central point of his argument. And certainly he did not propose that the possession of wealth itself became, for sixteenth- and seventeenth-century Christians, a sign of divine election. His minimal contention was that Protestants interpreted work as a divine calling and insisted on ascetic behavior as an outward expression of pure motives, thereby encouraging disciplined economic activity. With that contention no Puritan preacher would have disagreed. Weber then argued that the dispositions of restraint, diligence, and self-control engendered by this Protestant ethic were perfectly suited to the spirit of rationalized capitalism that was emerging in the West.[61]

Of course, the promotion of vigilance and industry was no uniquely Puritan or Protestant theme. Opponents of the Puritans often proclaimed the same values, as did promoters and entrepreneurs who displayed little interest in the Protestant ethic of work as a means of glorifying God. Praise for the values of labor could be heard from New England to Virginia, and it took a variety of forms. The promoters of Virginia praised "sober and thrifty passions and desires" and claimed that the dream of material accumulation itself made settlers "industrious and vigilant." From Maryland came word that "vigilant industrious care" was a trait highly esteemed even by people whose deepest commitment was to the promise of riches. But Weber would not have been reluctant to acknowledge that more than one kind of colonial American exalted the virtues of disciplined labor and frugality.[62]

Puritan preachers worried more than others that wealth could be a distraction from the main business of living, and their worries drew them into conflicts. As early as 1637 an English trader observed to John Winthrop that "many in your plantations discover much pride, as appeareth by the letters we receive from them, wherein some of them write over to us for lace . . . cutwork coifes; and others, for deep stammell dyes, and some of your own men tell us that many of you go finely clad." Before long the preachers were feeling obliged to tell the settlers in the Bay Colony that they were "a Plantation Religious, not a plantation of trade." But the merchants apparently saw no conflict between their prayers and their profits. If we can judge by the mounting intensity of clerical jeremiads against pomp and display during the second half of the century, a host of wealthy colonists cherished worldly success and fine fashions.[63]

To most American colonists, clerical denunciations of wealth and display undoubtedly would have sounded churlish and odd. Surely most came to America with the hope that they might follow the admonition of the promoter George Alsop: "Dwell here, live plentifully, and be rich." At the very inception of European settlement, therefore, Americans expounded two conflicting visions of the land. Some saw it as a religious utopia, a place of transcendent significance, a city upon a hill, and a light to the nations. They spoke of covenants, communities, and the service of God. But most of the colonists probably shared a different dream. Their America was a place where men and women could grow rich and live plentifully, and we can assume that they had little patience for preachers who tried to convince them otherwise.[64]

The praise of work and wealth must have at least helped to create the ethos in which wealthy men could claim to be great men. The recent work of social historians has shown the extent to which economic mobility could undermine the prevailing ideal of a well-ordered society. When former servants asserted their status as gentlemen, the old ideals of order and hierarchy began to lose their original force. But the former servants, having accumulated wealth and reputation, then appealed to the old and familiar ideals to justify their own self-assertion. By thus revising the definition of a great man so that wealth began to count as much as family lineage once had, the new great men of America ensured that a reverence for great men would long endure.[65]

Epilogue

The colonists' location on the periphery of European civilization found symbolic expression in the wigwams, huts, and hovels in which they lived during their first months in New England or Virginia. Even after decades of settlement, the physical appearance of the colonial landscape could display the harshness and crudeness of early America. New Englanders constructed well-built wooden houses, usually stretched out along a broad street or dispersed through the countryside (only rarely clustered around a meeting-house). But elsewhere the landscape was bleaker. In Middlesex County in Virginia most farm families lived in cramped, unpainted frame houses, located about a half-mile to five miles from each other, often in disrepair, with floors of earth or planks. In Maryland they built small box frame houses sided with clapboard and plastered with clay, sometimes with a lower floor of dirt and an upper one of planks. After forty years of settlement, the town of St. Mary's, the capital, consisted of thirty-odd houses, "very mean and little," spread five miles along a river. On the frontier of New Spain, the Spanish built adobe structures with flat roofs constructed of log rafters that were laid with branches and covered with clay. And the native American landscape often seemed, to Europeans, the bleakest of all. Jean de Brébeuf warned prospective visitors to Huronia that "we shall receive you in a Hut, so mean that I have scarcely found in France one wretched enough to compare it with; that is how you will be lodged." Both in the colonies and among the native Americans, the physical structures often conveyed a sense of impermanence and deprivation.[1]

The material landscape reflected also the cultural diversity. This was true

155

especially of the sacred spaces that colonists and native Americans constructed to give symbolic shape to their religious perceptions. The Pueblos dug their rectangular kivas deep into the dry soil and rock; the Hurons constructed longhouses from saplings and branches; the Powhatans in Virginia sought out high places to build arbor houses, each sixty feet long, to house the images of their kings and spirits and tombs of their leaders, and these buildings were so holy, wrote John Smith, that only "the Priests and Kings dare come into them."[2]

Europeans could hold strong convictions about their own sacred buildings. On the remote mesa of Acoma in New Mexico, Franciscan missionaries built from stone and adobe the austere church of St. Esteban (c. 1642), bare and dark inside but decorated with richly painted corbels and rafters and filled with colorful images. In New France the Jesuits consecrated at Sainte-Marie-aux-Hurons a wooden chapel and cemetery that contained the sacred relics of missionary martyrs, and they guarded zealously against any desecration of the spot.[3] Like the Swedish Lutherans on the Delaware River who distinguished themselves from their Dutch Calvinist neighbors by decorating their church with an altar painting, a silver altar cloth, and bells, other seventeenth-century colonists often made their religious buildings symbolize their cultural identity.[4]

Sacred architecture marked the lines of division between English Protestants. Anglicans in Smithfield, Virginia, for example, built in 1632 an English Gothic "Old Brick Church," complete with wall buttresses and lancet windows under round arches. The building bespoke a sense of ease about the authority of tradition, and the colonists also had no reservations about locating the symbolic focal point of the building at the end of a long nave, at an altar where they received the sacrament, though the architecture and the sacramental focus bore subtle suggestions of the medieval and Catholic past. In contrast the Puritans in Hingham, Massachusetts, erected a four-square clapboard meetinghouse with neither nave nor altar. Its symbolic center was a pulpit surrounded by oak benches, and its stark simplicity indicated the Puritan conviction that holiness resided not in external spaces but in a spiritual inwardness that drew its inspiration from the primitive biblical past and therefore supposedly transcended the flow of later tradition.

Sacred structures could symbolize something other than what the colonists intended. The congregation in New Amsterdam erected in 1633 a new building, simple and plain in keeping with the spirit of Dutch Calvinism, but within a decade it stood in a state of delapidation, prompting one Captain DeVries to complain that "it was a shame that the English should see, when they passed, nothing but a mean barn in which public worship was performed." Other Dutch communities in New Netherland exhibited a stronger sense of piety and a keener appreciation of the symbolic. The inhabitants of Flatbush planned a building in the form of a cross, a concession to tradition

156

that would have scandalized a New England Puritan. But the Dutch generally refused to nurture the sense for sacred structures that was evident in the Pueblo kivas of the Southwest, the Catholic chapels of New France and New Spain, the Lutheran church in New Sweden, or the Anglican churches in Virginia. This was partly because the Dutch, like the New England Puritans, were Calvinists, uncomfortable with too much external symbolism; it was also partly because they had more interest in commerce than in piety. The American colonists not only encountered a diverse landscape but also accentuated its diversity through the shaping of their sacred buildings.[5]

Despite the diversity one scene dominated the human landscape of colonial America: it was a land of small farms. The buildings and docks of Boston and New Amsterdam testified to the commercial links with Europe maintained by merchants and traders, but most colonists lived on farms, some content with subsistence farming, others—probably the greater number—eager to tap the profits in a larger capitalist market. And a considerable proportion of American intellectual life consisted of messages delivered to the ordinary people who worked on those farms.

The colonists lived during a period when the language of learning, diplomacy, and worship was rapidly shifting from Latin to the vernacular. The learned sometimes spoke only to each other, but even then, since they spoke so often in the vernacular, the unlearned could sometimes overhear. The learned also spoke directly to the unlearned through sermons, political speeches, lay exhortations (sometimes by dissenters), missionary homilies, catechetical instructions, public proclamations, and devotional writings designed to be read aloud. Indeed the unlearned often ventured to speak to one another, even on topics traditionally restricted to the educated. The translation of the Bible into the vernacular languages embodied the expectation that ordinary men and women on the farms would ponder deep mysteries, and the clergy addressed their messages mainly to those people. What percentage of the population listened and what differences it made to them we can never measure with precision, but it tells us something important about colonial culture to observe that the intellectual elite usually addressed themselves to a popular audience.

The learned addressed their messages not simply to ordinary people in the settlements but also to a similar audience in Europe and England. Conscious of their dependence on continued immigration, promoters directed their appeals to ordinary people in the homelands. Convinced of the rightness of their religious vision, Puritan preachers shipped back sermons designed to move a populace. Sometimes educated colonists wrote for an elite in the core culture; they produced letters to the Royal Society, narratives for diplomats and officers of the court, and treatises by theologians designed to be read by other theologians. But more often they directed their writings to a wider audience.

They spoke also to native Americans. The shape of the colonial cultures resulted from more than merely a series of dialogues among Europeans. The colonists looked not only eastward, back to Europe, but also westward toward the cultures they found in America. The missionaries in New Spain and New France wrote little more than catechisms, dictionaries, sermons, and narratives describing and interpreting their encounter with the people they called Indians; the English devoted a far smaller proportion of their cultural energies to the conversation with native Americans, but even they produced dictionaries, catechisms, and a translation of the Bible.

The conversation was more than one-sided. The oral cultures of the native Americans and Africans also formed part of the larger picture of seventeenth-century American thought. And the native Americans had the numerical strength to engage the Europeans and challenge their values and ideas. Africans and native Americans in the seventeenth century were probably as ethnocentric as Europeans; the Indians found the colonists to be disgustingly hairy and laughingly inept. They admired the technical superiority and material comfort of the European societies, and they often sought an exchange of technical skills, learning about weaponry and tools while teaching how to fertilize the ground with fish, how to make snowshoes, how to make warm pelt garments, and how to survive in the forests. But they also confronted the Europeans in debates about religion, the use of the land, and the superiority of their own cultures.[6]

To an impressive extent, early American thought continually reflected the pervasiveness of confrontation and conflict: Catholic missionaries in conflict with native American religious traditions; Puritan clergy justifying the New England way against critics at home and in England; dissenters confronting religious establishments; magistrates and proprietors confuting the upstart subjects who were confuting them. And the conflicts generated a persisting flow of persuasive discourse—sermons, pamphlets, and treatises intended to change the way other people acted and lived.

Intellectual life in early America flourished as part of a great practical enterprise. Promoters, historians, preachers, missionaries, medicine men, religious dissenters, and practical politicians created the patterns of early American thought. They wrote and spoke within a mosaic of multiple societies and traditions: Pueblos and conquistadors, English and Dutch, East Anglians and West Country settlers, and dozens of others. No overarching idea united them; no consensus prevailed among them. Yet one pattern did mark the public expression of thought in early America; from New Spain to New England, when seventeenth-century Americans dealt with ideas, they were usually intent on persuading somebody to do something.

Notes and References

Chapter 1: Persuasion

1. Cotton Mather, *Magnalia Christi Americana; Or, The Ecclesiastical History of New England* (New York: Russell and Russell, 1967), 2:115–16, 117; Cotton Mather, *Just Remembrances* (Boston, 1715), ii.

2. John Leverett, "Book of Latin Orations, 1688," Harvard University archives, in Samuel Eliot Morison, *Harvard College in the Seventeenth Century* (Cambridge: Harvard University Press, 1936), 2:433.

3. Ibid., 434.

4. Ibid., 420–21.

5. Ibid., 434.

6. This account of ideas and institutions in Europe is drawn from Robert Mandrou, *From Humanism to Science, 1480–1700*, trans. Brian Pearce (Atlantic Highlands, N.J.: Humanities Press, 1979), 124, 184, 223; Mark H. Curtis, *Oxford and Cambridge in Transition, 1558–1642* (Oxford: Clarendon Press, 1959), 70, 235, 227–60; Samuel Eliot Morison, *The Founding of Harvard College* (Cambridge: Harvard University Press, 1935), 29, 120, 126, 190; Hugh Trevor-Roper, "The Culture of the Baroque Courts," in *Europäische Hofkultur im 16. und 17. Jahrhundert*, ed. August Buck, et al. (Hamburg: Dr. Ernst Hauswedell & Co., 1981), 1:11–23; Walter E. Houghton, Jr., "The English Virtuoso in the Seventeenth Century," *Journal of the History of Ideas* 3 (1942):51–73, 190–219.

7. Walter J. Ong, *Orality and Literacy* (London and New York: Methuen, 1982), 43; Morison, *Founding of Harvard College*, 3–39.

8. Hanna H. Gray, "Renaissance Humanism: The Pursuit of Eloquence," *Journal of the History of Ideas* 24 (1963): 497–514.

9. Curtis, *Oxford and Cambridge in Transition*, 110.

10. Miriam Usher Chrisman, "From Polemic to Propaganda: The Development of Mass Persuasion in the Late Sixteenth Century," *Archiv für Reformationsgeschichte* 73 (1982):175–95; R. W. Scribner, *For the Sake of Simple Folk* (Cambridge: Cambridge University Press, 1981), 1–13, 59–147.

11. D. W. Meinig, *The Shaping of America* (New Haven: Yale University Press, 1986), 1:83.

12. Marc Simmons, *New Mexico* (New York: W. W. Norton, 1977), 66.

13. Meinig, *Shaping of America*, 109–117.

14. U.S. Department of Commerce, Bureau of the Census, *Historical Statistics of the United States: Colonial Times to 1957* (Washington, D.C.: Government Printing Office, 1960), 756.

15. David Steven Cohen, "How Dutch Were the Dutch of New Netherland?" *New York History* 62 (1981):43–60; Oliver A. Rink, "The People of New Netherland: Notes on the Non-English Immigration to New York in the Seventeenth Century," *New York History* 62 (1981):5–22.

16. David Grayson Allen, *In English Ways* (Chapel Hill: University of North Carolina Press, 1981), 3–14, 163–80.

17. Bureau of the Census, *Historical Statistics*, 756; Meinig, *Shaping of America*, 83.

18. Bernard Bailyn, "The Challenge of Modern Historiography," *American Historical Review* 87 (1982):1–24.

19. "Letter of John Pory, 1619," in *Narratives of Early Virginia 1606–1625*, ed. Lyon Gardiner Tyler (New York: Charles Scribner's Sons, 1907), 286.

20. Thomas Hooker, *A Survey of the Summe of Church-Discipline* (London, 1648), Preface; John Winthrop, Jr., to Sir Robert Moray, 20 September 1664, *Collections of the Massachusetts Historical Society*, 5th ser., 8 (1882):90–91 (cited hereafter as *MHSC*); Thomas Shepard, Jr., to John Winthrop, Jr., 8 March 1668/69, Winthrop MSS, XVIII, 59, cited by Peter N. Carroll, *Puritanism and the Wilderness* (New York: Columbia University Press, 1969), 86.

21. Louis Hartz, *The Founding of New Societies* (New York: Harcourt, Brace & World, 1964), 6–23; R. Cole Harris, "The Simplification of Europe Overseas," *Annals of the Association of American Geographers* 67 (1977): 469–83.

22. James T. Lemon, "Early Americans and Their Social Environment," *Journal of Historical Geography* 6 (1980):115–31; Robert D. Mitchell, "American Origins and Regional Institutions: The Seventeenth-Century Chesapeake," *Annals of the Association of American Geographers* 73 (1983):404–20.

23. Jack P. Greene and J. R. Pole, eds., *Colonial British America* (Baltimore: Johns Hopkins University Press, 1984), 14.

24. Raymond Phineas Stearns, *Science in the British Colonies of America* (Urbana: University of Illinois Press, 1970), 117–38, 176–82; Lewis Perry, *Intellectual Life in America* (New York: Franklin Watts, 1984), 12–35.

25. Samuel Eliot Morison, "The Harvard School of Astronomy in the Seventeenth Century," *New England Quarterly* 7 (1934):3–24; Marion Barber Stowell, *Early American Almanacs* (New York: Burt Franklin, 1977), 44; Rosa Lockwood, "The Scientific Revolution in Seventeenth-Century New England," *New England Quarterly* 52 (1980):76–95.

26. Sacvan Bercovitch, ed., Introduction to *The American Puritan Imagination* (Cambridge: Cambridge University Press, 1974), 3; Harrison T. Meserole, ed., Introduction to *Seventeenth-Century American Poetry* (New York: New York University Press, 1968), xix.

27. Rosemary M. Laughlin, "Anne Bradstreet: Poet in Search of Form," *American Literature* 42 (1970):1–17; Ann Stanford, "Anne Bradstreet," in *Major Writers of Early American Literature*, ed. Everett Emerson (Madison: University of Wisconsin Press, 1972), 37; Robert Henson, "Form and Content of the Puritan Funeral Elegy," *American Literature* 32 (1960):11–27.

28. Richard Beale Davis, "The Gentlest Art in Seventeenth-Century Virginia," in *Literature and Society in Early Virginia, 1608–1840* (Baton Rouge: Louisiana State University Press, 1973), 43–62.

29. Rush Welter, *Popular Education and Democratic Thought in America* (New York: Columbia University Press, 1962), 20; Walter Ong, *Rhetoric, Romance, and Technology* (Ithaca: Cornell University Press, 1971), 51; James Axtell, *The School upon a Hill* (New Haven: Yale University Press, 1974), 184–85.

30. J. H. Kennedy, *Jesuit and Savage in New France* (Hamden, Conn.: Archon Books, 1970), 11; Morison, *Harvard College*, 1:172.

31. *New Englands First Fruits* (London, 1643), in Morison, *Founding of Harvard College*, 435–36.

32. Ibid., 436; Ong, *Orality and Literacy*, 43; Morison, *Founding of Harvard College*, 3–39; Ong, *Rhetoric, Romance, and Technology*, 28.

33. Samuel Eliot Morison, *The Puritan Pronaos* (New York: New York University Press, 1936), 54, 65, 80, 96; William Heard Kilpatrick, *The Dutch Schools of New Netherland and Colonial New York* (Washington, D.C.: Government Printing Office, 1912), 98–99, 197; Richard Beale Davis, *Intellectual Life in the Colonial South, 1585–1763* (Knoxville: University of Tennessee Press, 1978), 1:275, 277, 282, 349, 355.

34. Kenneth A. Lockridge, *Literacy in Colonial New England* (New York: W. W. Norton, 1974), 13; Rhys Isaac, "Books and the Social Authority of Learning: The Case of Mid-Eighteenth Century Virginia," in *Printing and Society in Early America*, ed. William L. Joyce, David D. Hall, Richard D. Brown, and John B. Hency (Worcester, Mass.: American Antiquarian Society, 1983), 231; David D. Hall, "The Uses of Literacy in New England, 1600–1850," in *Printing and Society*, 20; Bernard Bailyn, *Education in the Forming of American Society* (New York: Random House, 1960), 28.

35. David D. Hall, "A World of Wonders: The Mentality of the Supernatural in Seventeenth-Century New England," *Seventeenth-Century New England*, 63 (1984):239–74; Jon Butler, "Magic, Astrology, and the Early American Religious Heritage, 1600–1760," *American Historical Review* 84 (1979):317–46; John Putnam Demos, *Entertaining Satan* (New York: Oxford University Press, 1982); Keith Thomas, *Religion and the Decline of Magic* (New York: Charles Scribner's Sons, 1971); Morison, *Puritan Pronaos*, 240.

36. Hugh T. Lefler, "Promotional Literature of the Southern Colonies," *Journal of Southern History* 33 (1967):11–13; Antonio Espejo, "Account of the Journey to the Provinces and Settlements in New Mexico, 1583," in *Spanish Exploration in the Southwest*, ed. Herbert Eugene Bolton, (New York: Charles Scribner's Sons, 1916), 190, 194; Thomas West, "The Relation of the Lord De-La-Ware," in *Narratives of Early Virginia*, 209–14; John Smith, *A Map of Virginia*, in *Narratives of Early Virginia*, 118.

37. John Parker, *Books to Build an Empire* (Amsterdam: N. Israel, 1965), 13–23;

David S. Shields, "Exploratory Narratives and the Development of the New England Passage Journal," *Essex Institute Historical Collections* 120 (1984):42. For bibliographical listings, see Charles Evans, *American Bibliography*, vol. 1:1639–1720 (Chicago: Blakely Press, 1903); George Watson Cole, *A Catalogue of Books Relating to the Discovery and Early History of North and South America* (New York: Peter Smith, 1951); Thomas D. Clark, *Travels in the Old South* (Norman: University of Oklahoma Press, 1956); and David B. Quinn, ed., *New American World* (New York: Arno Press and Hector Bye, 1979).

38. Frederick Lewis Weis, *The Colonial Clergy of the Middle Colonies, New York, New Jersey, and Pennsylvania, 1628–1776* (Worcester, Mass.: American Antiquarian Society, 1957); Frederick Lewis Weis, *The Colonial Clergy of Maryland, Delaware, and Georgia* (Baltimore: Genealogical Publishing Co., 1978); Frederick Lewis Weis, *The Colonial Clergy of Virginia, North Carolina, and South Carolina* (Boston: Publications of the Society of the Descendants of the Colonial Clergy, 1955); Frederick Lewis Weis, *Colonial Clergy and Colonial Churches of New England* (Baltimore: Genealogical Publishing Co., 1977); Maynard Geiger, *Biographical Dictionary of the Franciscans in Spanish Florida and Cuba (1528–1841)* (Paterson, N.J.: St. Anthony Guild Press, 1940); Lucy L. Wenhold, ed., "A 17th Century Letter of Gabriel Diaz Vara Calderon, Bishop of Cuba," *Smithsonian Miscellaneous Collections*, 95 (1936):2–14.

39. R. G. Thwaites, ed., *The Jesuit Relations and Allied Documents* (Cleveland: Burrows Brothers, 1896–1901), 5:195, 6:243; James Axtell, *The Invasion Within* (New York: Oxford University Press, 1985), 87–88; Roger Williams, *A Key into the Language of America* (London, 1643), *Publications of the Narragansett Club* (cited hereafter as PNC) (Providence, R.I.: Providence Press Co., 1866), 83.

40. Harry S. Stout, *The New England Soul* (New York: Oxford University Press, 1986), 13–50; Weis, *Colonial Clergy and the Colonial Churches of New England*, 143; Edwin Scott Gaustad, *Historical Atlas of Religion in America* (New York: Harper & Row, 1962), 2–3; Patricia U. Bonomi and Peter R. Eisenstadt, "Church Adherence in the Eighteenth-Century British American Colonies," *William and Mary Quarterly*, 3d ser., 39 (1982):263.

41. Samuel Stone, "The Whole Body of Divinity in a Catecheticall Way Handled by Mr. Samuel Stone" (1656). Baird Tipson graciously provided portions of his typescript of Stone's unpublished treatise.

42. George Selement, "Publication and the Puritan Minister," *William and Mary Quarterly*, 3d ser., 37 (1980):219–41.

43. Gerald F. DeJong, *The Dutch Reformed Church in the American Colonies* (Grand Rapids, Mich.: William B. Eerdmans Publishing Co., 1978), 30; "Extracts from the Annual Letters of the English Province of the Society of Jesus," in *Narratives of Early Maryland, 1633–1684*, ed. Clayton Colman Hall (New York: Charles Scribner's Sons, 1910), 122–23.

44. "Proceedings of the Virginia Assembly, 1619," in *Narratives of Early Virginia*, 273; Lawrence A. Cremin, *American Education* (New York: Harper & Row, 1972), 154; Winton U. Solberg, *Redeem the Time* (Cambridge: Harvard University Press, 1977), 119, 174, 207.

45. George Alsop, *A Character of the Province of Maryland*, in *Narratives of Early Maryland, 1633–1684*, 358.

Chapter 2: Promoters

1. [Robert Johnson], *Nova Britannia* (London, 1609), 3–4, 5, 12.

2. "Letters of Juan Ponce de Leon to the Cardinal of Tortosa and to King Charles I," in *New American World*, 1:245; Gonzalo Fernandez de Oviedo, *Historia general y natural*, in *New American World*, 264.

3. Alvar Núñez Cabeza de Vaca, *The Narrative of Alvar Núñez Cabeza de Vaca*, ed. Frederick W. Hodge, in *Spanish Explorers in the Southern United States 1528–1543*, ed. Frederick W. Hodge and Theodore H. Lewis (New York: Charles Scribner's Sons, 1907), 13, 29, 34, 111, 120.

4. Marcos de Niza, "A Relation of the Reverend Father Frier Marco de Nica," in *New American World*, 1:347, 348; David B. Quinn, *North America from Earliest Discovery to First Settlements* (New York: Harper & Row, 1975), 194–95.

5. Antonio de Mendoza to Charles V, 17 April 1540, in *New American World*, 1:359–60.

6. Pedro de Castañeda, *Narrative of the Expedition to Cibola*, in *New American World*, 1:373; Francisco Vásquez de Coronado to Antonio de Mendoza, 8 March 1540, in *New American World*, 1:426.

7. de Castañeda, *Narrative*, 1:366.

8. "The Narrative of the Expedition of Hernando de Soto, by the Gentleman of Elvas," ed. T. Hayes Lewis, in *Spanish Explorers*, 133–34.

9. Ibid., 142, 148, 179, 215, 267, 270.

10. Philipe de Escalante and Hernando Barrado, "Brief and True Account of the Exploration of New Mexico, 1583," in *Spanish Exploration in the Southwest, 1542–1706*, 157; Espejo, "Account of the Journey to the Provinces and Settlements of New Mexico, 1583," in *Spanish Exploration*, 190; Antonio de Ascensión, "A Brief Report of the Discovery in the South Sea," in *Spanish Exploration*, 112, 114, 117.

11. "Fray Francisco de Escobar's Diary of the Oñate Expedition to California, 1605," in *Don Juan de Oñate* ed. George P. Hammond and Agapito Rey (Albuquerque: University of New Mexico Press, 1953), 1026.

12. Espejo, "Account," 190; "Escobar's Diary," 1029.

13. "True Account of the Expedition of Oñate toward the East," in *Spanish Exploration*, 265–67.

14. Jacques Cartier, "The Third Voyage of Discovery," in *New American World*, 1:330, 332; Jean Ribault, "The True Discoverie of Terra Florida," in *New American World*, 2:289; "René de Laudonniére's Account of the First French Settlement at Charlesfort," in *New American World*, 2:294–307.

15. Samuel de Champlain, "Voyages and Discoveries in New France," in *Voyages of Samuel de Champlain, 1604–1618*, ed. W. L. Grant (New York: Charles Scribner's Sons, 1907), 265.

16. Richard Eden, *The Decades of the New Worlde or West India*, in *New American World*, 1:227; D. B. Quinn, C. E. Armstrong, and R. A. Skelton, "The Primary Hakluyt Bibliography," in *The Hakluyt Handbook*, ed. D. B. Quinn (London: Hakluyt Society, 1974), 2:471, 525, 527; Parker, *Books to Build an Empire*, 13–16.

17. Howard Mumford Jones, *O Strange New World* (1952; reprint ed., Wesport, Conn.: Greenwood Press, 1982), 43.

18. Sir Walter Raleigh, *The Discovery of the Large, Rich, and Beautiful Empire of Guiana*, ed. Sir Robert H. Schomburgk (London: Hakluyt Society, 1848), v, xiii; Louis B. Wright, ed., *The Elizabethans' America* (Cambridge: Harvard University Press, 1966), 27–28.

19. Thomas Hariot, *A Briefe and True Report of the New Found Land of Virginia*, in *The Roanoke Voyages, 1584–1590*, ed. David B. Quinn (London: Cambridge University Press for the Hakluyt Society, 1955), 2:324–50, 372–79; Wayne Franklin, *Discoverers, Explorers, Settlers* (Chicago: University of Chicago Press, 1979), 105–13.

20. W. P. D. Wightman, *Science in a Renaissance Society* (London: Hutchinson & Co., 1972), 109.

21. Hariot, *Briefe and True Report*, 320–21.

22. Ibid., 320, 322–24, 382.

23. Ralph Lane, "An Extract of Master Ralph Lane's Letter to Mr. Richard Hakluyt," in Richard Hakluyt, *The Principal Navigations Voyages Traffiques and Discoveries of the English Nation* (Glasgow: James MacLehose and Sons, 1904), 8:319; John Brereton, *A Brief and True Relation of the Discoverie of the North Part of Virginia*, in *The English New England Voyages 1602–1608*, ed. David B. Quinn and Alison M. Quinn (London: Hakluyt Society, 1983), 159, 193; James Rosier, *A True Relation of the Most Prosperous Voyage Made in This Present Yeare 1605*, in *New American World*, 3:377.

24. Alexander Brown, ed., *The Genesis of the United States* (New York: Russell and Russell, 1964), 1:30–31; Philip L. Barbour, ed., *The Jamestown Voyages under the First Charter, 1606–1609* (Cambridge: Cambridge University Press for the Hakluyt Society, 1969), 1:79, 100, 104, 76.

25. Barbour, ed., *Jamestown Voyages*, 1:144–45.

26. Alden T. Vaughan, "The Evolution of Virginia History: Early Historians of the First Colony," in *Perspectives on Early American History*, ed. Alden T. Vaughan and George Athan Billias (New York: Harper & Row, 1973), 9–39; Philip L. Barbour, *The Three Worlds of Captain John Smith* (Boston: Houghton Mifflin, 1964), 3–73.

27. John Smith, *A True Relation of Such Occurrences and Accidents of Noate, as Hath Hapned in Virginia*, in *Narratives of Early Virginia, 1606–1625*, 31, 71, 36–37, 66.

28. Smith, *True Relation*, 32; [Johnson], *Nova Britannia*, 12; John Parker, "Religion and the Virginia Colony 1609–10," in *The Westward Enterprise*, ed. K. R. Andrews, N. P. Canny, and P. E. H. Hair (Detroit: Wayne State University Press, 1979), 245–70.

29. Smith, *A Map of Virginia*, in *Narratives*, 98, 116, 118.

30. Ibid., 97, 136.

31. Ibid., 118, 123, 128.

32. John Smith, *A Description of New England* (London: Humfrey Townes, 1616), in *Tracts and Other Papers*, ed. Peter Force (New York: Peter Smith, 1947), 2:6, 22, 24.

33. Ibid., 23, 1, 21.

34. John Smith, *New Englands Trials* (London: William Jones, 1622) in *Tracts and Other Papers*, 2:23.

35. John Smith, *The Generall Historie of Virginia, New England, and the Summer Isles* (London, 1624), Preface.

36. Edward Maria Wingfield, "A Discourse of Virginia," in *Travels and Works of Captain John Smith* ed. Edward Arber (Edinburgh: John Grant, 1910), 1:lxxxiii, lxxxix; Richard Rich, *Newes from Virginia* (London, 1610), Preface; Alexander

Whitaker, *Good Newes from Virginia*, in *American Christianity*, ed. H. Shelton Smith, Robert T. Handy, and Lefferts A. Loetscher (New York: Charles Scribner's Sons, 1960), 1:46.

37. William Strachey, *The Historie of Travaile into Virginia Britannia*, ed. R. H. Mayor (London: Printed for the Hakluyt Society, 1869), Epistle to the Reader, 22.

38. Ibid., 2, 19, 16.

39. Quinn, *New American World*, 5:346–47.

40. Ralph Hamor, *A True Discourse of the Present State of Virginia*, ed. A. L. Rowse (Richmond: Virginia State Library, 1957), n.p.

41. Ibid., 2, 13, 24, 42, 46.

42. Edmund S. Morgan, "The First American Boom: Virginia 1618 to 1630," *William and Mary Quarterly*, 3d ser., 28 (1971):169–98.

43. William Bullock, *Virginia Impartially Explained* (London, 1649), n.p.; William Berkeley, *A Discourse and View of Virginia* (London, 1663), 3; Edward Bland, *The Discovery of New Brittaine* (London, 1651), n.p., 15.

44. Andrew White, *A Relation of the Successefulle Beginnings of the Lord Baltemore's Plantation in Mary-Land*, *Old South Leaflets* (Boston: Directors of the Old South Work, n.d.), 7:8; *A Perfect Description of Virginia* (London, 1649), in *Tracts and Other Papers*, 2:6, 7, 8, 11; J. A. Leo Lemay, *Men of Letters in Colonial Maryland* (Knoxville: University of Tennessee Press, 1972), 19.

45. David Minter, "John Hammond," in *American Writers before 1800: A Biographical and Critical Dictionary*, ed. James A. Levernier and Douglas R. Wilmes (Westport, Conn.: Greenwood Press, 1983), 2:705–6.

46. John Hammond, *Leah and Rachel, Or, the Two Fruitfull Sisters Virginia and Maryland* (London, 1656), in *Tracts and Other Papers*, 3:14:7, 17.

47. Francis Higginson, *New Englands Plantation*, 3d ed. (London, 1630), *Massachusetts Historical Society Proceedings* 62 (1929): 307 (cited hereafter as MHSP).

48. "Deputy Governor Dudley's Letter to the Right Honorable, My Very Good Lady, the Lady Bridget, Countess of Lincoln," in Alexander Young, ed., *Chronicles of the First Planters of the Colony of Massachusetts Bay* (Boston: Charles C. Little and James Brown, 1846), 310, 324.

49. Cited by Carroll, *Puritanism and the Wilderness*, 51, 56; Everett Emerson, ed., *Letters from New England* (Amherst: University of Massachusetts Press, 1976), 214, 215.

50. "Dudley's Letter," 324.

51. Higginson, *New Englands Plantation*, 306; Higginson, "Some Brief Collections out of a Letter That Mr. Higginson Sent to His Friends at Leicester," in *The Founding of Massachusetts*, ed. E. S. Morgan (Indianapolis: Bobbs-Merrill, 1964), 11; Edward Winslow, *Good Newes from New England* (London, 1624), *MHSC*, 2d ser., 9 (1822), 75; Hammond, *Leah and Rachel*, 10.

52. Thomas Morton, *New English Canaan*, in *Tracts and Other Papers*, 2:5; George B. Cheever, ed., *The Journal of the Pilgrims at Plymouth, in New England, in 1620* (New York: John Wiley, 1848), 96; William Wood, *New England's Prospect* (1634), ed. Alden T. Vaughan (Amherst: University of Massachusetts Press, 1977), 15; Alsop, *Character of the Province of Maryland*, in *Narratives of Early Maryland*, 342, 340.

53. Alsop, *Character of the Province of Maryland*, 355, 356.

54. Wood, *New England's Prospect*, 19–20.

55. John Josselyn, *An Account of Two Voyages to New England* (London, 1675), *MHSC*, 3d ser. (1833):234, 235, 311; John Josselyn, *New-Englands Rarities Discovered* (London, 1672), in *Archaeologia Americana* 4 (1860):138; Stearns, *Science in the British Colonies*, 141.

56. Adriaen Van der Donck, *A Description of the New Netherlands*, ed. Thomas F. O'Donnell (Syracuse: Syracuse University Press, 1968), 10; Francis Higginson, "A True Relation of the Last Voyage to New England," *MHSP* Thomas Morton, *New English Canaan* (London, 1632), in Force, ed., *Tracts and Other Papers*, 2:3.

57. Andrew White, "A Briefe Relation of the Voyage Unto Maryland," in *Narratives of Early Maryland*, 37; Josselyn, *Account of Two Voyages*, 240–92, and *New England Rarities*, 141–71; Wood, *New England's Prospect*, 33–57; Smith, *Map of Virginia*, 83.

58. Alsop, *Character of the Province of Maryland*, 344; Higginson, "True Relation of the Last Voyage," 290; Evelyn Page, *American Genesis* (Boston: Gambit, 1973), 192–207.

59. Page, *American Genesis*, 208; Daniel Denton, *A Brief Description of New York* (London, 1670), 19.

60. Higginson, "True Relation of the Last Voyage," 312, 319; Morton, *New English Canaan*, 64; Denton, *Brief Description of New York*, 19; Josselyn, *Account of Two Voyages*, 333.

61. Higginson, "Some Brief Collections out of a Letter," 154; Karen Ordahl Kupperman, "Climate and Mastery of the Wilderness in Seventeenth-Century New England," in *Seventeenth-Century New England*, 3–37; Cecelia Tichi, *New World, New Earth* (New Haven: Yale University Press, 1979), 10, 49.

62. John Smith, *Advertisements for the Unexperienced Planters of New-England, or Any Where* (London, 1631), *MHSC*, 3d. ser., 3 (1833):12; Edward Winslow, *Good News from New England, Chronicles of the Pilgrim Fathers*, ed. Alexander Young (Boston: Charles C. Little and James Brown, 1844), 294, 372.

63. Alsop, *Character of the Province of Maryland*, 365, 369; Josselyn, *Account of Two Voyages*, 293; "Observations by Master George Percy, 1607," in *Narratives of Early Virginia*, 6; White, "Briefe Relation," 87; Smith, *True Relation*, 39; John Lederer, *The Discoveries of John Lederer*, ed. William P. Cumming (Charlottesville, Va.: University of Virginia Press, 1958), 29; Andrew White, "A Relation of Maryland," in *Narratives of Early Maryland*, 86, 88; White, "Briefe Relation," 44; Cheever, ed., *Journal of the Pilgrims*, 96; "Letter of the Reverend Jonas Michaelius, 1628," in *Narratives of New Netherland*, 126, 127; Andrew White, "An Account of the Colony of the Lord Baron Baltimore," in *Narratives of Early Maryland*, 7.

64. Loren E. Pennington, "The Amerindian in English Promotional Literature," in *Westward Enterprise*, 175–94.

65. Higginson, "True Relation of the Last Voyage," 317; Wood, *New England's Prospect*, 95; White, "Relation of Maryland," 83; Hammond, *Leah and Rachel*, 20; Berkeley, *Discourse and View of Virginia*, 3.

66. Higginson, *New-Englands Plantation*, 316; Morton, *New English Canaan*, 13; Denton, *Brief Description of New York*, 7.

67. Higginson, "True Relation of the Last Voyage," 316.

68. Denton, *Brief Description of New York*, 7.

69. Hammond, *Leah and Rachel*, 18, 15.

70. Ibid., 9, 15–16; See also Berkeley, *Discourse and View of Virginia*, 3–4.

71. Alsop, *Character of the Province of Maryland*, 348, 349; Denton, *Brief Description of New York*, 20; Cheever, *Journal of the Pilgrims*, 30; Edward Winslow, *Hypocrisie Unmasked, Chronicles of the Pilgrim Fathers*, 387; Wood, *New England's Prospect*, 58; Higginson, "True Relation of the Last Voyage," 317.

72. Edmund S. Morgan, *American Slavery, American Freedom* (New York: W. W. Norton, 1975), 180–250; citation from Timothy H. Breen, *Puritans and Adventurers* (New York: Oxford University Press, 1980), 112; Darrett B. Rutman and Anita H. Rutman, *A Place in Time* (New York: W. W. Norton, 1984), 20–38.

73. Russell R. Menard, "Population, Economy, and Society in Seventeenth-Century Maryland," *Maryland Historical Magazine* 79 (1984):71–92; Russell R. Menard, "Maryland's 'Time of Troubles': Sources of Political Disorder in Early St. Mary's," *Maryland Historical Magazine* 76 (1981):124–40; Darrett B. Rutman, *Winthrop's Boston* (New York: W. W. Norton, 1972), 68–163.

Chapter 3: The Persuasive Past

1. Increase Mather, *A Brief History of the Warr with the Indians in New England* (Boston, 1676), in *So Dreadfull a Judgment*, ed. Richard Slotkin and James K. Folsom (Middletown, Conn.: Wesleyan University Press, 1978), 81, 82; William Bradford, *Of Plymouth Plantation, 1620–1647*, ed. Samuel Eliot Morison (New York: Alfred A. Knopf, 1963), 3; Nathaniel Morton, *New Englands Memoriall*, ed. Howard J. Hall (New York: Scholars' Facsimiles and Reprints, 1937), "To the Reader."

2. Morison, *Puritan Pronaos*, 133–51; Philip Alexander Bruce, *Institutional History of Virginia in the Seventeenth Century* (New York: G. P. Putnam's Sons, 1910), 1:402–41; Louis B. Wright, *The First Gentlemen of Virginia* (San Marino: Huntington Library, 1940), 117–54; David D. Hall, "The World of Print and Collective Mentality in Seventeenth-Century New England," in *New Directions in American Intellectual History*, ed. John Higham and Paul K. Conkin (Baltimore: Johns Hopkins University Press, 1979), 174; Hall, "Uses of Literacy in New England," 1–47.

3. Wingfield, "Discourse of Virginia," xci; Smith, *Description of New England*, 18; Morgan Godwin, *The Negro's and Indians Advocate, Suing for their Admission into the Church* (London, 1680), n.p.; Nathaniel Ward, *The Simple Cobbler of Aggawam in America* (London, 1647), in Force, *Tracts and Other Papers*, 3:13; Emerson, *Letters from New England*, 162.

4. Gaspar Perez de Villagra, *History of New Mexico* (1610), trans. Gilberto Espinosa, ed. F. W. Hedge (Los Angeles: Quivira Society, 1933), 41, 272.

5. Smith, *Generall Historie*, 8, 16, 19, 51, 59, 107.

6. Berkeley, *Discourse and View of Virginia*, 3; Breen, *Puritans and Adventurers*, 164–95.

7. William Sherwood, "Virginia's Deploured Condition," *MHSC*, 4th ser. (Boston, 1871), 9:162–76; [John Cotton?], "The History of Bacon's and Ingram's Rebellion, 1676," in *Narratives of the Insurrections*, ed. Charles M. Andrews (New York: Charles Scribner's Sons, 1915), 53, 62; "A True Narrative of the Late Rebellion in Virginia, By the Royal Commissioners, 1677," in *Narratives of the Insurrections*, 105–41. See Wilcomb E. Washburn, *The Governor and the Rebel* (Chapel Hill: University of North Carolina Press, 1957), 1–4, 167–75.

8. Herschel Baker, *The Race of Time* (Toronto: University of Toronto Press,

1967), 64; [Richard Mather], *An Apologie of the Churches in New-England for Church-Covenant* (London, 1643), 33. See Dwight Bozeman's study of Puritan primitivism, *To Live Ancient Lives*, (Chapel Hill: University of North Carolina Press, 1988). I am grateful to him for permitting me to read his manuscript.

9. Cited by Baker, *Race of Time*, 35–36, 37–38.

10. Martin Luther, *Lectures on Genesis, Luther's Works*, ed. Jaroslav Pelikan (St. Louis: Fortress Press, 1958), 1:231; Thomas M. Davis, "The Traditions of Puritan Typology," in *Typology and Early American Literature*, ed. Sacvan Bercovitch (Amherst: University of Massachusetts Press, 1972), 11–45.

11. Thomas Hooker, *The Covenant of Grace Opened* (London, 1649), 63; Samuel Willard, *A Compleat Body of Divinity in Two Hundred and Fifty Expository Lectures on the Assembly's Shorter Catechism* (Boston, 1726), 31–33.

12. Willard, *Compleat Body*, 32, 33; John Cotton, *The Churches Resurrection* (London, 1642), 7.

13. John Whitgift, *The Works of John Whitgift* (Cambridge, 1853), 1:208, 315, 316, 322, 369, 469–70, 3:94.

14. John Cotton, *A Brief Exposition with Practical Observations upon the Whole Book of Canticles* (London, 1655), 27; [John Winthrop], "Generall Considerations for the Plantation in New England," in *Chronicles*, 276; John Underhill, *News from America* (London, 1638), *MHSC*, ser. (1837):6:4, 25; Bozeman, *"Live Ancient Lives,"* chap. 5.

15. "Copy of a Letter from Mr. Cotton to Lord Say and Seal in the Year 1636," in *Puritan Political Ideas, 1558–1794*, ed. Edmund S. Morgan (Indianapolis: Bobbs-Merrill, 1965), 168–69; Thomas Shepard, *Subjection to Christ in All His Ordinances and Appointments* (London, 1652), 124.

16. Thomas Shepard, *A Defense of the Answer Made unto the Nine Questions Sent from England* (London, 1645), 2; Richard Mather, *Church-Government and Church Covenant Discussed* (London, 1643), 9.

17. Shepard, *Defense of the Answer*, 73, 88, 191; Mather, *Church-Government and Church Covenant Discussed*, 9, 23; John Cotton, *The Way of Congregational Churches Cleared* (London, 1648), 94; Mather, *Apologie of the Churches in New-England*, 1, 3, 5; John Cotton, *The Way of the Churches of Christ in New-England* (London, 1645), 3.

18. Hooker, *Survey of the Summe of Church-Discipline*, Preface, 1:5, 11, 45, 221, 3:20.

19. Paul R. Lucas, *Valley of Discord* (Hanover, N.H.: University Press of New England, 1976), 23–65.

20. Samuel Danforth, *A Brief Recognition of New Englands Errand into the Wilderness* (1671), in *The Wall and Garden*, ed. A. W. Plumstead (Minneapolis: University of Minnesota Press, 1968), 61.

21. Samuel Mather, *The Figures or Types of the Old Testament* (1683; reprint ed., London, 1705), 52, 75, 155.

22. Cotton, *Brief Exposition on Canticles*, 27; Thomas Shepard, *Theses Sabbaticae. Or the Doctrine of the Sabbath* (London, 1649), 27, 133.

23. [John Cotton], *The Result of a Synod at Cambridge in New England, Anno 1646* (London, 1654), 21–25.

24. John Cotton, *The Bloudy Tenent, Washed, and Made White in the Bloud of the Lambe* (London, 1647), 73; John Cotton, *Singing of Psalmes a Gospel-Ordinance* (London, 1647), 23–24.

25. John Cotton, *Of the Holinesse of Church-Members* (London, 1650), 80.

26. Shepard, *Theses Sabbaticae*, 1:135, 2:15.

27. Roger Williams, *Mr. Cottons Letter Lately Printed, Examined, and Answered* (London, 1644), *PNC*, 1st ser. (Providence, R.I.: Providence Press Co., 1866), 1:76; *Master John Cotton's Answer to Master Roger Williams*, ed. J. Lewis Diman, *PNC*, 2:144–45; Cotton, *The Bloudy Tenent, Washed*, 88.

28. Cotton, *The Bloudy Tenent, Washed*, 68, 72, 73.

29. John Cotton, *The Grounds and Ends of the Baptisme of the Children of the Faithfull* (London, 1647), 4; Hooker, *Survey of the Summe of Church-Discipline*, 1:9.

30. Hooker, *Survey of the Summe of Church-Discipline*, 1:2; Cotton, *Way of the Churches of Christ*, 72–73; Cotton, *Grounds and Ends*, 167.

31. Shepard, *Subjection to Christ in All His Ordinances*, 124; Bozeman, *To Live Ancient Lives*, chap. 6.

32. G. B. Warden, "The Rhode Island Civil Code of 1647," in *Saints and Revolutionaries*, ed. David D. Hall, John M. Murrin, and Thad W. Tate (New York: W. W. Norton, 1984), 143; George Lee Haskins, *Law and Authority in Early Massachusetts* (New York: Macmillan, 1960), 5; Bradford, *Of Plymouth Plantation*, 411.

33. Bozeman, *To Live Ancient Lives*, chaps. 2–6.

34. Thomas Hooker, *The Soules Union with Christ*, in Hooker, *The Soules Exaltation* (London, 1638), 35; John Cotton, *An Exposition upon the Thirteenth Chapter of the Revelation* (London, 1655), 118.

35. Bradford, *Of Plymouth Plantation*, 3, 46, 63; Peter Gay, *A Loss of Mastery* (New York: Vintage Books, 1968), 32.

36. Bradford, *Of Plymouth Plantation*, 296.

37. Ibid., 3; David Levin, "William Bradford: The Value of Puritan Historiography," in *Major Writers of Early American Literature*, ed. Everett Emerson (Madison: University of Wisconsin Press, 1972), 11–31; Bradford, *Of Plymouth Plantation*, 63, 89; Robert Daly, "William Bradford's Vision of History," *American Literature* 44 (1973):557–69.

38. Bradford, *Of Plymouth Plantation*, 118.

39. Ibid., 14, 164, 204, 253.

40. Ibid., 24, 164, 177, 222; David Levin, "Review of Peter Gay, *A Loss of Mastery*," *History and Theory* 7 (1968):389; Alan B. Howard, "Art and History in Bradford's *Of Plymouth Plantation*," *William and Mary Quarterly*, 3d ser., 28 (1971):253.

41. Bozeman, *To Live Ancient Lives*, chaps. 7–9; Bernard Capp, "The Millennium and Eschatology in England," *Past and Present* 57 (1972):156–62.

42. John Cotton, *A Brief Exposition of the Whole Book of Canticles or, Song of Solomon* (London, 1642), 10; James F. Maclear, "New England and the Fifth Monarchy," *William and Mary Quarterly*, 3d ser., 32 (1975):223–60; Thomas Allen, "To the Reader," in Cotton, *Exposition upon the Thirteenth Chapter of the Revelation*, n.p.

43. Cotton, *Exposition upon the Thirteenth Chapter of the Revelation*, 22, 93; John Cotton, *The Pouring Out of the Seven Vials, Or an Exposition, of the 16. Chapter of the Revelation* (London, 1642), 1–16; Cotton, *The Churches Resurrection*, 20, 21.

44. Maclear, "New England and the Fifth Monarchy," 234–36; Hooker, *Survey of the Summe of Church-Discipline*, Preface; Cotton, *Exposition upon the Thirteenth Chapter of the Revelation*, 34–35; Shepard, *Clear Sun-shine of the Gospel*, 30.

45. Cited by Maclear, "New England and the Fifth Monarchy," 237; Johnson, *Johnson's Wonder-Working Providence*, 25.

46. Johnson, *Johnson's Wonder-Working Providence*, 137.

47. Ibid., 24, 146, 270–71; Sacvan Bercovitch, "The Historiography of Johnson's *Wonder-Working Providence*," *Essex Institute Historical Collections* 104 (1968):138–61.

48. Johnson, *Johnson's Wonder-Working Providence*, 4; John Davenport, Epistle to the Reader, in Increase Mather, *The Mystery of Israel's Salvation Explained and Applyed* (London, 1669), n.p.

49. Williston Walker, ed., *The Creeds and Platforms of Congregationalism* (Boston: Pilgrim Press, 1960), 304, 312; David M. Scobey, "Revising the Errand: New England's Ways and the Puritan Sense of the Past," *William and Mary Quarterly*, 3d ser., 41 (1984):3–31.

50. William Stoughton, *New England's True Interest*, in *The Puritans*, ed. Perry Miller and Thomas H. Johnson (1938; reprint ed., New York: Harper & Row, 1963), 1:243, 246; Sacvan Bercovitch, "New England's Errand Reappraised," in *New Directions*, 85–104.

51. Richard S. Dunn, "John Winthrop Writes His Journal," *William and Mary Quarterly*, 3d ser., 41 (1984):185–212.

52. Morton, *New Englands Memoriall*, ii, 197, "To the Reader."

53. Ibid., "To the Reader."

54. Bradford, *Of Plymouth Plantation*, 320; Morton, *New Englands Memoriall*, 197–98.

55. Kenneth B. Murdock, "William Hubbard and the Providential Interpretation of History," *Proceedings of the American Antiquarian Society* 52 (1942):15–37; Thomas Shepard, Jr., *Eye Salve* (Cambridge, Mass., 1673), 16–17.

56. Urian Oakes, *New England Pleaded With* (Cambridge, Mass., 1673), 23; Increase Mather, *Brief History of the Warr with the Indians*, 81–82.

57. Increase Mather, *Brief History of the Warr with the Indians*, 113.

58. Charles H. Lincoln, ed., *Narratives of the Indian Wars 1675–1689* (New York: Charles Scribner's Sons, 1913), 5; John Easton, "A Relacion of the Indyan Ware, by Mr. Easton of Roade Isld, 1675," in *Narratives of the Indian Wars*, 11, 15–17.

59. Increase Mather, *Brief History of the Warr with the Indians*, 81; [Nathaniel Saltonstall], *The Present State of New-England with Respect to the Indian War* (1675), in *Narratives of the Indian Wars*, 35, 40, 49.

60. Increase Mather, *Brief History of the Warr with the Indians*, 82, 84.

61. Ibid., 125.

62. Ibid., 104, 179, 117, 187.

63. William Hubbard, *The Happiness of a People in the Wisdome of Their Rulers* (Boston, 1676), 38; William Hubbard, *A Narrative of the Indian Wars in New England* (Stockbridge, Mass.: Herman Willard, 1803; reprinting of *A Narrative of the Troubles with the Indians*), 359–60.

64. Murdock, "William Hubbard and the Providential Interpretation of History," 17; Hubbard, *Narrative of the Indian Wars*, 171, 172, 177, 184, 253.

65. Ibid., "Epistle Dedicatory," n.p. (1677 ed.), 254 (1803 ed.).

66. Increase Mather, *A Relation of the Troubles Which Have Hapned in New England, By Reason of the Indians There* (Boston, 1677), in *Early History of New England*, ed. Samuel G. Drake (Albany: J. Munsell, 1864), "To the Reader," 48, 238–39; Richard Mather to ?, 9 November 1655, *MHSC*, 4th ser. (Boston, 1868), 8:232.

67. Benjamin Tompson, *New Englands Crisis* (Boston, 1676), in *So Dreadfull a Judgment*, 218; Thomas Wheeler, *A Thankfull Remembrance of Gods Mercy* (Cambridge,

Mass., 1676), in *So Dreadfull a Judgment*, 244, 248; Mary Rowlandson, *The Sovereignty and Goodness of God* (Cambridge, 1682), in *So Dreadfull a Judgment*, 352, 353.

68. Rowlandson, *Sovereignty and Goodness of God*, 359, 365.

69. Increase Mather, *A Relation of the Troubles*, 48.

70. William Hubbard, *General History of New England*, *MHSC*, 2d ser. (Cambridge, Mass., 1815), 6:661.

71. Ibid., 6:676.

Chapter 4: Persuasion Across Cultures

1. Fray Alonso de Benavides, *The Memorial of Fray Alonso de Benavides 1630*, trans. Mrs. Edward E. Ayer (Chicago: n.p., 1916), 11, 28, 50.

2. Ibid., 50–52.

3. Quinn, ed., *New American World*, 5:70.

4. Lewis Hanke, *Bartolomé de las Casas* (The Hague: Martinus Nijhoff, 1951), 19–33; Juan Friede, "Las Casas and Indigenism in the Sixteenth Century," in *Bartolomé de Las Casas in History*, ed. Juan Friede and Benjamin Keen (De Kalb: Northern Illinois University Press, 1971), 127–234.

5. Bartolomé de Las Casas, *In Defense of the Indians*, trans. Stafford Poole (De Kalb: Northern Illinois University Press, 1974), 19–22, 39, 302; Lewis Hanke, *Bartolomé de Las Casas, Historian* (Gainesville: University of Florida Press, 1952), 13–45.

6. Fray Gregorio de Beteta, "The Mission of Fray Luis Cancer to Florida as Told By Beteta," in *New American World*, 2:190–97; Antonio de la Ascensión, "Brief Report of the Discovery," 133; France V. Scholes, *Church and State in New Mexico, 1610–1650* (Albuquerque: University of New Mexico Press, 1937).

7. Robert Ricard, *The Spiritual Conquest of Mexico* (Berkeley: University of California Press, 1966), 104, 181, 194.

8. Hammond and Rey, eds., *Don Juan de Oñate*, 1:47, 65, 110, 129.

9. Ibid., 77, 335; Frederick Webb Hodge, George P. Hammond, and Agapito Rey, eds., *Fray Alonso de Benavides' Revised Memorial of 1634* (Albuquerque: University of New Mexico Press, 1945), 62, 69; Edward H. Spicer, *Cycles of Conquest* (Tucson: University of Arizona Press, 1962), 288; Andrew O. Wiget, "Truth and the Hopi," *Ethnohistory* 29 (1982):181–99.

10. Elsie Clews Parson, *Pueblo Indian Religion* (Chicago: University of Chicago Press, 1939), 1:309; Henry Warner Bowden, "Spanish Missions, Cultural Conflict and the Pueblo Revolt of 1680," *Church History* 44 (1975):217–28; Estevan de Perea, "True Report of the Great Conversion," in *Benavides' Revised Memorial*, 214; Spicer, *Cycles of Conquest*, 153; Alfonso Ortiz, "Ritual Drama and the Pueblo World View," in *New Perspectives on the Pueblos*, ed. Alfonso Ortiz (Albuquerque: University of New Mexico Press, 1972), 142; Alfonso Ortiz, "San Juan Pueblo," in *Southwest*, ed. Alfonso Ortiz, *Handbook of North American Indians*, (Washington, D.C.: Smithsonian Institution, 1979), 9:279.

11. Hammond and Rey, *Don Juan de Oñate*, 1:140; Spicer, *Cycles of Conquest*, 385.

12. Smith, Handy, and Loetscher, *American Christianity*, 1:24; Hammond and Rey, *Don Juan de Oñate*, 110.

13. Ortiz, "Ritual Drama and the Pueblo World View," 137; Parson, *Pueblo Indian Religion*, 1:493.

14. Henry Warner Bowden, *American Indians and Christian Missions* (Chicago: University of Chicago Press, 1981), 50–51; Spicer, *Cycles of Conquest*, 380, 387.

15. Hammond and Rey, *Don Juan de Oñate*, 46; Hodge, Hammond, and Rey, *Benavides' Revised Memorial*, 53, 73; Perea, "True Report of the Great Conversion," 220.

16. Hodge, Hammond, and Rey, *Benavides' Revised Memorial*, 61, 71; Lincoln Bruce Speiss, "Church Music in Seventeenth-Century New Mexico," *New Mexico Historical Review* 40 (1965):5–21.

17. Parson, *Pueblo Indian Religion*, 1:393; Don L. Roberts, "The Ethnomusicology of the Eastern Pueblos," in *New Perspectives on the Pueblos*, 244.

18. White, "Pueblo of Santa Ana, New Mexico," 66; Albert H. Schroeder, "Rio Grande Ethnohistory," in *New Perspectives on the Pueblos*, 51; Perea, "True Report of the Great Conversion," 218; Hammond and Rey, *Don Juan de Oñate*, 147.

19. Hammond and Rey, *Don Juan de Oñate*, 158; Perea, "True Report of the Great Conversion," 215; Hodge, Hammond, and Rey, *Benavides' Revised Memorial*, 83; Edward P. Dozier, *The Pueblo Indians of North America* (New York: Holt, Rinehart, and Winston, 1970), 48; Marc Simmons, "History of Pueblo-Spanish Relations to 1821," in *Handbook of North American Indians*, 9:182; Spicer, *Cycles of Conquest*, 158, 424, 507.

20. Perea, "True Report of the Great Conversion," 217; Hodge, Hammond, and Rey, *Benavides' Revised Memorial*, 66; Wiget, "Truth and the Hopi," 185.

21. Hodge, Hammond, and Rey, *Benavides' Revised Memorial*, 176; Charles W. Hackett, ed., *Revolt of the Pueblo Indians of New Mexico and Otermin's Attempted Reconquest, 1680–1682* (Albuquerque: University of New Mexico Press, 1942), 8:25; Spicer, *Cycles of Conquest*, 159.

22. Hackett, ed., *Revolt of the Pueblo Indians*, 9:235.

23. Ibid., 8:62.

24. Ibid., 9:213.

25. Ibid., 8:26, 45, 102, 117, 177, 195.

26. Ibid., 9:247, 225, 240, 248, 239.

27. Bruce Trigger, *The Children of Aataentsic* (Montreal: McGill-Queens University Press, 1976), 1:75; Cornelius J. Jaenen, *Friend and Foe* (New York: Columbia University Press, 1976), 56; Conrad E. Heidenreich, "Huron," in *Northeast*, ed. Bruce Trigger, *Handbook of North American Indians*, 15:372.

28. Bowden, *American Indians and Christian Missions*, 73–74, 80; Trigger, *Children of Aataentsic*, 1:77; Bruce Trigger, *The Huron Farmers of the North* (New York: Holt, Rinehart, and Winston, 1969), 92; Heidenreich, "Huron," 373.

29. Trigger, *Huron Farmers of the North*, 96; James P. Ronda, "'We Are Well as We Are': An Indian Critique of Seventeenth-Century Christian Missions," *William and Mary Quarterly*, 3d ser., 34 (1977):66–82; Bowden, *American Indians and Christian Missions*, 75.

30. Thwaites, *Jesuit Relations*, 10:209, 15:179.

31. Cited by Axtell, *Invasion Within*, 50, 53.

32. James P. Ronda, "The European Indian: Jesuit Civilization Planning in New France," *Church History* 41 (1972):385–95; George R. Healy, "The French Jesuits and the Idea of the Noble Savage," *William and Mary Quarterly*, 3d ser., 15 (1958):150;

Thwaites, ed., *Jesuit Relations*, 8:161; Bruce Trigger, "The Jesuits and the Fur Trade," *Ethnohistory* 12 (1965):30–53.

33. Axtell, *Invasion Within*, 80–81, 101, 106; Thwaites, *Jesuit Relations*, 8:111.

34. Thwaites, *Jesuit Relations*, 6:177–81; Ronda, "The European Indian," 389; Ronda, "'We Are Well as We Are,'" 69–70.

35. Axtell, *Invasion Within*, 81–82, 88; Cornelius J. Jaenen, "Amerindian Views of French Culture in the Seventeenth Century," *Canadian Historical Review* 55 (1974):271.

36. Axtell, *Invasion Within*, 62.

37. Thwaites, *Jesuit Relations*, 83; Axtell, *Invasion Within*, 118–19; Wilfrid Jury and Elsie McLeod Jury, *Sainte-Marie among the Hurons* (Toronto: Oxford University Press, 1954), 4, 96.

38. Bowden, *American Indians and Christian Missions*, 75, 90; Trigger, *Children of Aataentsic*, 1:77; Trigger, *Huron Farmers of the North*, 92; Heidenreich, "Huron," 375.

39. Bowden, *American Indians and Christian Missions*, 69–70.

40. Axtell, *Invasion Within*, 125; Thwaites, *Jesuit Relations*, 27:143, 18:167.

41. Thwaites, *Jesuit Relations*, 60:137–39; Axtell, *Invasion Within*, 121; Jaenen, *Friend and Foe*, 47.

42. Thwaites, *Jesuit Relations*, 57:95, 16:247; Jaenen, "Amerindian Views of French Culture," 268–74.

43. Thwaites, *Jesuit Relations*, 61:37, 39:129–31; Jaenen, "Amerindian Views of French Culture," 274–76, and *Friend and Foe*, 56–57.

44. Thwaites, *Jesuit Relations*, 11:9, 10:17, 3:123; Ronda, "'We Are Well as We Are,'" 70; Trigger, "Jesuits and the Fur Trade," 45.

45. Trigger, "Jesuits and the Fur Trade," 46.

46. Neal Salisbury, *Manitou and Providence* (New York: Oxford University Press, 1982), 30, 36.

47. Williams, *Key into the Language of America*, 24, 111, 148, 157–58; William S. Simmons, *Cautantowwit's House* (Providence: Brown University Press, 1970), 50–62.

48. Williams, *Key into the Language of America*, 82, 148, 151; William S. Simmons, "Southern New England Shamanism: An Ethnographic Reconstruction," in *Papers of the Seventh Algonquian Conference, 1975*, ed. William Cowan (Ottowa: Carleton University, 1976), 218.

49. Williams, *Key into the Language of America*, 94, 148; Bowden, *American Indians and Christian Missions*, 103; Salisbury, *Manitou and Providence*, 238; Winslow, *Good Newes from New England*, 361.

50. Winslow, *Good Newes from New England*, 359; William S. Simmons, "Narragansett," in *Northeast*, 191; Williams, *Key into the Language of America*, 153, 197; Salisbury, *Manitou and Providence*, 35.

51. Morton, *New English Canaan*, 24; Henry W. Bowden and James P. Ronda, eds., *John Eliot's Indian Dialogues* (1671, reprint ed., Westport, Conn.: Greenwood Press, 1980), 87, 134; Winslow, *Good Newes from New England*, 356.

52. Winslow, *Good Newes from New England*, 357; [John Eliot?], *The Day-Breaking If Not the Sun-Rising of the Gospell with the Indians in New England* (London, 1647), *MHSC*, 3d ser. (1834), 4:20; Henry Whitfield, *Strength Out of Weakness* (London, 1652), *MHSC*, 3d ser. (1834), 4:186; Williams, *Key into the Language of America*, 213;

William S. Simmons, "Cultural Bias in New England Puritans' Perception of Indians," *William and Mary Quarterly*, 3d ser., 38 (1981):60; William S. Simmons, "Conversion from Indian to Puritan," *New England Quarterly* 52 (1979):197–218.

53. Winslow, *Good Newes from New England*, 116; Williams, *Key into the Language of America*, 152.

54. Morton, *New English Canaan*, 21; Wood, New England's Prospect, 100; Winslow, *Good Newes from New England*, 355; Simmons, "Cultural Bias in New England Puritans' Perception of Indians," 57–67.

55. Walker, *Creeds and Platforms*, 80.

56. Shepard, *Theses Sabbaticae*, 47; John Eliot and Thomas Mayhew, *Tears of Repentance* (London, 1653), *MHSC*, 3d ser. (1834), 4:117; James P. Walsh, "Holy Time and Sacred Space in Puritan New England," *American Quarterly* 32 (1980):87.

57. [Robert Cushman], "Reasons and Considerations Touching the Lawfulness of Removing out of England into the Parts of America," *Remarkable Providences, 1600–1760*, ed. John Demos (New York: George Braziller, 1972), 28; Axtell, *Invasion Within*, 155; Salisbury, *Manitou and Providence*, 180, 198; Ruth Barnes Moynihan, "The Patent and the Indians: The Problem of Jurisdiction in Seventeenth-Century New England," *American Indian Culture and Research Journal* 2 (1977–78):8–18. I am grateful to my colleague John Juricek for guidance on this difficult issue.

58. Axtell, *Invasion Within*, 139, 220; Robert Blair St. George, "'Set Thine House in Order': The Domestication of the Yeomanry in Seventeenth-Century New England," in *New England Begins*, 2:160–66.

59. Bradford, *Of Plymouth Plantation*, 97; Walsh, "Holy Time and Sacred Space in Puritan New England," 82, 87.

60. Shepard, *Theses Sabbaticae*, 3, 13.

61. John Norton, *The Answer to the Whole Set of Questions of the Celebrated Mr. William Apollonius*, trans. Douglas Horton (Cambridge: Harvard University Press, 1958), 144: Cotton, *Exposition upon the Thirteenth Chapter of the Revelation*, 117; E. Brooks Holifield, *The Covenant Sealed* (New Haven: Yale University Press, 1974), 139–68.

62. Cotton, *Exposition upon the Thirteenth Chapter of the Revelation*, 117; *The Whole Book of Psalmes Faithfully translated into English Metre* (Cambridge, Mass., 1640), n.p., 4; John Cotton, *Singing of Psalmes, A Gospel Ordinance* (London, 1647), 4, 5–17, 23.

63. [John White], *The Planters Plea* (London, 1630), in *Tracts and Other Papers*, 2:11; Francis Jennings, *The Invasion of America* (New York: W. W. Norton, 1976), 230; Axtell, *Invasion Within*, 218.

64. [Eliot], *Day-Breaking If Not the Sun-Rising of the Gospell*, 11, 15; Thomas Lechford, *Plain Dealing*, intro. Darrett B. Rutman (New York: Johnson Reprint Corporation, 1969), 55; Thomas Shepard, *The Clear Sun-Shine of the Gospel Breaking Forth upon the Indians of New England* (London, 1648), *MHSC*, 3d ser. (1834), 4:66; Wood, *New England's Prospect*, 96, 109; Salisbury, *Manitou and Providence*, 178; Henry Whitfield, *The Light Appearing More and More Towards the Perfect Day* (London, 1651), *MHSC*, 3d ser. (1834), 4:126; G. E. Thomas, "Puritans, Indians, and the Concept of Race," *New England Quarterly* 48 (1975):3–27.

65. [Eliot], *Day-Breaking If Not the Sun-Rising of the Gospell*, 4; Whitfield, *Strength out of Weakness*, 157; Whitfield, *Light Appearing More and More*, 120.

66. Whitfield, *Light Appearing More and More*, 133, 145; John Eliot, *The Glorious*

Progress of the Gospel, Amongst the Indians of New England (1649), *MHSC*, 3d ser. (1834), 4:82; Eliot, *Day-Breaking If Not the Sun-Rising of the Gospell*, 7; Bowden and Ronda, *John Eliot's Indian Dialogues*, 72, 104.

67. Cited by Axtell, *The Invasion Within*, 233; Shepard, *Clear Sun-Shine of the Gospel*, 47, 56–57; Eliot, *Glorious Progress of the Gospel*, 86–87; Bowden and Ronda, *John Eliot's Indian Dialogues*, 65, 71, 75, 84, 92.

68. Eliot, *Glorious Progress of the Gospel*, 88; Shepard, *Clear Sun-Shine of the Gospel*, 49–50; Eliot, *Day-Breaking If Not the Sun-Rising of the Gospell*, 15; Neal Salisbury, "Red Puritans: The 'Praying Indians' of Massachusetts Bay and John Eliot," *William and Mary Quarterly*, 3d. ser., 31 (1974):27–54.

69. Shepard, *Clear Sun-Shine of the Gospel*, 39; Whitfield, *Strength out of Weakness*, 171; Whitfield, *Light Appearing More and More*, 131; Axtell, *Invasion Within*, 141.

70. Bowden and Ronda, 66, 147; Shepard, *Clear Sun-Shine of the Gospel*, 25.

71. Bowden and Ronda, *John Eliot's Indian Dialogues*, 88; Shepard, *Clear Sun-Shine of the Gospel*, 51; Eliot, *Day-Breaking If Not the Sun-Rising of the Gospel*, 13.

72. Bowden and Ronda, *John Eliot's Indian Dialogues*, 95.

73. Cited by Jennings, *Invasion of America*, 241, 277; cited by Axtell, *Invasion Within*, 48.

74. Eliot and Mayhew, *Tears of Repentance*, 229, 231, 233, 234, 243, 246, 254.

75. John Winthrop, *Winthrop's Journal: "History of New England," 1630-1649*, ed. James Kendall Hosmer (New York: Charles Scribner's Sons, 1908), 2:124; Winslow, *Good Newes from New England*, 350; Simmons, "Conversion from Indian to Puritan," 202; Eliot, *Glorious Progress of the Gospel*, 77–78, Whitfield, *Light Appearing More and More*, 111.

76. Morton, *New English Canaan*, 18; Elise M. Brenner, "To Pray or to Be Prey: Strategies for Cultural Autonomy of Massachusetts Praying Town Indians," *Ethnohistory* 27 (1980):135–52; James Axtell, "Some Thoughts on the Ethnohistory of Missions," *Ethnohistory* 29 (1982):35–41.

77. Shepard, *Clear Sun-Shine of the Gospel*, 63.

78. John William Blake, ed., *Europeans in West Africa, 1450–1560* (London: Printed for the Hakluyt Society, 1942), 150–51; "The Second Voyage to Guinea" (1554), in Hakluyt, *Principal Navigations*, 6:167; Richard Jobson, *The Golden Trade* (London, 1623), 67.

79. Cited by Winthrop Jordan, *White over Black* (Baltimore: Penguin Books, 1969), 23; Jobson, *The Golden Trade*, 67; Albert Raboteau, *Slave Religion* (New York: Oxford University Press, 1978), 8, 9, 12; Samuel Purchas, "On the Religion and the Customs of the Peoples of Angola, Congo, and the Loango," in E. G. Ravenstein, ed., *The Strange Adventures of Andrew Battell* (London: For the Hakluyt Society, 1901), 73; John C. Inscoe, "Carolina Slave Names: An Index to Acculturation," *Journal of Southern History* 49 (1983):527–54; Roger Bastide, *African Civilisations in the New World*, trans. Peter Green (London: C. Hurst, 1967), 117.

80. Morgan Godwin, *The Negro's and Indians Advocate* (London, 1680), 33; Raboteau, *Slave Religion*, 13, 70; Jobson, *Golden Trade*, 57, 67; Ravenstein, *Strange Adventures*, 49.

81. Sidney W. Mintz and Richard Price, *An Anthropological Approach to the Afro-American Past* (Philadelphia: Institute for the Study of Human Issues, 1976), 1–26.

82. Wesley Frank Craven, *White, Red, and Black* (Charlottesville: University

Press of Virginia, 1971), 77; David Brion Davis, *The Problem of Slavery in Western Culture* (Ithaca: Cornell University Press, 1966), 8, 129; Jordan, *White over Black*, 63, 66, 73.

83. T. H. Breen and Stephen Innes, *"Myne Owne Ground"* (New York: Oxford University Press, 1980), 17.

84. Godwin, *Negro's and Indians Advocate*, 36; Winthrop Jordan, "Modern Tensions and the Origins of American Slavery," *Journal of Southern History* 28 (1962):18–30; "The Representation of New Netherland," in *Narratives of New Netherland*, 330, 364; Breen and Innes, *"Myne Owne Ground,"* 68–109.

85. Breen and Innes, *"Myne Owne Ground,"* 87; Hugh Hastings, ed., *Ecclesiastical Records of New York* (Albany: James B. Lyon, 1901), 1:548; Davis, *Problem of Slavery in Western Culture*, 98, 210; Godwin, *Negro's and Indians Advocate*, 140.

86. Godwin, *Negro's and Indians Advocate*, 19, 20, 36, 44, 124.

87. Ibid., 11, 13, 38–39, 40.

88. Ibid., 128; Davis, *Problem of Slavery in Western Culture*, 169.

89. Davis, *Problem of Slavery in Western Culture*, 144, 304; Jordan, *White over Black*, 194.

90. Godwin, *Negro's and Indians Advocate*, 39; Davis, *Problem of Slavery in Western Culture*, 118.

Chapter 5: Theologies of Persuasion

1. John Thomas Albro, *Life of Thomas Shepard*, *The Works of Thomas Shepard* (Boston: Doctrinal Tract and Book Society, 1853), 1:xxvi; Thomas Shepard, *The Parable of the Ten Virgins Opened and Applied* (London, 1660), 130; Shepard, *Subjection to Christ*, A3.

2. Edmund S. Morgan, ed., *The Diary of Michael Wigglesworth, 1653–1657* (New York: Harper & Row, 1965), V–viii; George Selement, *Keepers of the Vineyard* (Lanham, Md.: University Press of America, 1984), 1–97.

3. David D. Hall, "Understanding the Puritans, in *The State of American History*, ed. Herbert J. Bass (Chicago: Quadrangle Books, 1970), 330–49; George Marsden, "Perry Miller's Rehabilitation of the Puritans: A Critique," *Church History* 39 (1970):91–105; David D. Hall, "Religion and Society: Problems and Reconsiderations," in *Colonial British America*, 317–44; Michael McGiffert, "American Puritan Studies in the 1960s," *William and Mary Quarterly*, 3d ser., 27 (1970):36–37.

4. Albro, *Life of Thomas Shepard*, 27.

5. John Calvin, *Institutes of the Christian Religion*, ed. John T. McNeill, trans., Ford Lewis Battles (Philadelphia: Westminster Press, 1960), 1:183–228, John Norton, *The Orthodox Evangelist* (London, 1654), 51.

6. Norton, *Orthodox Evangelist*, 213.

7. Ibid., 19; Thomas Hooker, *The Saints Dignitie and Dutie* (London, 1651), 8; Thomas Hooker, *Heavens Treasury Opened in a Fruitfull Exposition of the Lord's Prayer* (London, 1645), 12.

8. Norton, *Orthodox Evangelist*, 35, 39, 40, 48, 49, 50; Hooker, *Saints Dignitie and Dutie*, 3–75.

9. Thomas Hooker, *The Unbelievers Preparing for Christ* (London, 1638), 160; Thomas Hooker, *The Soules Effectual Calling to Christ* (London, 1637), 64; Shepard, *Parable of the Ten Virgins*, 32; Norton, *Orthodox Evangelist*, 49.

10. Hooker, *Unbelievers Preparing for Christ*, 2; Thomas Hooker, *The Christians Two Chiefe Lessons* (London, 1640), 203; Thomas Hooker, *The Application of Redemption By the Effectual Work of the Word and Spirit of Christ for the Bringing Home of Lost Sinners to God, The Ninth and Tenth Books* (London, 1657), 197; Thomas Hooker, *The Soules Preparation for Christ, Or a Treatise of Contrition* (London, 1632), 40, 73; Thomas Hooker, *The Soules Implantation* (London, 1637), 61; John Cotton, *The Way of Life* (London, 1641), 134; Hooker, *Saints Dignitie and Dutie*, 135; Shepard, *Parable of the Ten Virgins*, 193.

11. Charles Lloyd Cohen, *God's Caress* (New York: Oxford University Press, 1986), 164; Morgan, *Diary of Wigglesworth*, 107–11; George Selement, "The Meeting of Elite and Popular Minds at Cambridge, New England, 1638–1645," *William and Mary Quarterly*, 3d. ser., 41 (1984):32–48.

12. Morgan, *Diary of Wigglesworth*, 123–25.

13. Shepard, *Sound Believer*, 17, and *Parable of the Ten Virgins*, 2:631.

14. Norton, *Orthodox Evangelist*, 270–71; Thomas Hooker, *The Paterne of Perfection* (London, 1640), 232; Hooker, *Unbelievers Preparing for Christ*, 202; Cotton, *Way of Life*, 274.

15. Thomas Hooker, *The Application of Redemption By the Effectual Work of the Word, and Spirit of Christ, for the Bringing Home of Lost Sinners to God* (London, 1656), 135; Shepard, *Theses Sabbaticae*, 25; Thomas Shepard, *Certain Select Cases Resolved*, (London, 1650), 42; Norton, *Orthodox Evangelist*, 271.

16. Norman Fiering, *Moral Philosophy at Seventeenth-Century Harvard* (Chapel Hill: University of North Carolina Press, 1981), 110.

17. Fiering, *Moral Philosophy*, 128.

18. Hooker, *Paterne of Perfection*, 120, 150, *Application of Redemption*, 48, and *Soules Preparation for Christ*, 31–32, 123.

19. Shepard, *Parable of Ten Virgins*, 147; Hooker, *Soules Vocation*, 72, and *Christians Two Chiefe Lessons*, 248.

20. Norton, *Orthodox Evangelist*, 213; Hooker, *Application of Redemption*, 353, and *Unbelievers Preparing for Christ*, 126.

21. Hooker, *Application of Redemption*, 387; Norton, *Orthodox Evangelist*, 65, 74.

22. Norton, *Orthodox Evangelist*, 114.

23. Ibid., 214; Hooker, *Unbelievers Preparing for Christ*, 27; John Cotton, *A Brief Exposition with Practicall Observations upon the Whole Book of Ecclesiastes* (London, 1654), 65.

24. William Ames, *The Marrow of Sacred Divinity* (London, 1642), 51.

25. Shepard, *Subjection to Christ in All His Ordinances*, 55.

26. Peter Ramus, *The Logike of the Most Excellent Philosopher P. Ramus Martyr*, trans. M. Roll (London, 1581), 17–18; Walter J. Ong, *Ramus: Method and the Decay of Dialogue* (Boston: Harvard University Press, 1958), 136, 200, 270–92.

27. Robert Letham, "The *Foedus Operum*: Some Factors Accounting for Its Development," *Sixteenth Century Journal* 14 (1983):464–66.

28. Peter Bulkeley, *The Gospel-Covenant; Or the Covenant of Grace Opened* 2d ed. (London, 1651), 31–34, 114; Hooker, *Saints Dignitie and Dutie*, 33, 81, *Paterne of Perfection*, 210, and *Application of Redemption*, 25; John Cotton, *The Covenant of Gods Free Grace* (London, 1645), 11–13.

29. Michael McGiffert, "Grace and Works: The Rise and Division of Covenant Divinity in Elizabethan Puritanism," *Harvard Theological Review* 75 (1982):463–502.

30. Ibid., 492–95; William K. B. Stoever, *"A Faire and Easie Way to Heaven"* (Middletown, Conn.: Wesleyan University Press, 1978), 82; Jens C. Moeller, "The Beginnings of Puritan Covenant Theology," *Journal of Ecclesiastical History* 14 (1963):46–67; Michael McGiffert, "William Tyndale's Conception of Covenant," *Journal of Ecclesiastical History* 32 (1981):167–84; Michael McGiffert, "Covenant, Crown, and Commons in Elizabethan Puritanism," *Journal of British Studies* 20 (1980):32–52; Cohen, *God's Caress*, 56.

31. Thomas Hooker, *The Faithful Covenanter* (London, 1644), 13; Bulkeley, *Gospel-Covenant*, 102, 147.

32. Shepard, *Parable of the Ten Virgins*, 5, 28; John Cotton, *The New Covenant* (London, 1655), 21; Bulkeley, *Gospel-Covenant*, 129. See also Cotton, *The Way of Life*, 229, and *New Covenant*, 136; Calvin, *Institutes*, 2:354–62.

33. Bulkeley, *Gospel-Covenant*, 56–61; Cotton, *Covenant of Gods Free Grace*, 11–13; Hooker, *Application of Redemption*, 25.

34. Hooker, *The Christians Two Chiefe Lessons*, 211, 213.

35. Norton, *Orthodox Evangelist*, 85; Hooker, *Soules Vocation*, 199.

36. Charles E. Hambrick-Stowe, *The Practice of Piety* (Chapel Hill: University of North Carolina Press, 1982), 54–90.

37. Hooker, *Soules Vocation*, 514, 608; Bulkeley, *Gospel-Covenant*, 313, 323, 324; Shepard, *Parable of the Ten Virgins*, 130.

38. Cotton, *New Covenant*, 18, 29; Shepard, *Certain Select Cases Resolved*, 13; Hooker, *Unbelievers Preparing for Christ*, 40; Bulkeley, *Gospel-Covenant*, 80, 382. See also Shepard, *Sound Believer*, 167, and see Michael McGiffert, "The Problem of the Covenant in Puritan Thought: Peter Bulkeley's *Gospel Covenant*," *New England Historical and Genealogical Register* 130 (1976):107–29, for a slightly different view of Bulkeley.

39. Bulkeley, *Gospel-Covenant*, 383.

40. Thomas Hooker, *The Covenant of Grace Opened* (London, 1649), 2, 20, 41–44; Thomas Shepard, *The Church Membership of Children and Their Right to Baptisme* (Cambridge, Mass., 1663), 2, 6; John Cotton, *The Grounds and Ends of the Baptisme of the Children of the Faithfull* (London, 1647), 43, 53, 54.

41. Walker, *Creeds and Platforms of Congregationalism*, 224; Cotton, *Grounds and Ends of the Baptisme*, 125, 145–46, and *Of the Holinesse of Church-Members*, 19, 41.

42. Albro, *Life of Thomas Shepard*, clxxxvii; Giles Firmin, *The Real Christian* (London, 1670), 2, 8; Thomas Shepard, *The First Principles of the Oracles of God* (London, 1650), 77.

43. Thomas Hooker, "To the Reader," in John Rogers, *The Doctrine of Faith* (London, 1632; 1st ed., 1627), n.p.; Cotton, *Way of Life*, 12, and *New Covenant*, 25; Bulkeley, *Gospel-Covenant*, 334–35, 370.

44. Hooker, *Soules Implantation*, 61, 68–69; Cotton, *Way of Life*, 139; Firmin, *Real Christian*, 55; Shepard, *Sound Believer*, 94.

45. Shepard, *First Principles of the Oracles of God*, 77; Hooker, *Soules Humiliation*, 112; Firmin, *Real Christian*, 108; Hooker, *Unbelievers Preparing for Christ*, 33, *The Saints Guide* (London, 1645), 160, and *The Soules Ingrafting into Christ* (London, 1638), 6; Shepard, *Sound Believer*, 125.

46. Hooker, *The Christians Two Chiefe Lessons*, 251, and *Soules Vocation or Effectual Calling to Christ*, 344; Cohen, *God's Caress*, 87, n.35; David D. Hall, ed., *The Antinom-*

ian Controversy, 1636–1638 (Middletown, Conn.: Wesleyan University Press, 1968), 177; Cotton, *Way of Congregational Churches Cleared*, 76; Norton, *Orthodox Evangelist*, 166.

47. John Hart [Jasper Heartwell], *The Firebrand Taken Out of the Fire* (London, 1654), 119, 124, 148; Cohen, *God's Caress*, 84–85, 87 n.35, Norton, *Orthodox Evangelist*, 166, 168.

48. Hooker, *Unbelievers Preparing for Christ*, 2, 8, 10, *Application of Redemption*, 151, and *Soules Vocation*, 289, 338.

49. Shepard, *Certain Select Cases Resolved*, 42–43, and *First Principles of the Oracles of God*, 289; Hambrick-Stowe, *Practice of Piety*, 197–241.

50. Hall, *Antinomian Controversy*, 26, 29, 30.

51. Ibid., 30.

52. Cotton, *Way of Congregational Churches Cleared*, 53; Hall, *Antinomian Controversy*, 32.

53. Hall, *Antinomian Controversy*, 85, 87, 92, 107, 144.

54. Ibid., 76, 102; Stoever, *"Faire and Easie Way to Heaven,"* 34–80.

55. Hall, *Antinomian Controversy*, 85, 104.

56. Ibid., 183, 186.

57. Ibid., 80.

58. Hall, *Antinomian Controversy*, 143; Stoever, *"Faire and Easie Way to Heaven,"* 34–57.

59. Hall, *Antinomian Controversy*, 122.

60. Michael McGiffert, ed., *God's Plot* (Amherst: University of Massachusetts Press, 1972), 74; Hall, *Antinomian Controversy*, 417; Johnson, *Wonder-Working Providence*, 125; Jonathan Mitchell and Thomas Shepard, Jr., "To the Reader," in Shepard, *Parable of the Ten Virgins*, n.p.

61. Willard, *Compleat Body*, 119–21, 123.

62. Ibid., 118, 122, 123.

63. William Ames, *Of Conscience, and the Cases Thereof* (London, 1643), 1:13–14. Gail Thain Parker, "Jonathan Edwards and Melancholy" *New England Quarterly* 41 (1968):195, 197.

64. Shepard, *Parable of the Ten Virgins*, 147; Willard, *Compleat Body*, 211; Hooker, *Survey of the Summe*, 160.

65. Hooker, *Saints Guide*, 94–95, 97; Thomas Shepard, *The Sincere Convert*, in *Works*, 1:10; Hooker, *Unbelievers Preparing for Christ*, 87; Norton, *Orthodox Evangelist*, 1; Thomas Hooker, *An Exposition of the Principles of Religion* (London, 1645), 1–2, and *Heavens Treasury Opened* (London, 1644), 6.

66. Willard, *Compleat Body*, 33–40, 592–98.

67. John Davenport, *The Saints Anchor-Hold* (London, 1682), 34, 52, 62.

68. Walker, *Creeds and Platforms of Congregationalism*, 330; Jonathan Mitchell, "An Answer to the Apologetical Preface," in [Richard Mather], *A Defense of the Answer and Arguments of the Synod Met at Boston in the Year 1662* (Cambridge, Mass., 1644), 44–45; John Davenport, *Another Essay for the Investigation of the Truth* (Cambridge, Mass., 1663), 29–30; Increase Mather, *A Call from Heaven to the Present and Succeeding Generations* (Boston, 1679), 31.

69. Increase Mather, *Returning unto God the Great Concernment of a Covenant People* (Boston, 1680), 8; Samuel Willard, *The Duty of a People That Have Renewed Their Cov-*

enant with God (Boston, 1680), 5; Robert C. Pope, *The Half-Way Covenant* (Princeton: Princeton University Press, 1969), 241.

70. Hall, *Faithful Shepherd*, 249–69; Increase Mather, *Returning unto God*, 8.

Chapter 6: Dissenters

1. [Nathaniel Ward], *The Simple Cobler of Aggawam in America* (London, 1647), in *Tracts and Other Papers*, 3:9–10.

2. Michael R. Watts, *The Dissenters* (Oxford: Oxford University Press, 1978), 7–26.

3. John Taylor, *A Swarm of Sectaries and Schismatiques* (London, 1641), 7, cited by ibid., 80.

4. Philip F. Gura, *A Glimpse of Sion's Glory* (Middletown, Conn.: Wesleyan University Press, 1984), 32, citing anon., *A Blow at the Root* (London, 1650), 151–52.

5. Roger Williams, *Mr Cotton's Letter Lately Printed, Examined and Answered* (London, 1644), *PNC*, 1st ser., 6 vols. (Providence, R.I.: Providence Press, 1866), 1:97.

6. Morton, *New English Canaan*, 118; Bradford, *Of Plymouth Plantation*, 206; Morton, *New Englands Memoriall*, 76.

7. Morton, *New Englands Memoriall*, 76; Hubbard, *General History*, xv, 117; David D. Hall, "John Cotton's Letter to Samuel Skelton," *William and Mary Quarterly*, 3d ser., 22 (1965):478–85.

8. Winthrop, *Journal*, 1:62, 168; Williams, *Mr. Cotton's Letter*, 94.

9. Williams, *Mr. Cotton's Letter*, 91; John Cotton, *A Letter of Mr. John Cotton Teacher of the Church in Boston in New England to Mr. Williams* (London, 1643), *PNC*, 1:24; Morton, *New Englands Memoriall*, 79; Winthrop, *Journal*, 1:157; Edmund S. Morgan, *Roger Williams* (New York: Harcourt, Brace, and World, 1967), 3–27.

10. Roger Williams, *The Bloudy Tenent of Persecution, for Cause of Conscience, Discussed, in a Conference betweene Truth and Peace* (London, 1644), *PNC*, 3:334; Cotton, *Letter of Mr. John Cotton's*, 14–21; Williams, *Mr. Cotton's Letter*, 74–90; C. Leonard Allen, "'The Restauration of Zion': Roger Williams and the Quest for the Primitive Church" (Ph.D. diss., University of Iowa, 1984).

11. Morton, *New Englands Memoriall*, 79, 82; Winthrop, *Journal*, 1:149; Williams, *Mr. Cotton's Letter*, 105; Morgan, *Roger Williams*, 29–33.

12. Winthrop, *Journal*, 1:116–17, 154; Morgan, *Roger Williams*, 122; Williams, *Bloudy Tenent of Persecution*, 119.

13. Williams, *Bloudy Tenent of Persecution*, 77, 97, 119, 129, 146.

14. Ibid., 354; Cotton, *Bloudy Tenent, Washed*, 68; Roger Williams, *The Bloody Tenent Yet More Bloody by Mr. Cottons Endeavour to Wash It White in the Blood of the Lambe* (London, 1652), *PNC*, 4:450; W. Clark Gilpin, *The Millenarian Piety of Roger Williams* (Chicago: University of Chicago Press, 1979), 40–42.

15. Williams, *Bloudy Tenent of Persecution*, 250; Sacvan Bercovitch, "Typology in Puritan New England: The Williams-Cotton Controversy Reassessed," *American Quarterly* 19 (1967):166–91.

16. Roger Williams, *The Hireling Ministry None of Christs* (London, 1652), *The Complete Writings of Roger Williams*, ed. Perry Miller (New York: Russell and Russell, 1963), 7:158, 160; Roger Williams, *Queries of Highest Consideration* (London, 1644), *PNC*, 2:21, 29.

17. Hall, ed., *Antinomian Controversy*, 268, 272, 308.

18. Emery Battis, *Saints and Sectaries* (Chapel Hill: University of North Carolina Press, 1962), 249–89; Johnson, *Wonder-Working Providence*, 192.

19. Hall, *Antinomian Controversy*, 308.

20. Ibid., 264, 302, 306.

21. Ibid., 264, 326, 333, 235.

22. Ibid., 333, 339, 216.

23. Johnson, *Wonder-Working Providence*, 129; Williams cited by Edward Winslow, *Hypocrisie Unmasked* (London, 1646), 55–56.

24. Winslow, *Hypocrisie Unmasked*, 7, 56; Gura, *Glimpse of Sion's Glory*, 278–300.

25. Gura, *Glimpse of Sion's Glory*, 292; "Samuel Gorton's Letter to Nathanial Morton, Warwick, June 30th, 1669," in *Tracts and Other Papers*, 4:3.

26. Winslow, *Hypocrisie Unmasked*, 7, 49, 58; Gura, *Glimpse of Sion's Glory*, 295; Samuel Gorton, *Simplicities Defence against Seven-Headed Policy* (London, 1646), 27, 68, 104, 109.

27. Gura, *Glimpse of Sion's Glory*, 104, 119.

28. Nathaniel Shurtleff, ed., *Records of the Governor and Company of the Massachusetts Bay in New England* (Boston: W. White, 1854–61), 1:85.

29. Charles Francis Adams, *Antinomianism in the Colony of Massachusetts Bay, 1636–1638* (Boston: Prince Society, 1894), 183–84; Winslow, *Hypocrisie Unmasked*, 26; Winthrop, *Journal*, 1:297; William G. McLoughlin, *New England Dissent, 1630–1833* (Cambridge: Harvard University Press, 1971, 1:16.

30. John Clark, *Ill Newes from New England* (London, 1652), 13.

31. Cited by McLoughlin, *New England Dissent*, 1:21; Isaac Backus, *A History of New England with Particular Reference to the Baptists* (1777–95, reprint ed., Newton, Mass.: Backus Historical Society, 1871), 1:290, 292.

32. Francis Howgill, *The Popish Inquisition Newly Erected in New-England* (London, 1659), 11, 48; Melvin B. Endy, Jr., *William Penn and Early Quakerism* (Princeton: Princeton University Press, 1973), 60, 68.

33. Endy, *William Penn and Early Quakerism*, 55, 82; Arthur J. Worrall, *Quakers in the Colonial Northeast* (Hanover, N.H.: University Press of New England, 1980), 36–37.

34. Roger Williams, *George Fox Digg'd Out of His Burrowes* (Boston, 1676), *PNC*, 5:49, 102.

35. Williams, *Mr. Cotton's Letter*, 31, 53, 96; Williams, *Bloudy Tenent of Persecution*, 243.

36. Hall, *Antinomian Controversy*, 309; Clark, *Ill Newes from New-England*, 3, 49–51.

37. Howgill, *Popish Inquisition*, 17; Worrall, *Quakers in the Colonial Northeast*, 19.

38. Williams, *George Fox Digg'd Out*, 266.

39. Thomas Shepard, *New Englands Lamentations for Old Englands Present Errours* (London, 1645), 2; Gilpin, *Millenarian Piety of Roger Williams*, 143; Johnson, *Wonder-Working Providence*, 127, 173.

40. McLoughlin, *New England Dissent*, 1:56; "Samuel Gorton's Letter to Nathanial Morton," 14.

41. Roger Williams, *The Hireling Ministry None of Christs* (London, 1652), in *Complete Writings*, 7:163, 167; Williams, *George Fox Digg'd Out*, 146.

42. Winthrop, *Journal*, 1:116; Hall, *Antinomian Controversy*, 314; Gura, *Glimpse of Sion's Glory*, 297; Thomas Shepard, Preface to George Phillips, *Reply to a Confutation of some Grounds for Infants Baptisme* (London, 1645), n.p.

43. John Cotton, *The True Constitution of a Particular Visible Church, Proved by Scripture* (London, 1642), 6; Larzer Ziff, ed., *John Cotton on the Churches of New England* (Cambridge: Harvard University Press, 1968), 112.

44. Hall, *Faithful Shepherd*, 48–71.

45. Demos, *Entertaining Satan*, 78, 247.

46. Morgan, *American Slavery, American Freedom*, 152; Smith, Handy, and Loetscher, *American Christianity*, 1:37.

47. Hall, *Antinomian Controversy*, 209; Winslow, *Hypocrisie Unmasked*, 9–34, 42–43.

48. Hugh Barbour, "From the Lamb's War to the Quaker Magistrate," *Quaker History* 55 (1966):3–23; Worrall, *Quakers in The Colonial Northeast*, 28–29; James Bowden, *The History of the Society of Friends in America* (London: Charles Gilpin, 1850) 1:273; Smith, Handy, and Loetscher, *American Christianity*, 1:176.

49. John Childe, *New Englands Jonas Cast Up at London* (London, 1647), in *Tracts and Other Papers*, 4:9, 12; Gura, *Glimpse of Sion's Glory*, 304–28.

50. Jonathan M. Chu, *Neighbors, Friends, and Madmen* (Westport, Conn.: Greenwood Press, 1985), 59–84; Bowden, *History of the Society of Friends in America*, 1:154.

51. Hall, *Antinomian Controversy*, 206, 365; Johnson, *Wonder-Working Providence*, 132, 186; Gura, *Glimpse of Sion's Glory*, 299; Bowden, *History of the Society of Friends*, 1:40, 42, 126–40; Mary Maples Dunn, "Saints and Sisters: Congregational and Quaker Women in the Early Colonial History," *American Quarterly* 30 (1978): 582–601; Lyle Koehler, "The Case of the American Jezebels," *William and Mary Quarterly*, 3d ser., 31 (1974):55–78.

52. Winthrop, *Journal*, 2:138; McLoughlin, *New England Dissent*, 1:16; Williams, *George Fox Digg'd Out*, 19; Dunn, "Saints and Sisters," 596.

53. Cotton, *The Bloudy Tenent, Washed*, 12, 22, 33.

54. John Norton, *The Heart of N-England Rent at the Blasphemies of the Present Generation* (Cambridge, Mass., 1659), 51–53; Hubbard, *Happiness of a People*, 38.

55. Benavides, *Memorial of Fray Alonso de Benavides*, 69; Scholes, *Church and State in New Mexico*, 9, 17, 86, 128.

56. "Articles, Lawes, and Orders, Divine Politique, and Martiall for the Colony of Virginia" (London, 1612), in *Tracts and Other Papers*, 3:10, 17; Davis, *Intellectual Life in the Colonial South*, 2:633, 646; J. P. Kennedy and H. R. McIlwaine, eds., *Journals of the House of Burgesses of Virginia* (Richmond: n.p., 1905–15), 1:13, 36; John D. Krugler, "'With Promise of Liberty in Religion': The Catholic Lords Baltimore and Toleration in Seventeenth-Century Maryland, 1634–1692," *Maryland Historical Magazine* 79 (1984):21–43.

57. William Hening, ed., *The Statutes at Large; Being a Collection of All the Lawes of Virginia* (New York: n.p., 1810–23), 2:517; Breen, *Puritans and Adventurers*, 180.

58. Cynthia Z. Stiverson and Gregory A. Stiverson, "The Colonial Retail Book Trade: Availability and Affordability of Reading Material in Mid-Eighteenth-Century Virginia," in *Printing and Society in Early America*, 139–40; William H. Seiler, "The Church of England as the Established Church in Seventeenth-Century Virginia," *Journal of Southern History* 15 (1949):478–508; Kenneth L. Carroll, "Quakerism

on the Eastern Shore of Virginia," *Virginia Magazine of History and Biography* 74 (1966):170–89; Darrett B. Rutman, "The Evolution of Religious Life in Early Virginia," *Lex et Scientia* 14 (1978):190–214.

59. Albert Cook Myers, ed., *Narratives of Early Pennsylvania, West New Jersey, and Delaware, 1630–1707* (New York: Charles Scribner's Sons, 1912), 121, 150; Amandus Johnson, *The Swedish Settlements on the Delaware, 1638–1664* (Baltimore: Genealogical Publishing Co., 1969), 1:205, 366; Amandus Johnson, *The Instructions for Johan Printz: Governor of New Sweden* (Philadelphia: Swedish Colonial Society, 1930), 33, 150, 155, 163; Thomas Campanius Holm, *Description of the Province of New Sweden*, trans. Peter S. DuPonceau (1834, reprint ed., Milwood, N.Y.: Kraus Reprint Co., 1975), 92.

60. DeJong, *Dutch Reformed Church in the American Colonies*, 34.

61. Jameson, *Narratives of New Netherland*, 260; Hastings, *Ecclesiastical Records of New York*, 1:396–97; Frank Melville Kerr, "The Reverend Richard Denton and the Coming of the Presbyterians," *New York History* 21 (1940):180–86.

62. Smith, Handy, and Loetscher, *American Christianity*, 1:72–74; Hastings, *Ecclesiastical Records of New York*, 1:400.

63. Jameson, *Narratives of New Netherland*, 302.

64. Ibid.; Philip Sandler, "Earliest Jewish Settlers in New York," *New York History* 36 (1955):39–50.

65. Smith, *Religion and Trade in New Netherland*, 231–34.

66. Backus, *History of New England*, 1:249; Jameson, *Narratives of New Netherland*, 400; Carl N. Everstine, "Maryland's Toleration Act: An Appraisal," *Maryland Historical Magazine* 79 (1984):99–116.

67. "Instructions to the Colonists by Lord Baltimore, 1633," in *Narratives of Early Maryland*, 16; Everstine, "Maryland's Toleration Act," 99–116; Krugler, "'With Promise of Liberty in Religion,'" 21–43; Menard, "Population, Economy, and Society in Seventeenth-Century Maryland," 71–92.

68. Kenneth L. Carroll, "Elizabeth Harris: The Founder of American Quakerism," *Quaker History* 57 (1968):96–111; Kenneth L. Carroll, "Persecution of the Quakers in Early Maryland (1658–1661)," *Quaker History* 53 (1964):67–80; Krugler, "'With Promise of Liberty in Religion,'" 36.

Chapter 7: Rulers

1. "The Magistrates of Gravesend to the Directors at Amsterdam" (1651), in *Documents Relative to the Colonial History of the State of New York*, ed. E. B. O'Callaghan (Albany, N.Y.: Weed, Parson, & Co., 1856), 2:155; "Petition of the Commonalty of New Netherland to the States General" (1649), in *Documents*, 1:166.

2. Norton, *Heart of N-England Rent*, 30–31.

3. Ibid., 30; Alsop, *Character of the Province of Maryland*, 354; Hubbard, *Happiness of a People*, 10.

4. Norman H. Dawes, "Titles as Symbols of Prestige in Seventeenth-Century New England," in *Class and Society in Early America*, ed. Gary B. Nash (Englewood Cliffs, N.J.: Prentice-Hall, 1970), 89–99.

5. Rutman and Rutman, *A Place in Time*, 129; Rowland Berthoff, *An Unsettled People* (New York: Harper & Row, 1971), 88; Kenneth A. Lockridge, *A New England Town* (New York: W. W. Norton, 1970), 16; G. M. Brydon, *Virginia's Mother Church*

and the Political Conditions Under Which It Grew (Richmond: Virginia Historical Society, 1947), 23; Karin Calvert, "Children in American Family Portraiture, 1670 to 1810," *William and Mary Quarterly*, 3d ser., 39 (1982):87–113; Hening, *Statutes at Large*, 1:127, 146.

6. Norton, *Heart of N-England Rent*, 39–40; *Winthrop Papers* (Boston: Massachusetts Historical Society, 1943), 4:162; Berkeley, *Discourse and View of Virginia*, 8; John C. Rainbolt, "The Alteration in the Relationship between Leadership and Constituents in Virginia, 1660–1720," *William and Mary Quarterly*, 3d ser., 27 (1970):416, 426; William A. Reavis, "The Maryland Gentry and Social Mobility, 1637–1676," *William and Mary Quarterly*, 3d ser., 14 (1957):425.

7. "Complaint from Heaven with a Huy and a Crye and a Petition out of Virginia and Maryland" (1676), *Archives of Maryland* (Baltimore: Maryland Historical Society, 1887), 5:135; Cheever, *Journal of the Pilgrims at Plymouth*, 21; Hooker, *Survey of the Summe*, 188.

8. "Complaint from Heaven," 135, 138; J. Mills Thornton III, "The Thrusting Out of Governor Harvey: A Seventeenth-Century Rebellion," *Virginia Magazine of History and Biography* 76 (1968):19.

9. Jonathan Mitchell, *Nehemiah on the Wall in Troublesome Times* (Cambridge, Mass., 1671), 12; Langdon G. Wright, "Local Government and Central Authority in New Netherland," *New-York Historical Society Quarterly* 57 (1973):15; Richard Green, *Virginia's Cure: Or an Advisive Concerning Virginia* (London, 1662), in *Tracts and Other Papers*, 3:4; George B. Curtis, "The Colonial County Court: Social Forum and Legislative Precedent," *Virginia Magazine of History and Biography* 85 (1977):274–88; Cheever, *Journal of the Pilgrims*, 30; Norton, *Heart of N-England Rent*, 30; "Complaint from Heaven," 141; John Langford, *Refutation of Babylon's Fall* (London, 1655), in *Narratives of Early Maryland*, 265; *Winthrop Papers*, 4:360; Johnson, *Wonder-Working Providence*, 124.

10. "Complaint from heaven," 138; "Copy of a Letter from Mr. Cotton to Lord Say and Seal in the Year 1636," in Thomas Hutchinson, *The History of the Colony and Province of Massachusetts Bay*, ed. Lawrence Shaw Mayo (Cambridge: Harvard University Press, 1936), 1:417; Johnson, *Wonder-Working Providence*, 207.

11. Cotton, *Exposition upon the Thirteenth Chapter of the Revelation*, 71.

12. Morgan, ed., *Puritan Political Ideas*, 36, 50, 51.

13. Winthrop, *Journal*, 2:238.

14. Stephen Foster, *Their Solitary Way* (New Haven: Yale University Press, 1971), 17; "Magistrates of Gravesend to the Directors at Amsterdam," 155; in Brown, *Genesis of the United States*, "Letter to William Pond" (1630), in John Demos, ed., *Remarkable Providences, 1600–1760* (New York: George Braziller, 1972), 74.

15. *Winthrop Papers*, 3:241, 432; Richard S. Dunn, *Puritans and Yankees* (Princeton: Princeton University Press, 1962), 75, 77; Jones, *Congregational Commonwealth*, 164.

16. Bradford, *Plymouth Plantation*, appendix IV, 370.

17. Brown, *Genesis of the United States*, 1:413; Berkeley, *Discourse and View of Virginia*, 3; Foster, *Their Solitary Way*, 17; *Winthrop Papers*, 3:437; Johnson, *Wonder-Working Providence*, passim.

18. "Certain Proposals Made by Lord Say, Lord Brooke, and Other Persons of Quality," in Hutchinson, *History*, 1:411–12.

19. [John Cotton], *An Abstract of the Lawes of New England* (London, 1641), in *Tracts and Other Papers*, 3:3; Richard L. Bushman, *From Puritan to Yankee* (Cambridge: Harvard University Press, 1967), 12.

20. "Copy of a Letter from Mr. Cotton to Lord Say and Seal," 415–16.

21. *Winthrop Papers*, 4:54, 383; "A Replye to the Answer Made to the Discourse about the Negative Vote," in Robert C. Winthrop, *Life and Letters of John Winthrop* (Boston: Little, Brown, 1895), 2:430, 435; Winthrop, *Journal*, 1:303.

22. Winthrop, *Journal*, 2:238.

23. Howard M. Chapin, ed., *Documentary History of Rhode Island* (Providence: Preston and Rounds, 1919), 1:100; Sydney V. James, *Colonial Rhode Island* (New York: Charles Scribner's Sons, 1975), 61–63; "The Fundamental Constitutions of Carolina," in *The Colonial Records of North Carolina*, ed. William L. Saunders (Raleigh: P. M. Hale, 1886), 1:188–89.

24. "Copy of a Letter from Mr. Cotton to Lord Say and Seal," 415; *Winthrop Papers*, 4:383; Haskins, *Law and Authority*, 44.

25. David S. Lovejoy, "Equality and Empire: The New York Charter of Libertyes, 1683," *William and Mary Quarterly*, 3d ser., 21 (1964):493–515.

26. Bernard Bailyn, "Politics and Social Structure in Virginia," in *Seventeenth-Century America: Essays in Colonial History*, ed. Morton Smith (Chapel Hill: University of North Carolina Press, 1959), 90–115.

27. David W. Jordan, "Maryland's Privy Council, 1637–1715," in *Law, Society, and Politics in Early Maryland*, ed. Aubrey C. Land, Lois Green Carr, and Edward C. Papenfuse (Baltimore: Johns Hopkins University Press, 1977), 65; Reavis, "Maryland Gentry and Social Mobility," 422; David W. Jordan, "Political Stability and the Emergence of a Native Elite in Maryland," in *The Chesapeake in the Seventeenth Century: Essays on Anglo-American Society and Politics*, ed. Thad W. Tate and David L. Ammerman (New York: W. W. Norton, 1979), 243–73.

28. Hening, *Statutes at Large*, 1:517, 537; *MHSP*, 58 (1924–25), 456–57; Foster, *Their Solitary Way*, 79.

29. Foster, *Their Solitary Way*, 90; Johnson, *Wonder-Working Providence*, 76; Jones, *Congregational Commonwealth*, 180; Dunn, *Puritans and Yankees*, 79.

30. O'Callaghan, *Documents*, 1:212, 213, 298, 309.

31. Ibid., 213.

32. Jones, *Congregational Commonwealth*, 71; Cotton, *Exposition upon the Thirteenth Chapter of the Revelation*, 72.

33. Jones, *Congregational Commonwealth*, 71; Cotton, *Exposition upon the Thirteenth Chapter of the Revelation*, 72; *Winthrop Papers*, 3:423; anon., *The Lord Baltemore's Case* (London, 1653), in *Narratives of Early Maryland*, 174.

34. *Winthrop Papers*, 4:170; Cheever, *Journal of the Pilgrims*, 30; Jones, *Congregational Commonwealth*, 79; Lockridge, *A New England Town*, 5–6.

35. Winthrop, *Journal*, 2:238; *Winthrop Papers*, 4:390; Mitchell, *Nehemiah on the Wall in Troublesome Times*, 25.

36. Winthrop, *Journal*, 1:74.

37. Ibid., 172; Bruce, *Institutional History*, 2:352; 468; Jordan, "Political Stability and the Emergence of a Native Elite in Maryland," 264; O'Callaghan, *Documents*, 1:310.

38. "Proceedings of the Virginia Assembly, 1619," in *Narratives of Early Virginia*,

277; Warren M. Billings, ed., *The Old Dominion in the Seventeenth Century* (Chapel Hill: University of North Carolina Press, 1975), 38, 51.

39. Aubrey C. Land, *Colonial Maryland* (Millwood, N.Y.: KTO Press, 1981), 38.

40. Menard, "Maryland's Time of Troubles," 136.

41. Anon., *Virginia and Maryland, Or, the Lord Baltamore's Printed Case, Uncased and Answered* (London, 1655), in *Tracts and Other Papers*, 2:12, 24; anon., *Lord Baltemore's Case*, 174; "Complaint from Heaven," 138.

42. Winthrop, *Journal*, 1:134.

43. Ibid.

44. *Winthrop Papers*, 4:383, 386.

45. Ibid., 360, 388.

46. Winthrop, *Journal*, 1:151, 196; *Abstract of the Lawes of New England*, 3–17; *Winthrop Papers*, 4:81; Timothy H. Breen, *The Character of the Good Ruler* (New Haven: Yale University Press, 1970), 71.

47. Haskins, *Law and Authority*, 128–30; Winthrop, *Journal*, 1:50.

48. Winthrop, *Journal*, 1:51.

49. Ibid., 2:213–16.

50. Ibid., 2:241; *Winthrop Papers*, 4:468, 474, 476.

51. Winthrop, *Journal*, 2:238, 242–43.

52. Warden, "Rhode Island Civil Code of 1647," 138–51.

53. Hutchinson, *History of New England*, 1:370.

54. Winthrop, *Journal*, 2:49; Rutman, *Winthrop's Boston*, 46; Foster, *Their Solitary Way*, 69.

55. Bruce, *Institutional History*, 2:358; Warren M. Billings, "The Growth of Political Institutions in Virginia, 1634 to 1676," *William and Mary Quarterly*, 3d ser., 31 (1974):225–42; Menard, "Maryland's Time of Troubles," 124; Land, *Colonial Maryland*, 62.

56. John Eliot, *The Harmony of the Gospels* (Boston, 1678), 34–35; Land, *Colonial Maryland*, 70.

57. Foster, *Their Solitary Way*, 128; Hooker, *Christians Two Chiefe Lessons*, 65.

58. Eliot, *Harmony of the Gospels*, 36; Cotton, *Practical Commentaries on the Epistle of John* (1658), 132, cited by David Shi, *The Simple Life* (New York: Oxford University Press, 1985), 11–12; Cotton, *Treatise of the Covenant of Grace*, 223; Hooker, *Paterne of Perfection*, 294; see Shepard, *Parable of the Ten Virgins*, 18.

59. Winthrop, *Journal*, 1:515–16; Bernard Bailyn, *The New England Merchants in the Seventeenth Century* (New York: Harper & Row, 1964), 42.

60. John Cotton, *Christ the Fountain of Life* (London, 1651), 119–20; Hooker, *Heavens Treasury Opened*, 115; Shepard, *Subjection to Christ in His Ordinances*, 120.

61. Max Weber, *The Protestant Ethic and the Spirit of Capitalism* (New York: Charles Scribner's Sons, 1958), 48–92, 155–83.

62. Berkeley, *Discourse and View of Virginia*, 4; Alsop, *Character of the Province of Maryland*, 349.

63. *Winthrop Papers*, 3:216, 403–3, cited by Shi, *Simple Life*, 15; Norton, *Heart of N-England Rent*, 58; Bailyn, *New England Merchants*, 134–42.

64. Alsop, *Character of the Province of Maryland*, 344.

65. Menard, "Maryland's Time of Troubles," 134; Rutman, *Winthrop's Boston*, 246.

Epilogue

1. James T. Lemon, "Spatial Order: Households in Local Communities and Regions," in *Colonial British America*, 86–122; Rutman and Rutman, *A Place in Time*, 121; Gloria L. Main, *Tobacco Colony* (Princeton: Princeton University Press, 1982), 147; Milton W. Brown, *American Art to 1900* (New York: Harry N. Abrams, 1977), 41–43; Thwaites, *Jesuit Relations*, X:89, 91, 93.

2. Smith, *Generall Historie*, 35.

3. Brown, *American Art to 1900*, 42; Jury and Jury, *Sainte-Marie among the Hurons*, 4, 96.

4. Brahe to Printz, 9 November 1642, in Johnson, *Instructions for John Printz*, 155; Myers, *Narratives of Early Pennsylvania, West New Jersey, and Delaware*, 122, 150.

5. Hastings, *Ecclesiastical Records of New York*, 1:163.

6. T. H. Breen, "Creative Adaptations: People and Cultures," in *Colonial British America*, 195–232.

Bibliographic Essay

The books with which to begin a study of seventeenth-century American thought are still Perry Miller, *The New England Mind: The Seventeenth Century* (rpt., Boston: Beacon Press, 1961; 1st ed., New York: Macmillan, 1939) and *The New England Mind: From Colony to Province* (Cambridge: Harvard University Press, 1953). Subject now to frequent criticism, Miller raised questions and offered thoughtful answers that have stimulated research for half a century. For the southern colonies, the nearest counterpart to Miller is Richard Beale Davis's encyclopedic *Intellectual Life in the Colonial South, 1585–1763*, 3 vols. (Knoxville: University of Tennessee Press, 1978), which contends that secular themes prevailed in early southern writing.

For the European intellectual background, see especially Robert Mandrou, *From Humanism to Science, 1480–1700*, trans. Brian Pearce (Atlantic Highlands, N.J.: Humanities Press, 1979). Useful analyses of rhetorical traditions appear in two books by Walter Ong: *Rhetoric, Romance, and Technology* (Ithaca: Cornell University Press, 1971) and *Ramus: Method and the Decay of Dialogue* (Cambridge: Harvard University Press, 1958). Samuel Eliot Morison also illumines the European setting in his *Harvard College in the Seventeenth Century*, 2 vols. (Cambridge: Harvard University Press, 1936).

Bernard Bailyn, *The Peopling of British North America* (New York: Alfred A. Knopf, 1986), examines the distinction between core and periphery. D. W. Meinig, *The Shaping of America*, 2 vols. (New Haven: Yale University Press, 1986), also presents an overarching synthesis using those concepts. For an illuminating treatment of diversity in one region, see David Grayson Allen, *In English Ways* (Chapel Hill: University of North Carolina Press, 1981).

To understand the arguments about literacy in colonial America, read Kenneth Lockridge, *Literacy in Colonial New England* (New York: W. W. Norton, 1974), and the essays in William L. Joyce, David D. Hall, Richard D. Brown, and John B. Hench, eds., *Printing and Society in Early America, 1600–1850* (Worcester, Mass.: American Antiquarian Society, 1983). Bernard Bailyn, *Education in the Forming of American Society* (New York: Vintage Books, 1960), argues for an expanded conception of learning; James Axtell, *The School upon a Hill* (New Haven: Yale University Press, 1974), follows Bailyn's suggestion and studies the transmission of values, as well as literacy.

The most useful study of colonial science is Raymond Phineas Stearns, *Science in the British Colonies of America* (Urbana: University of Illinois Press, 1970). Robert Daly, *God's Altar* (Berkeley: University of California Press, 1978), discusses the colonial poets. Samuel Eliot Morison, *The Puritan Pronaos* (New York: New York University Press, 1936), examines poets and scientists.

David Quinn, ed., *New American World*, 5 vols. (New York: Arno Press and Hector Bye, 1979), is an unusually helpful collection of early writings. They can be read in conjunction with Quinn's *North America from Earliest Discovery to First Settlement* (New York: Harper & Row, 1975). Three literary historians offer useful critical comments on the literature of discovery and exploration: Howard Mumford Jones, *O Strange New World* (1952, reprint ed., Westport, Conn.: Greenwood Press, 1982); Wayne Franklin, *Discoverers, Explorers, Settlers* (Chicago: University of Chicago Press, 1979); and Evelyn Page, *American Genesis* (Boston: Gambit, 1973).

Captain John Smith has elicited diverse responses from historians. His seeming exaggerations invited debunking, but Philip L. Barbour, *The Three Worlds of Captain John Smith* (Boston: Houghton Mifflin, 1964), Bradford Smith, *Captain John Smith* (Philadelphia: Lippincott, 1953), and Alden T. Vaughan, *American Genesis* (Boston: Little, Brown, 1975), confirm the authenticity of tales that earlier historians had accused Smith of inventing. Everett Emerson, *Captain John Smith* (New York: Twayne Publishers, 1971), focuses attention on Smith as a writer.

Some recent works in social history help readers understand the background of the promotional writings. Darrett B. Rutman, *Winthrop's Boston* (rpt., New York: W. W. Norton, 1972; 1st ed., Chapel Hill: University of North Carolina Press, 1965), argues that Puritan ideals had little influence on New England society. Darrett B. Rutman and Anita H. Rutman, *A Place in Time* (New York: W. W. Norton, 1984), contend for a redefinition of community in early Virginia. Edmund Morgan, *American Slavery, American Freedom* (New York: W. W. Norton, 1975), presents a bleak picture of a boom-and-bust society in Virginia as part of his investigation of the way slavery helped form American notions of freedom. Gloria L. Main, *Tobacco Colony* (Princeton: Princeton University Press, 1982), gives a realistic account of life in Maryland. One should also look at such New England community studies as John Demos, *A Little Commonwealth* (New York: Oxford University Press, 1970); Kenneth A Lockridge, *A New England Town* (New York: W. W. Norton, 1970), Sumner C. Powell, *Puritan Village* (Middletown, Conn.: Wesleyan University Press, 1963); and Philip J. Greven, Jr., *Four Generations* (Ithaca, N.Y.: Cornell University Press, 1970). Timothy Breen, *Puritans and Adventurers* (New York: Oxford University Press, 1980), provides helpful comparisons of social attitudes and practices in New England and the Chesapeake colonies.

Theodore Dwight Bozeman, *To Live Ancient Lives* (Chapel Hill: University of North Carolina Press, 1988), analyzes the primitivist view of the past in New England Puritanism and offers a reinterpretation of millennialism. Louis B. Wright, *The First Gentlemen of Virginia* (San Marino: Huntington Library, 1940), reveals the interest in history among wealthier Virginians. For the historiography of the Indian wars, see Richard Slotkin and James K. Folsom, *So Dreadfull a Judgment* (Middletown, Conn.: Wesleyan University Press, 1978). Wilcomb Washburn, *The Governor and the Rebel* (Chapel Hill: University of North Carolina Press, 1957), has good discussions of the writings that interpreted Bacon's Rebellion.

Bradford's *Of Plymouth Plantation* has drawn conflicting evaluations. Peter Gay, *A Loss of Mastery* (New York: Vintage Books, 1968), concludes that Bradford's piety led him to overlook historical complexity. David Levin, "William Bradford: The Value of Puritan Historiography," in *Major Writers of Early American Literature*, ed. Everett Emerson (Madison: University of Wisconsin Press, 1972), argues that the piety mandated inquiry into the complexity.

Perry Miller opened the debate over typology in Puritan thought in his *Roger Williams* (Indianapolis: Bobbs Merrill, 1953). For recent explorations of the topic, presenting an interpretation different from mine, see two books by Sacvan Bercovitch: *The Puritan Origins of the American Self* (New Haven: Yale University Press, 1975), and *The American Jeremiad* (Madison: University of Wisconsin Press, 1978). Bercovitch has also edited a collection of essays: *Typology and Early American Literature* (Amherst: University of Massachusetts Press, 1972).

James Axtell, *The Invasion Within* (New York: Oxford University Press, 1985), is the new standard for understanding relations among the Jesuits, Hurons, and Iroquois in New France and the Puritans and native Americans in the New England region. One should also consult Gary B. Nash, *Red, White, and Black* (Englewood Cliffs, N.J.: Prentice-Hall, 1974), Karen Kupperman, *Settling with the Indians* (Totowa, N.J.: Rowman and Littlefield, 1980), and W. F. Craven, *White, Red, and Black* (Charlottesville: University Press of Virginia, 1971). Henry Warner Bowden, *American Indians and Christian Missions* (Chicago: University of Chicago Press, 1981), extends his view to the Franciscans and Pueblos.

The starting point for any study of native American culture is *Handbook of North American Indians*, gen. ed. William C. Sturtevant, 20 vols. (Washington, D.C.: Smithsonian Institution, 1978–79). In looking at the Pueblos, I found valuable information and interpretation in Edward H. Spicer, *Cycles of Conquest* (Tucson: University of Arizona Press, 1962); Edward P. Dozier, *The Pueblo Indians of North America* (New York: Holt, Rinehart, and Winston, 1970); and Elsie Clews Parson, *Pueblo Indian Religion*, 2 vols. (Chicago: University of Chicago Press, 1939). Bruce Trigger clarifies Huron ideas about religion and society in *The Children of Aataentsic* (Montreal: McGill-Queens University Press, 1976) and *The Huron Farmers of the North* (New York: Holt, Rinehart, and Winston, 1969), as does Cornelius J. Jaenen, *Friend and Foe* (New York: Columbia University Press, 1976). A helpful guide to changes in the native American cultures of New England can be found in Neal Salisbury, *Manitou and Providence* (New York: Oxford University Press, 1982).

A thoughtful appraisal of methods to recover early African culture in the Americas can be found in Sidney W. Mintz and Richard Price, *An Anthropological Approach to the Afro-American Past* (Philadelphia: Institute for the Study of Human Issues, 1976). Albert Raboteau, *Slave Religion* (New York: Oxford University Press, 1978), offers careful judgments about cultural continuity between Africa and America. Early colonial attitudes toward Africans can be examined in Winthrop D. Jordan, *White over Black* (Chapel Hill: University of North Carolina Press, 1968), and David Brion Davis, *The Problem of Slavery in Western Culture* (Ithaca: Cornell University Press, 1966). Timothy H. Breen and Stephen Innes, *"Myne Owne Ground"* (New York: Oxford University Press, 1980), show black successes in preserving links to their ancient cultures while adapting to new ones.

The literature on Puritan theology is vast and sophisticated. Perry Miller, *Errand into the Wilderness* (Cambridge: Harvard University Press, 1956), viewed covenant theology as a domestication of Calvinism, a view that also permeated his *New England Mind*. David D. Hall summarizes more recent assessments in "Religion and Society: Problems and Reconsiderations," in *Colonial British America*, ed. Jack P. Greene and J. R. Pole (Baltimore: Johns Hopkins University Press, 1984).

The books that best interpret technical Puritan theology in New England are Ernest Lowrie, *The Shape of the Puritan Mind* (New Haven: Yale University Press, 1974), and William K. B. Stoever, *"A Faire and Easie Way to Heaven"* (Middletown, Conn.: Wesleyan University Press, 1978). Norman Fiering provides invaluable help with the philosphical background in his *Moral Philosophy at Seventeenth-Century Harvard* (Chapel Hill: University of North Carolina Press, 1981). Robert Middlekauff, *The Mathers* (New York: Oxford University Press, 1971), uses the Mather family to trace the changes in New England thought. E. Brooks Holifield, *The Covenant Sealed* (New Haven: Yale University Press, 1974), looks at covenantal thought in relation to sacramental disputes, while Robert E. Pope, *The Half-Way Covenant*

(Princeton: Princeton University Press, 1969), uses church records to challenge notions of religious decline.

The topic of conversion reappears throughout recent scholarly literature on Puritanism. Edmund Morgan, *Visible Saints* (Ithaca: Cornell University Press, 1965), explores the relationship between conversionist piety and the formation of churches. Michael McGiffert, ed., *God's Plot* (Amherst: University of Massachusetts Press, 1972), examines the piety of Thomas Shepard. Edmund Morgan, ed., *The Diary of Michael Wigglesworth, 1653–1657* (New York: Harper & Row, 1965), reprints valuable conversion narratives, as do George Selement and Bruce C. Woolley, eds., *Thomas Shepard's Confessions, Colonial Society of Massachusetts Collections* 58 (Boston: Colonial Society of Massachusetts, 1981). Charles Lloyd Cohen provides a satisfying account of the narratives in *God's Caress* (New York: Oxford University Press, 1986).

In his *Keepers of the Vineyard* (Lanham, Md.: University Press of America, 1984), George Selement discusses the pastoral preoccupations standing behind the sermons. For the history of the ministry in New England, the best book is David D. Hall, *The Faithful Shepherd* (Chapel Hill: University of North Carolina Press, 1972). Readers who prefer biographical approaches will appreciate Larzer Ziff, *The Career of John Cotton* (Princeton: Princeton University Press, 1962); Everett H. Emerson, *John Cotton* (New York: Twayne Publishers, 1965); and Sargent Bush, Jr., *The Writings of Thomas Hooker* (Madison: University of Wisconsin Press, 1980). Charles E. Hambrick-Stowe puts the theology in a new perspective in *The Practice of Piety* (Chapel Hill: University of North Carolina Press, 1982). And Harry Stout, *The New England Soul* (New York: Oxford University Press, 1986), uses unpublished sermon manuscripts to show that the theology changed little throughout the century.

The best studies of dissent are Philip F. Gura, *A Glimpse of Sion's Glory* (Middletown, Conn.: Wesleyan University Press, 1984), and David S. Lovejoy, *Religious Enthusiasm in the New World* (Cambridge: Harvard University Press, 1985). Emery Battis, *Saints and Sectaries* (Chapel Hill: University of North Carolina Press, 1962), studies the social dimensions of the Antinomian struggle. Lyle Koehler, *Search for Power* (Urbana: University of Illinois Press, 1980), sees gender issues underlying the dispute. David D. Hall provides documents and interpretation in his *The Antinomian Controversy, 1636–1638* (Middletown, Conn.: Wesleyan University Press, 1968).

In *Roger Williams* (Indianapolis: Bobbs-Merrill, 1953), Perry Miller challenged the depiction of Williams as a progressive democrat. Edmund Morgan, *Roger Williams* (New York: Harcourt, Brace, and World, 1967), emphasized Williams's consistency as a thinker. W. Clark Gilpin, *The Millenarian Piety of Roger Williams* (Chicago: University of Chicago Press, 1979), found eschatological themes at the center of Williams's dissent.

William McLoughlin offers thorough analyses of the Baptists in *New Eng-*

land Dissent, 1630–1833, 2 vols. (Cambridge: Harvard University Press, 1971). Still valuable, partly for its reprinting of original sources, is Isaac Backus, *A History of New England with Particular Reference to the Baptists*, 2 vols. (Newton, Mass.: Backus Historical Society, 1871). Melvin B. Endy, Jr., *William Penn and Early Quakerism* (Princeton: Princeton University Press, 1973), places Quakerism in a larger intellectual setting.

For unconventional forms of religion in England, see Keith Thomas, *Religion and the Decline of Magic* (New York: Charles Scribner's Sons, 1971). Other scholars have applied Thomas's methods to the colonies, but see the criticism in David D. Hall, "A World of Wonders: The Mentality of the Supernatural in Seventeenth-Century New England," *Seventeenth-Century New England, Colonial Society of Massachusetts Publications*, vol. 63 (Charlottesville: University Press of Virginia, 1984). The literature on witchcraft is voluminous; the best place to start is John P. Demos, *Entertaining Satan* (New York: Oxford University Press, 1982).

Instructive guides to political and social thought can be found in Jack P. Greene and J. R. Pole, eds., *Colonial British America* (Baltimore: Johns Hopkins University Press, 1984). For New England, see Stephen Foster, *Their Solitary Way* (New Haven: Yale University Press, 1971), and T. H. Breen, *The Character of the Good Ruler* (New Haven: Yale University Press, 1970). Richard S. Dunn has fine insights into the Winthrop dynasty in *Puritans and Yankees* (Princeton: Princeton University Press, 1962), and thousands of students gratefully read the lucid account of John Winthrop by Edmund S. Morgan, *The Puritan Dilemma* (Boston: Little, Brown, 1958). Morgan also illumined thought about the family in *The Puritan Family* (New York: Harper & Row, 1966). The best study of economic thought is still Bernard Bailyn, *The New England Merchants in the Seventeenth Century* (Cambridge: Harvard University Press, 1955). For political ideas in Virginia, see James Morton Smith, ed., *17th-Century America* (Chapel Hill: University of North Carolina, 1959), along with the essays in Thad W. Tate and David L. Ammerman, eds., *The Chesapeake in the Seventeenth Century* (New York: W. W. Norton, 1979).

Index

Aataentsic, 71
Act Concerning Religion, 131
Affections, 108
Africans, 7, 8, 63–64, 85–89
Almanacs, 10
Alsop, George, 17; *Character of the Province of Maryland, A*, 32, 38; on hierarchy, 135; on wealth, 153
Ames, William, 101; *Marrowe of Sacred Divinity, The*, 98
Anabaptists, 110, 112, 119, 129, 131
Antinomianism, 104–5, 111, 116–19, 124, 126
Architecture, 155–56
Arminianism, 95
Arminius, Jacobus, 95
Ascensión, Antonio de la, 21, 65
Astronomy, 10, 13
Austin, Ann, 120

Bacon, Nathaniel, 40–41, 136
Bacon's Rebellion, 40–41, 134, 136
Baltimore, Lord, 7, 112, 124, 131, 136, 151
Baptism, 55, 87, 101, 119–20, 130
Baptists, 101, 116, 119–20, 123, 126; General, 111; Particular, 111
Bay Psalm Book, The, 81
Baylie, Robert, 106
Bellingham, Richard, 122
Benavides, Alsonso de, 62–63, 128

Berkeley, William, 29, 128, 134, 146; *Discourse and View of Virginia, A*, 41
Bible, 42–52, 82, 117, 119, 149
Bland, Edward: *Discovery of New Brittaine, The*, 30
Body of Liberties, 148
Book of Common Prayer, The, 16, 113
Bozeman, Dwight, 50
Bradford, William, 32, 56, 61; *Of Plymouth Plantation*, 50–52
Bradstreet, Anne, 11, 53
Brahe, Tycho, 4
Brébeuf, Jean de, 72, 73, 155
Brereton, John: *Brief and True Relation of the Discoverie of the North Part of Virginia, A*, 24
Brewster, Margaret, 125
Brigden, Zechariah, 10
Brightman, Thomas, 53
Browne, Robert, 111
Browne, Samuel, 113
Bry, Theodor de, 24
Bulkeley, Peter: *Gospel Covenant, The*, 98–99, 101, 102, 127
Bullock, William, 29

California, 21
Calling, 152
Calvert, Cecil, 145–46
Calvin, John, 42, 91, 99, 101

Calvinism, 90–109, 110–11, 129, 156
Cambridge Platform, 45, 102
Cambridge University, 5
Cancer, Luis, 65
Carigonan, 73
Carolina, 22, 88, 131–32
Cartier, Jacques, 22
Cartwright, Thomas, 43
Castañeda, Pedro de: *Narrative of the Expedition to Cibola*, 20
Catholicism, 7, 12, 14–16, 64, 156; in Maryland, 30, 131; in New France, 15, 71–76; in New Spain, 64–70
Cautantowwit, 77–78
Ceremony, political, 145; *See* Sacred gesture
Champlain, Samuel de, 7, 22, 72
Charles I, of England, 39, 111
Charles I, of Spain, 19
Chatham, Catherine, 125
Chauncey, Charles, 49
Chepi, 78
Child, Robert, 125
Christ, 43–46, 93–94, 117–20, 125
Christina, Queen of Sweden, 4
Church, 3, 16, 44–47, 73, 79, 114
Church of England, 14
Cibola, 20, 22, 23
Civil War, England, 39, 111, 134; Maryland, 146
Civility, 82–83
Clarke, John: *Ill-Newes from New England*, 119, 121
Clergy, 14, 16; Protestant, 42–50, 79–85, 91–109, 113–14, 122–23; Catholic, 14, 16, 66–68, 72–76
Coddington, William, 141
Collins, John, 94
Columbus, Christopher, 6–7
Common good, 136–37
"Complaint from Heaven, A," 147
Complexity, in Europe, 3–8; in America, 9
Condemnation, as rhetorical strategy, 124
Congregationalism, 44, 79–85, *111–12*, 129, 131
Congregations, 15
Connecticut, 138–39, 140, 143–44; *See* Thomas Hooker, John Winthrop, Jr.
Consent, 144–45
Copernican theory, 10
Cotton, John, 40; *Keyes of the Kingdom of Heaven, The*, 123; *Of the Holinesse of Church Members*, 47; on antinomians, 104, 117;

on conversion, 94; on covenant, 99, 101, 106; on church, 114; on democracy, 140; on interpretation, 42, 43, 49; on law, 49, 148; on millennium, 53; on prophesying, 123; on preparation, 102–3; on rulers, 138–39, 142, 144, 147; on sacred gestures, 80; on separatism, 113; on toleration, 115, 127; on typology, 46–48, 115; on sanctification, 105; on union with Christ, 105; on wealth, 150–51, 152; *Singing of Psalms a Gospel Ordinance, The*, 81
Cotton, John, of Virginia, 11, 41
Covenant, 97–102; civil, 144; conditional, 100, 106; external, 101; internal, 101; of grace, 99, 100; of works, 99, 117
Covenant renewal, 109
Credibility, as problem, 18–38
Cushman, Robert, 32

Dale, Thomas, 29, 128
Danforth, Samuel: *Astronomic Description of the Late Comet or Blazing Star, An*, 13; "New Englands Errand," 45
Davenport, John, 55, 109
Davis, Richard Beale, 11
Democracy, 140
Demos, John, 124
Denton, Daniel: *Brief Description of New York, A*, 34
Denton, Richard, 129
Descartes, René, 3
Diaz, Melchior, 20
Discovery narratives, 14
Disputations, 12
Dissent, 110–32
Dominicans, 65
Donck, Adriaen van der: *Description of the New Netherlands, A*, 34
Drake, Joan, 103
Dudley, Thomas, 31–32
Dunster, Henry, 12, 120
Dutch Reformed church, 14, 112, 129–30

Easton, John: "Relacion of the Indyan Warre, A," 57
Edmundson, William, 88
Educated ministry, 122–23
El Dorado, 23
Eliot, Sir Thomas: *Governour, The*, 5

Eliot, John, mission of, 81–82, 84; on millennium, 54; on wealth, 151; *Tears of Repentance*, 84
Elite, 13, 91
Elizabeth I, 111
Endecott, John, 122, 151
Enjalrean, Jean, 75
Escobar, Francisco, 21
Espejo, Antonio de, 14, 21
European background, 2–6
Eusebius, 40

Fenner, Dudley: *Sacra Theologia*, 99
Fiering, Norman, 95
Fifth Monarchists, 55, 111
Firmin, Giles, 102–3
Fisher, Mary, 120
Fiske, John, 11
Fitch, James, 109
Florida, 7, 15, 20
Fox, George, 88
Foxe, John: *Acts and Monuments*, 52
Franciscans, 15, 20–21, 62–70, 156
Free will, 96–97
Fundamental Constitutions of Carolina, 88

Gassendi, Pierre, 3
Gates, Sir Thomas, 29
General Baptists, 111
Gentleman of Elvas: *Narrative*, 21, 24
Gentility, 139
Gilbert, Sir Humphrey, 23
Godwin, Morgan, 40, 87–89
Gookin, Samuel, 58
Goold, Thomas, 120
Gorton, Samuel, 118–19, 123–24, 125–26
Grammar Schools, 11, 12
Great men, 133–54
Guale Revolt, 64

Hakluyt, Richard, 23
Halfway Covenant, 55
Hammond, John: *Leah and Rachel*, 30, 32, 37, 41
Hamor, Ralph, 29
Hariot, Thomas, 35; *Briefe and True Report, A*, 23–24
Harris, Elizabeth, 131
Harrison, Robert, 111
Harvard College, 1–3, 10, 12, 40, 95–96
Harvey, John, 136, 146

Hennepin, Louis, 72, 73
Hiacoomes, 82, 84
Hierarchy, 135–36, 139–42
Higginson, Francis, 34, 35, 36; *New-Englands Plantation*, 31–32
Hingham, Mass., 125, 140
Hispaniola, 7
History, 39–61; *See* Sacred time
Hobbes, Thomas, 4
Holmes, Obadiah, 121–22
Hooker, Thomas, on self-denial, 103
Hooker, Thomas, 9, 94, 100; on affliction, 151; on consent, 144; on conversion, 93; on covenant, 99–101; on interpretation, 42, 48–49; on millennium, 53; on politics, 143–44, 148; on preparation, 102, 103–4; on public good, 136; on reason, 108; on wealth, 152; on will, 96; *Survey of the Summe*, 44
Hubbard, William: *Narrative of the Troubles*, 59; *General History*, 61
Human nature, Puritan views, 93–95
Humanism, 5–6
Huronia, 71–76
Hutchinson, Anne, 104, 111, 116–18; on prophesying, 123; on Scripture, 117; on suffering, 121
Hutchinson, Thomas, 150

Incarnation, 93, 106, 115
Independents. *See* Congregationalists
Indians. *See* Native Americans
Ingle, Richard, 146
Inquisition, in New Mexico, 128
Institutions, as settings for thought, 3–4, 9, 11, 13
Intellectualism, 96
Interpretation, biblical, 42–49
Islam, 85
Israel, imitated, 45; as type, 47

Jeremiads, 55
Jesuit Relations, 15
Jesuits, 7, 12, 14, 15, 16, 64, 72–76, 156; in Maryland, 30, 131
Jews, in Puritan theology, 45–46, 53–54, 55, 81, 82; in New Netherland, 130
Jogues, Isaac, 7, 129
Johnson, Anthony, 87
Johnson, Edward, 18, 106–7, 117, 118, 137; *Wonder-Working Providence*, 54–55

Johnson, Robert, 18
Josephus, 40
Josselyn, John, 33, 34, 37
Junius, Francis, 47

Kachinas, 68
Keayne, Robert, 147, 152
Kepler, Johann, 4
Kieft, Willem, 143
King Philip's War, 40, 57, 85, 134
Kivas, 66

Laity, 94, 123
Land, Indian conceptions of, 66, 71, 77,
   79; English conceptions of, 36, 58, 79–
   80; Spanish conceptions of, 67; *See*
   Sacred space
Landscape, depicted, 33–35
Las Casas, Bartolomé de: *Very Brief Account*,
   65
Laud, William, 44
Laudonniére, René de, 22, 23, 24
Law, civil, 49; codified, 150; Mosaic, 49,
   148
Lawes and Liberties, 150
Le Caron, Joseph, 72
Lechford, Thomas, 53
Leibniz, 4
LeJeune, Paul, 73
Léon, Juan Ponce de, 7, 19
Levellers, 111
Liberty, 137
Literacy, 12–13
Locke, John, 88
Luther, Martin, 42, 91
Lutherans, 14, 112, 129, 130, 156–57

Magistrates, power of, 46, 148–50
Malebranche, Nicolas, 3
Manitous, 77
Maryland, 7, 38; political and social
   thought in, 136, 141–42, 146–47;
   promotion of, 30, 32–33, 34; toleration
   in, 131
Massachusetts Bay, 8, 9, 10, 27, 31; dissent
   in, 110–27; promotion of, 27, 31–33, 35–
   37; political and social thought in, 135–
   42, 147–53; history in, 42–61; missions
   in, 76–84; theology in, 90–109
Mather, Cotton, 61

Mather, Increase, on history, 39, 57–60; on
   reform, 109; *Mystery of Israel's Salvation,*
   The, 55; *Relation of the Troubles Which Have*
   Hapned in New England, The, 60
Mather, Richard, 81; *Summe of Certain*
   Sermons, The, 127
Mayflower Compact, 137, 144
Mayhew, Thomas, Jr., 78, 82, 84
Megapolensis, Johannes, 129
Melancholy, 107–8
Mendoza, Antonio de, 20
Mennonites, 130
Mesmes, Henri de, 4
Millennialism, 52–55, 82, 116
Miracles, 13
Mitchell, Jonathan, 55, 94, 120
Moody, Joshua, 15
Moody, Deborah, 119, 126
Morton, Nathaniel: *New Englands*
   Memoriall, 56
Morton, Thomas, 34; *New English Canaan,*
   The, 32, 113; on Indians, 79, 85; on
   Puritans, 113
Music. *See* Sacred sound

Nanoba, Don Pedro, 70
Native Americans, 6, 14, 15, 22, 63, 157;
   Algonkian-speaking, 23, 64, 76–85;
   Hurons, 71–76; Pequots, 51, 84;
   conversion of, 26, 28, 35–36, 58–61, 62–
   85; described, 19, 20, 35; extermination
   of, 65; in Virginia, 25; Massachuset, 78;
   Narraganset, 77; Powhatans, 29, 36;
   Pueblos, 63–70; Roanokes, 23
Nature, 33–35
Negative voice, 145–48
New England, 8, 9, 10, 31; dissent in, 110–
   28; history in, 42–61; missions in, 76–84;
   political and social thought in, 135–42,
   147–53; promoters of, 27, 31–33, 35–37;
   theology in, 90–109
New France, 7, 14, 22, 155; mission to,
   71–76
New Haven, 16
New Mexico, 7, 11, 15, 141; history of, 40;
   mission to, 62–70; inquisition in, 128;
   promoted, 21, 22; 64–70; *See* New Spain
New Netherland, 7, 12, 14, 19, 87;
   political and social thought in, 141, 143;
   toleration in, 129–30; *See* New York

New Spain, 7, 8, 11, 15, 19, 40, 64–70; *See* New Mexico
New Sweden, 8, 14, 129, 156–57
New York, 14, 37, 38, 71, 141; *See* New Netherland
Niza, Marcos de, 20
Norton, John, 92, 96, 97; on Arminianism, 95; on hierarchy, 136; on human nature, 93; on order, 134–35; on toleration, 127; *Orthodox Evangelist, The*, 127

Oakes, Urian, 1–2, 57
Oñate, Juan de, 7, 22, 66
Onderha, 71
Ononharoia, 74
Oviedo, Gonzalo Fernández de, 19
Oxford University, 5, 24

Paradox of grace, 93, 109
Parker, Thomas, 53
Particular Baptists, 111
Pauline theology, 51, 97, 100, 126
Peacham, Henry: *Compleat Gentleman, The*, 4
Percy, Henry, 4
Perfect Description of Virginia, A, 30
Periphery, 6, 8
Perkins, William, 99, 137–38
Perrault, Julien, 72
Perry, George, 25
Piumbukhou, 83
Plagues, interpreted, 36
Plokhoy, Pieter, 130
Plutarch, 40
Plymouth, 19, 32, 37, 38, 50–52
Pocahontas, 29
Poetry, 10–11
Polhemus, Johannes, 16
Political theory, 133–54
Popé, El, 70
Pory, John, 8
Powhatan, 29
Powwows, 78
Prayer, by converts, 83
Preparation for salvation, 102–4
Presbyterianism, 45, 111, 128–29, 131
Prideaux, Matthew: *Introduction for Reading, An*, 40
Primitivism, 41–49, 114, 119–20, 126
Printing, 16, 91, 128
Printz, John, 129

Promoters, 14, 18–38
Prophesying, 123
Proportional interpretation, 48–49
Protestant Ethic, 152–53
Providence, 32, 36, 41, 51–52, 54–55, 58–59, 60, 90, 92
Psalms, 46, 81, 131
Psychology, Puritan, 95–97, 107–9
Ptolemaic theory, 10
Pueblo Revolt, 70
Pueblos, 63–70
Puritanism, 9, 14, 41, 79–85, 90–109, 110–28
Pynchon, William: *Meritorious Price of our Redemption, The*, 125; on magisterial discretion, 148

Quakers, 57, 88, 111, 112, 120–21, 126, 134; in Carolina, 132; in Maryland, 131; in New Netherland, 130; in Rhode Island, 131; in Virginia, 128, 129; on learning, 123; on ministry, 123; on suffering, 122; on women, 126; rhetoric of, 125

Race, 88; *See* Africans, Native Americans
Raleigh, Sir Walter, 23, 24, 30; *History of the World*, 40, 42
Ramus, Petrus, logic of, 44, 98
Recollects, 72, 75
Reforming Synod, 109
Revitalization prophets, 76
Rhetoric, 5, 11, 73, 100, 102, 124; among Native Americans, 5, 15
Rhode Island, 11, 88, 131; democracy in, 140; dissenters in, 116, 118–19, 121; toleration in, 131; *See* Baptists, Roger Williams
Ribault, Jean, 22
Rich, Richard: *Newes from Virginia*, 28
Roanoke Island, 23–24
Robinson, John, 138
Rodríguez, Augustín: "Brief and True Account of the Exploration of New Mexico, A," 21
Rolfe, John, 29, 87
Rome, history of, 40
Rosier, James: *True Relation of the Most Prosperous Voyage, A*, 24
Rous, John, 122
Rowlandson, Mary, 60–61

Royal Society, 4, 10, 157
Royal University of Mexico, 12

Sabbath, 16, 47, 80, 83
Sacraments, 55, 73, 75, 87, 101, 119, 130
Sacred gesture, 63; African, 86; French Catholic, 75–76; Huron, 71, Narraganset, 77–78; Pueblo, 69; Puritan, 80–81; Spanish Catholic, 69
Sacred sound, 63; African, 86; French Catholic, 75; Huron, 71, 75; Narraganset, 78–79; Pueblo, 68; Puritan, 81; Spanish Catholic, 68
Sacred space, 63, 156; African, 85; French Catholic, 72–73; Huron, 71; Narraganset, 77; Pueblo, 66–67; Puritan, 79; Spanish Catholic, 66
Sacred time, 63; African, 85–86; French Catholic, 75; Huron, 71; Narraganset, 78; Pueblo, 67; Puritan, 80; Spanish Catholic, 67
Saffin, John, 11
Saint Esteban, Acoma, 156
Sainte-Marie-aux-Hurons, 156
Saltmarsh, John, 122
Saltonstall, Nathaniel: *Present State of New England, The*, 57–58
Sanctification, 105
Sandys, George: *Metamorphoses*, 11
Scholastics, 91
Scott, Katherine, 119
Self-denial, 103
Selyns, Henricus, 87
Separatism, 111–16, 119, 124, 126
Sermons, 15, 16, 93
Shepard, Thomas, 94; on affections, 108; on antinomians, 104, 106; on biblical interpretation, 43; on covenant, 98, 101; on millennium, 54; on ministry, 122; on persuasion, 90; on preparation, 102–3; on primitive church, 44; on Sabbath, 80; on sacred space, 79; on typology, 47; *Parable of the Ten Virgins, The*, 104, 127; *Theses Sabbaticae*, 80, 127
Shepard, Thomas, Jr., 9, 57
Sherwood, William, 41
Simplification, 9
Singing, 46; *See* Sacred sound
Skelton, Samuel, 113
Slander, 124
Slavery, 7, 33, 65, 86–89

Smith, John, 14, 30, 35, 36, 40, 156; *Description of New England, A*, 27; *Generall Historie of Virginia, New England, and the Summer Isles, The*, 27, 41; *Map of Virginia, A*, 26, 28; *New Englands Trials*, 27; *True Relation of Such Occurences and Accidents of Noate, as Hath Hapned in Virginia, A*, 25; *True Travels, The*, 25
Soto, Hernando de, 20–21
Soul, 95–96, 107–9; Huron views of, 74
Spiritism, 116–18, 120–21
Stone, John, 96
Stone, Samuel, 15
Stoughton, Israel, 147
Strachey, William: *Historie of Travaile into Virginia Britannia, The*, 28
Stukeley, Thomas, 23
Stuyvesant, Peter, 129, 130, 143, 145
Suffering, described, 121–22
Symonds, Samuel, 54

Theocracy, 141
Theology, 15, 41, 42–54, 90–109
Thou, Jacques-Auguste de, 4
Titles, 135
Toleration, 112, 127–32; John Cotton on, 115; Roger Williams on, 115
Tompson, Benjamin, 11, 60
Twiller, Wouter Van, 143
Typology, 34, 45–48, 81, 115

Underhill, John, 43
Union with Christ, 104–5, 117
Ursinus, Zacharias, 99
Ursulines, 75

Vaca, Alvar Núñez Cabeza de: *Relation*, 19
vacuum domicilium, 79
Vane, Henry, 117
Vásquez de Coronado, Don Francisco, 20
Vernacular, 157
Villagra, Gaspar Pere de: *History of New Mexico, The*, 40
Virginia, 7, 14, 16, 18, 19; description of, 37; history in, 40–41; political and social thought in, 136, 138–39, 141, 145–46, 153; promotion of, 22–26, 27–31, 34, 36–37; slavery in, 87; toleration in, 128–29
Virginia Company, 8, 19, 25, 26, 29
Virtuosos, 4
Vizcaino, Sebastián, 21

Vocation, 137–38
Voluntarism, 95–96
Voting, ideas about, 141

Ward, Nathaniel, 40, 110, 136, 148
Wardel, Lydia, 125
Warr, Lord De la, 14, 138, 139
Warton, Edward: *New England's Present Sufferings*, 57
Wealth, ideas about, 150–54
Weber, Max, 152–53
Wheeler, Thomas: *Thankful Remembrance*, 60
Whitaker, Alexander: *Good Newes from Virginia*, 28
White, Andrew, 30, 34, 36
White, John, 24
Whitgift, John, 43
Wigglesworth, Mary, 94
Wigglesworth, Michael: *Day of Doom, The*, 11
Will, in Harvard disputations, 95–96
Willard, Samuel, on affections, 108; on interpretation, 42; on persuasion, 109; on reason, 108; on soul, 107
Williams, Roger, 15, 111, 125, 141; on baptism, 119; on church, 114; on Indians, 77, 78; on learning, 123; on primitivism, 114–16; on Quakers, 121; on separatism, 112, 113–14; on suffering, 121, 122; on typology, 47, 115; dissent of, 113–16; poetry of, 11
Wilson, Deborah, 125
Wingfield, Edward Maria, 40; "Discourse of Virginia, A," 28
Winslow, Edward, 84, 125; *Good News from New England*, 32, 35; on Indians, 77, 78
Winthrop, John, 43, 84, 124, 142, 153; "Discourse on Arbitrary Government, A," 149–50; "History of New England," 56; on antinomians, 117; on consent, 144–45; on democracy, 140; on government, 141, 147, 150; on liberty, 138; on negative voice, 145–48; on order, 137
Winthrop, John, Jr., 9, 10, 13, 138–39, 142
Women, 71; and dissent, 126; ideas of, 60–61, 94, 104, 116–18, 121, 123, 125; Quakers, 120, 131
Wood, William, 33, 34, 36; *New England's Prospect*, 32; on Indians, 79; poetry of, 11
Work, ideas about, 152–53
Wycliffe, John, 110

Yeardley, George, 29